1992

THE RIGHT TO
PRIVACY

Gays, Lesbians, and
the Constitution

THE RIGHT TO PRIVACY

Gays, Lesbians, and the Constitution

Vincent J. Samar

TEMPLE UNIVERSITY PRESS
Philadelphia

TEMPLE UNIVERSITY PRESS, PHILADELPHIA 19122
COPYRIGHT © 1991 BY TEMPLE UNIVERSITY. ALL RIGHTS RESERVED
PUBLISHED 1991
PRINTED IN THE UNITED STATES OF AMERICA

The paper used in this publication meets the minimum
requirements of American National Standard for Information
Sciences—Permanence of Paper for Printed Library Materials,
ANSI Z39.48-1984 ∞

Library of Congress Cataloging-in-Publication Data
Samar, Vincent Joseph, 1953–
    The right to privacy : gays, lesbians, and the Constitution /
Vincent J. Samar.
        p.   cm.
    Includes bibliographical references and index.
    ISBN 0-87722-796-9
    1. Privacy, Right of—United States.   2. Homosexuality—
Law and legislation—United States.   3. Sex and law—United
States.   I. Title.
KF1262.S26   1991
342.73'0858—dc20
[347.302858]   90-21937
                                                           CIP

FOR MOM,
THE MEMORY OF DAD,
AND JOHN KVEDARAS

Contents

Preface

This book has two major purposes. The first is to lay the theoretical foundation for a general right to privacy. What does privacy mean and how is the right to privacy justified? Is there an underlying principle uniting various applications of the right? When privacy conflicts with another right, how does one decide which right takes precedence? And how does privacy relate to the government's 'compelling interest' in protecting the health and welfare of its citizens? In Part One, I address these issues.

In Part Two, I take up the question of how a philosophical justification becomes a legal justification. In applying the theory, I pay particular attention to lesbian and gay issues because the privacy problems confronting these groups have generally been underappreciated in the literature and because these groups are representative of other ostracized or marginalized groups. Moreover, I believe that analyzing lesbian and gay privacy issues, along with issues such as abortion, surrogate motherhood, drug testing, and the right to die, will illustrate the common constitutional-ethical underpinnings of all these issues.

Perhaps now more than ever, the legal right to privacy is a focal point of criticism in American jurisprudence. In part, this might be explained by the recent rise in conservatism in the United States, especially on the questions of abortion and gay rights. More fundamentally, the criticisms center on the line of cases beginning with the 1965 Supreme Court decision that extended the right to privacy to allow a married couple to obtain contraceptives and the subsequent cases that further extended the right to include a woman's choice to have an abortion and a minor's claim to be able to receive contraceptives without parental consent. Never was the right to privacy debate more clearly present than in the summer of 1988 when the United States Senate took up President Reagan's nomination of Robert Bork to a seat on the Supreme Court. The controversy that precipitated the failure of that appointment has recently been rekindled with the United States Supreme Court's decision to limit the progeny of its 1973 landmark abortion case, *Roe v. Wade.*[1]

What makes the criticisms especially plausible is that the legal right to privacy seems to have developed in three separate areas of the law, with no clear conceptual links. Indeed, this concern has given rise to arguments over whether the right to privacy ranges over several distinct, very loosely connected concepts or there exists a single, univocal concept of privacy. Unfortunately, the holders of the latter view have never been able to produce a satisfactory definition applicable in all three areas of the law in which the right to privacy has been recognized.

Two other fundamental questions that have been particularly difficult for the courts in having to justify the various extensions of the right to privacy are: first, What is the justification for the right in a democratic society? and, second, How can one clearly specify the degree of protection of the right, relative to other rights with which it may conflict? When the courts could not answer these questions, they associated the right to privacy with various fundamental interests of society (such as the protection of marital intimacy or procreative choice) without ever making clear precisely how the right is related to these interests. This has caused many scholars to believe that the right to privacy (at least in its recent extensions) is merely a judicial attempt at social engineering rather than a natural exposition of a long-standing legal tradition.

No doubt part of the frustration that underlies the criticisms from both the normative and the conceptual sides concerns the difficulty courts and legal scholars have had in making sense of claims relating to ultimate rights. This difficulty can be appreciated if one recognizes that in areas of the law not involving fundamental rights, judicial decisions are evaluated in terms of their consistency with past-case precedents or underlying statutory policies, as revealed by a statute's legislative history.

Where fundamental rights are involved, however, often no such precedents and only very few articulated policy interests exist. Consequently, if judicial decisions in this area are to be evaluated, it must be a conceptual or a normative analysis, depending on whether the problem is one of clarifying a concept or of choosing among various theories of what government should do. In either instance, one is faced with having to resolve difficult philosophical questions that usually transcend the traditional bounds of legal expertise. Since this book is concerned with the meaning and justification of the legal right to privacy, I combine methods of philosophical analysis with traditional legal analysis in order to understand the law of privacy.

In doing so, I take cognizance of the political context in which judicial decisions, especially constitutional decisions (because of their greater symbolic importance), arise. As Alexander Bickel reminds us, such decisions ultimately rely on acceptance.[2] This is especially true where the new principle is likely to unearth an existing social order,[3] such as the roles assigned to men and women. Still, the likelihood of controversial decisions being accepted in societies like ours, especially where they are potentially very far-reaching, is increased if they are based coherently on solid principles that ultimately support self-rule.[4] Hence, even where values compete, I assume there is a cognitive psychological disposition toward favoring autonomy. With this notion in the background, let us begin to lay the groundwork for a philosophical/legal discussion about the meaning and justification of legal privacy.

In the Introduction, I set forth some current history for this discussion by briefly reviewing the role of politics in and the relationship of the doctrine of original intent to the Bork nomination. In Chapter 1, I specify the objects (types of cases) that have been subsumed under the legal concept of privacy. I also delineate the areas of the law where those objects appear, clarifying the different interests at stake. In Chapter 2, I show that most of the objects identified in Chapter 1 fall under one of two privacy concepts: a private act or a private state of affairs. I also suggest that what is really at stake in all privacy cases is the concept of a private act that in some cases would be possible only were there in existence a private state of affairs. In Chapter 3, I assume the concept of privacy specified in Chapter 2 to ask whether a Western democratic society can justify a fundamental right or norm that will protect the objects the concept subsumes. In arguing that such a norm does exist, I establish a connection between the right to privacy and the fundamental value of autonomy in Western democracies. In addition, I argue that the connection gives rise to criteria for resolving conflict of rights situations, as well as situations in which the state has a more compelling interest to protect than individual privacy. In Chapter 4, I take up the epistemological question of why a philosophically justified privacy norm should carry any weight in a legal system and show what is wrong with two recent approaches—an interpretative and a utilitarian—to the issue of privacy. In Chapter 5, I illustrate how the conceptual and normative analyses of Chapters 2 and 3 might be applied to the privacy issues associated with the openly gay teacher, gay and lesbian parenting and marriages, surrogate motherhood, testing and screening for AIDS (Acquired Immune Deficiency Syndrome), adult consensual sodomy statutes, abortion, the rise of computer data banks and electronic funds transfer services, the possession and use of pornography and drugs in the home, employer drug and alcohol testing, and the right to die. In the Epilogue, I take up the ultimate question of the justification of autonomy itself.

It should be noted that works by David Richards also touch some of the topics discussed herein.[5] However, in respect to privacy, my work goes beyond what Richards has been able to achieve. First, I show the conceptual connections between the different areas of the law where privacy has been recognized. Second, I provide a much more detailed specification of how Mills's harm principle can be relied upon to identify those acts that are (at least) prima facie self-regarding. Third, I suggest that the system of privacy I construct would be justified even if one refused to adopt a contractarian model, so long as one concedes the values underlying the right to vote in Western democracies.

I expect that the analysis provided in this book will be of interest not only to philosophers and legal scholars but also to judges and lawyers, political scientists, and persons concerned about human rights in general. The law of privacy is clearly lacking in both conceptual clarity and a noncontroversial justification of the right to privacy. Consequently, if I have contributed to making the law in this area clearer and the importance of the right more fully understood, the effort in writing this book has been well worthwhile.

Before I take up my thesis on privacy, some comments about style should be made. I use the terms *gay* and *lesbian* in preference to *homosexual* where I am not discussing activity or stating somebody else's ideas. In this, I support the efforts of many gay and lesbian activists to be identified by names we choose for ourselves. Also, I use single quotation marks when referring to a word or phrase that has special legal or philosophical meaning.

The primary goal of this work is to situate the concept and justification of privacy in a philosophical/legal framework that transcends narrow historical considerations. However, new laws and court decisions put the consideration of any legal problem in an ever-changing arena. The issues discussed here—privacy and many of its subsidiary topics—are particularly dynamic forces in late twentieth-century America. Therefore, this book, which is current as of winter 1991, reveals and makes use of the history of legal privacy at the time of publication, but the reader must take into account the changes that continue to inform and shape our lives.

This book is an outgrowth of my doctoral dissertation at the University of Chicago. I am indebted to many people who have been very willing to hear and express comments on the ideas contained herein. In particular, I would like to express my special appreciation to the chairman of my graduate committee, Alan Gewirth, of the University of Chicago philosophy department, and my other two readers, Russell Hardin of the University of Chicago philosophy and political science departments and Cass Sunstein of the University of Chicago School of Law. I would also like to acknowledge Michael O. Sawyer, professor of political science at Syracuse University, for being an unofficial reviewer, and Bruce

Barton and Howard Kaplan for their many helpful suggestions on various aspects of this work. I want also to acknowledge the research contributions from Jeannine Thoms and Kathleen Needham, as well as the insightful questions of many of my students. Finally, I want to thank John Kvedaras, my partner in life, whose continued love and support (and occasional editing and typing skills) allowed me to complete this venture.

THE RIGHT TO
PRIVACY

Gays, Lesbians, and the Constitution

Introduction
A WORD ABOUT
POLITICS AND
ORIGINAL INTENT

To a substantial extent, this book is about doctrine and the important political points courts can make by emphasizing doctrine. Court decisions that might be questionable or controversial are frequently offered as merely interpretations of the law. Judicial (and some political) conservatives, in particular, make much of this claim. Therefore, by showing that on their own terms, politically hot decisions like *Bowers v. Hardwick*[1] (which upheld a state's right to prohibit by criminal statute adult consensual homosexual activity in the home) do not comport with existing law, we expose the underlying political agenda that motivated the decision. Herein lies the real debate on the Senate's rejection of President Reagan's nomination of Robert Bork to the Supreme Court in the summer of 1988.

What made the Bork nomination so important was the effect it could have had on the current and future makeup of the Court. With the retirement of Justice Powell in 1987, the Court was left with eight voting members. Justices Brennan, Marshall, Blackmun, and Stevens (the so-called liberal justices) were strong supporters of civil rights and liberties. Justices Rehnquist, White, O'Connor, and (except for First Amendment free speech) Scalia (the "conservatives") tend to vote against civil rights and civil liberties protections. Of the four liberals, all are over eighty except Justice Stevens, who is over seventy; whereas, of the four conservatives, only one is over seventy. Consequently, given the ages of the justices and the conservatism of the president, potential approval of the Bork nomination signaled a conservative majority on the Court well into the next century. As it turned out, the Bork nomination failed, but Justice Kennedy, who was confirmed in his place, has shown strong signs of being almost as conservative. Similarly, if Judge David H. Souter, President Bush's nominee to replace retiring Justice Brennan, turns out to be as conservative as the Reagan appointees (Bush has stated that Souter is a strict constructionist), then the controversy over Bork will have been just the beginning of an ongoing series of political battles between the president and Congress for control over the doctrinal direction of the Supreme Court.[2] In light of these events, many civil rights advocates may still see realized their concern that Bork's judicial conservatism was not merely an unwillingness to extend civil rights and civil liberties protections to heretofore unprotected groups but was an active commitment to undo those extensions that had already been made.

The Bork nomination was also controversial because, as a result of these concerns, the Senate evaluated the ideology of the nominee as well as his general character and credentials (as is traditional). In essence, many senators saw themselves deciding whether or not the Court was going to continue to defend the civil rights and civil liberties that previous courts had protected for the last quarter century.

Since the Supreme Court decides cases by majority vote, the appointment of the fifth member could be expected to determine the Court's stance on such important issues as abortion, affirmative action, the right of a gay or lesbian person not to be excluded from military service because of sexual orientation, and how police carry out arrests, searches and seizures, and interrogations. No doubt it was hoped that President Reagan would appoint to this position a judicial moderate (as Justice Kennedy was at first thought to be); certainly he would not have appointed a liberal. Powell was, after all, a moderate. With a moderate on the Court, decisions would still steer to the right but would probably not be significantly different from those the Court had rendered in the past several years.

In this scenario, the decisions likely to be handed down probably would not have opened any new doors for gays or lesbians, as the decision in *Bowers v. Hardwick* attests. Still, it was hoped that on more mainstream issues the appointment of a moderate at least would represent no major retreat from established pro-abortion or affirmative action policies.

Robert Bork strongly contrasted with this idea of a judicial moderate. Based on an academic writing in the *Indiana Law Review*,[3] in which he criticizes a case invalidating private racially restrictive covenants, as well as several other statements from his past, many feared Bork would go beyond the usual limit of not extending rights. The concern was that he would help forge an activist conservative majority and that he, Rehnquist, and Scalia would take the lead in dismantling many of the existing civil rights and liberties. According to the July 13, 1987, edition of the *Recorder*, Judge Bork—as a Yale University faculty member—opposed a policy in the 1970s prohibiting law firms from recruiting on campus unless they pledged not to discriminate against job candidates on the basis of sexual orientation. He also criticized a case that threw out a poll tax and another that voided a literacy test requirement for voting eligibility,[4] both requirements that allegedly limited the access of many Afro-Americans to the polls. In 1985, he took the minority view in a case in which the Washington, D.C., Court of Appeals held a savings and loan association liable for sexual harassment. Two years before *Hardwick* was decided, Bork wrote the majority opinion in *Dronenburg v. Zech*,[5] in which he states that lesbians and gay men have no constitutional right to privacy for sexual expression—even in the confines of their own bedrooms—and that the military can prescribe regulations requiring the discharge of any person declared to be a homosexual or engaging in same-sex relationships. What worried people was not the rationale that Bork used in any one of these decisions but the collective insensitivity demonstrated to the needs of minority and other marginalized groups. Bork could not find any persuasive reason to protect the interests of the minority in any of these cases.

Bork has always claimed that the basis for his opinions is the doctrine of original intent. Briefly stated, the doctrine holds that justices, when deciding cases involving constitutional law, must not look beyond what the Founding Fathers intended. In other words, if the Founding Fathers (also called the framers) had a certain interpretation of equality that excluded blacks, women, gays, or lesbians, then any gains made by any of these groups must be made solely through the political process. Although in the long run it is necessary to gain acceptance in the political and social arenas if rights are ultimately to survive,[6] in the short run, women and minorities must turn to the courts because the other branches of government are effectively closed to them. One cannot progress in making legitimate political interests heard, especially against institutionalized prejudice, when any attempt at getting the word out is likely to lead to loss of job, residence, or personal status.

The rationale of the doctrine of original intent is that by confining the Court to the framers' understanding of the Constitution, Bill of Rights, and Fourteenth Amendment, one avoids the possibility that the Court, which is not directly accountable to the people (since the justices are appointed to life tenure), will seek to impose its own values independent of the representative process. On a superficial reading, the doctrine makes democratic sense. The problem arises in what is to constitute the original intent of the framers.

Ronald Dworkin has noted that the framers of our Constitution had abstract beliefs about equality, liberty, and equal protection under the laws.[7] Their intentions concern the value concepts that are explicitly stated in the Constitution or can be inferred either from the Constitution or from the scheme of government it creates. In many instances, these concepts need to be filled in by broader moral views, which in turn will arise from our deeper reflection about human beings and the relation of government to society. Like us, the framers had concrete beliefs about society, some of which they wrote into the Constitution itself. These included political compromises such as the idea that a negro slave would count as three-fifths of a white man for purposes of determining the number of representatives in Congress.[8] Other areas were left without such specifications. It is reasonable to infer that the framers understood that many of these beliefs might change as we became more fully aware of our own nature and the nature of society. Consequently, they left many specifics out of the Constitution so that the document could be open to continuing interpretation over subsequent generations.

Let us imagine that the Supreme Court today is asked to decide a case involving blacks and public education, much like *Brown v. Board of Education*,[9] which held that separate but equal education is inherently unconstitutional. Should the justices look to the framers' abstract intentions (their basic value concepts) or to their concrete intentions (what they understood the world to be like)? The question becomes important in contexts where the framers did not write into the Constitution their concrete beliefs but gave only abstract expressions (such as equal protection of the laws) of what they intended. The question is further complicated if all our empirical evidence shows that certain of the framers' concrete understandings of the world (such as their beliefs about the marginal humanity of negro slaves) were seriously mistaken.

In *The Tempting of America*, Bork states that the decision in *Brown v. Board of Education* was necessary to insure equality and that this becomes apparent once one realizes that the only choice is between equality and segregation.[10] To stay in keeping with his notion of original intent, Bork claims that the deeper purpose of the Fourteenth Amendment requires this result. But if *Brown* can be justified on what is essentially a principle of morality, why not other rights? No justification could be based in a private morality, for that varies from person to person and group to group and does not involve the kind of neutral principles necessary for governing a pluralistic society. Still, if Bork can find a public morality for *Brown*, why can there not be a public morality for privacy? For example, should there not be a justification to use contraceptives, to allow a woman the right to choose an abortion, or to allow lesbian and gay persons the right to engage in intimate and fulfilling sexual relations in the home?

If *Brown* is indeed distinguished from these other areas, it cannot be because the decision was well received when it was handed down. At that time, much of society had not yet come to accept desegregated schools, nor would they for some time thereafter.[11] Moreover, there would be little concern for why the *Brown* decision was right (beyond a professorial interest) if the majority of society had accepted the decision at the time. If Bork can accept the *Brown* decision, why does he object to courts' considering philosophical discussions on privacy issues?[12] It appears that Bork is able to pick and choose according to his own political agenda, independent of any theory (liberal or conservative) of judicial interpretation.

There are many constitutional interpretation cases like *Brown* in which the Constitution provides only abstract intentions as a basis for deciding the case. Consequently, we should not try to decide these cases by guessing which intentions (abstract or concrete) the framers might have wanted the justices to consider when making decisions. Indeed, it does not appear that the framers had in mind the type of intention that was to guide constitutional interpretations. Whether or not they did is unimportant. Why be so concerned about the framers' intention at all? Why not simply adopt the interpretation that provides the best fit with that portion of the existing law taken as settled or, as a matter of political morality, which reproduces the rights people actually have? After all, most people will assent to the elaboration of an idea (even in a way they may not previously have thought) if they believe that it more exactly captures what they were originally aiming at, not necessarily what they may have specifically had in mind.[13] The point is that there is a choice about which theory of interpretation to follow. When a judge adopts a particular theory of interpretation, he or she is making a substantive political decision based on a particular conception of representative government. Consequently, the question of which conception should be chosen is properly a question for political inquiry and debate. This does not entail that such a question need necessarily be unanswerable. All that it entails is that the determination of the answer need not, as Bork seems to think, be governed by the concrete intentions of the framers.

In light of this, it makes sense to argue that a justice of the Supreme Court should not try to deduce concrete intentions not stated in the Constitution. Our conception of human nature has changed since the framers' days. Psychology, sociology, political science, and anthropology have given us a much better sense of what we are. With this picture has come a different understanding of society and of how human beings live in society. The old concepts are still with us, but the knowledge we have acquired since the days of the Founding Fathers has given us a deeper appreciation of them. Consequently, the views that might have led the framers to think of Afro-Americans as less than full persons and women as the property of men are no longer appropriate. What has changed is not so much values (given a sufficient degree of generality) as our understanding of how to apply those values.

This is particularly true for lesbians and gay men, for whom the principal constitutional questions are of privacy and of equal protection under the laws. If there are sound reasons for thinking that adults' consensual sexual acts do not impinge on the rights of others (as I will and others have argued), then such acts are not the business of the state. Indeed, it would be morally and legally wrong for the Supreme Court not to extend the protection of the right to privacy to lesbians and gay men. To say (as Bork would probably say) that this is not what the framers had in mind misses the distinction between abstract and concrete beliefs and overlooks a history of psychological and sociological insight into the nature of the human condition. At the same time, this position ignores the fact that our theories of constitutional interpretation are inevitably political. Bork ignored such questions and became an unacceptable candidate for the Supreme Court. I choose not to ignore these issues. I will approach the subject of privacy first from the point of view of what the law is and then from what it should be.

PART
ONE
THEORY

THE OBJECTS OF
LEGAL PRIVACY

1

Can a gay or lesbian person validly claim that the constitutional right to privacy is violated when he or she is forced from a job because of sexual orientation or when the state enacts a sodomy statute prohibiting sexual relations among same-sex individuals? Does a person with AIDS or a person who is HIV positive have the constitutional right not to be forced into quarantine or to have his or her body tattooed or name included on a governmental list of infected and potentially dangerous individuals if no other person is endangered? Does a woman have the constitutional right to privacy to have an abortion? Should an employee be able to refuse drug and polygraph tests, at least when he or she is not in a sensitive position requiring split-second judgments that affect life or property? Should a person be able to view pornographic material in exclusively adult settings? These questions and many others have been and will continue to be before the courts. One reason they are so controversial is that we do not have a clear understanding of the scope and content of privacy or why we are justified in protecting it as a right.

Analyzing Privacy

After a century of development of the right to privacy in American law, the parameters of privacy and the arguments for its protection are still unclear. Never has this problem been more acute than in the past twenty years when the law of privacy has been interpreted to protect not only certain states of affairs but also certain human actions. In this period, the Supreme Court first recognized a married couple's right to obtain contraceptives,[1] a person's right to possess pornography in his or her home,[2] and a woman's right to an abortion.[3] The problem is that these cases do not appear prima facie to have anything in common with prior privacy cases in the areas of the Fourth Amendment and tort law. Consequently, it is unclear what makes these cases privacy cases. Similarly, it is unclear what criteria should be relied upon when classifying a new case as a privacy case. Yet the Supreme Court has held that the right being asserted in each of these cases was privacy. What justification, if any, could the Court have for grouping these very different kinds of cases under the single rubric "privacy"? The search for a justification is the search for a method to decide cases not yet before a court and to evaluate decisions the courts have already made.

Since privacy is a right that one person claims against another or claims against the government and not a duty owed to society imposed by statute or case law, it will help to begin this discussion with a more general understanding of what is meant by a right. To this end, I follow Alan Gewirth (with one amendment that will be explained shortly), who treats discussions about rights as discussions concerning one or more aspects of the following paradigm:

A has a right to X against B by virtue of Y[4]

This is an appropriate paradigm to use in this analysis because it allows us not only to specify the various actors who are involved in a privacy claim but also to separate what the claim is about from the justification for the claim.

According to Gewirth, A represents the subject of the right, X the object, B the respondent, and Y the reason or justification for asserting the right. This view is similar to the position taken by Joel Feinberg that rights are a kind of claim against persons, except that it leaves open the possibility of rights against institutions (for example, government) or persons in their institutional capacities only (for example, judges or prosecutors). On the other hand, the view is substantially different from the position taken by McCloskey and Robert Nozick, who treat rights essentially as entitlements (that is, as rights *to* rather than rights *against*).[5] Certainly, legal rights are also rights against, and privacy, in the way we will deal with it, is a legal right. Since privacy is a right that courts have recognized against persons and institutions, the most useful perspective for us is the Gewirthian one. Applying his paradigm to the questions asked at the outset, we get

Gay/lesbian person		
Person with AIDS		(state)
A woman	has a right to privacy against	(employer)
An employee		(other person)
A person at home		

where the specification of the privacy right will vary with the issue under consideration. Examples would include not to be fired from a job because one is openly gay or lesbian, not to be prohibited from engaging in same-sex sexual relations in the home, to have an abortion, and not to be forced by one's employer to take a drug or polygraph test. Still, it is apparent that the paradigm is insufficient, for it does not tell us anything about the nature of the right being claimed or in what setting the right is recognized.[6] To rectify this limitation, we can modify the paradigm at "a right." The substitute phrase preferred here because of its greater precision might be termed a "U-V right," where U means the institutional setting in which the right is based and V the type of right that is being claimed.

The significance of this substitution can be seen by comparing two situations in which very different kinds of rights are being asserted. In the first situation, Ted and Jim are walking down the street.[7] At about the same time, they both notice a ten-dollar bill lying on the pavement. Each decides to pick up the bill and in doing so lays claim to the right to pick it up. Yet both Ted and Jim are making the same claim, with presumably the same justification. Consequently, nothing inherent in either claim puts the other under an obligation or duty to refrain from interfering or to assist his counterpart in retrieving the ten dollars. If that is true, then what kind of right is the right to pick up the ten dollars? It cannot be anything more than what Wesley Hohfeld describes as a privilege—that is, both A and B are at liberty (free) to pick up the ten dollars.[8]

The claim in this situation is very different from the claim that is asserted when Jane claims the right to have an abortion. In this second situation, Jane's claim is intended to prescribe certain very definite duties on the state, namely, to refrain from interfering with her action. If that is true, then the right Jane is claiming is substantially different from the right described in the first situation. Consequently, one is inclined to speak of Jane as having asserted a claim-right, that is, a right from which duties follow,[9] to distinguish it from the above liberty-right.

Applying the paradigm to the situations specified at the outset of this chapter, we see that what is asserted is a claim-right. For in each of the situations cited, the person intends to be generally free from the intrusion of either the state or other persons to exercise those rights. In other words, the person expects others to be under a duty not to interfere with his or her privacy.

Still, claims like those asserted above also have to be made from within an institutional setting, the second element in the U-V configuration. By institutional setting is meant the complete set of principles, precedents, and methods of analysis usually assumed in the context of a given institution, such as etiquette, law, or (depending upon what one means by institution) possibly morality, that provide the justification for a rights claim. For example, the institutional setting of the law in the United States includes the federal and state constitutions, statutes, cases, administrative rules, ordinances, authoritative treatises, and judicial interpretations. The institutional setting differs from the justification of the right in that the latter refers to the specific reason or reasons that lead one to believe, within the given institutional context, that the right in question really does obtain. For fundamental constitutional rights, as will be shown below, the justification may extend beyond a strictly legal theory of fit (to existing cases) to encompass political morality.

Gewirth's paradigm now takes the following form:

A has a U-V right to X against B by virtue of Y.

Applying it to our original privacy assertions, we note that each has the nature of a claim-right and that, where the state is the respondent, the institutional context is usually constitutional law. Privacy claims against private persons appear in other legal areas. Still to be specified, however, is the justificatory basis for these right claims within their various institutional contexts.

Two questions remain. First, in the situation of Jane's claiming the right to an abortion, why did B translate into *state?* The answer to this question lies in the fact that the institutional setting for her claim was the Constitution, not merely the law. This suggests that Jane had an interest in being protected against a form of intrusion by the state only. Perhaps the state had passed a statute prohibiting abortions. In that case, only an appeal to a higher law (the Constitution) could overturn the state statute. In other words, constitutional rights are claimed against the government directly or against a person or group acting under color of law. Consequently, it is safe to assume that B will mean state, referring to some government policy, statute, rule, or regulation, whenever a constitutional right is asserted. Second, the amended analysis still does not clarify the basis upon which the courts classified various objects (types of cases) as falling under the rubric privacy, nor does it specify what other objects might also be classified under privacy. To understand the kinds of cases that courts have grouped under this term, we first turn to the extension of the legal concept of privacy. (The distinction between term and concept is not important here.)

It might be thought that the right to privacy here is nothing more than the right to act as the winning party did in those cases that afforded it recognition. But this is to rob privacy of its legitimacy as a legal concept capable of giving direction to courts when deciding new cases and to scholars when critiquing past cases. To avoid triviality and to lend legal legitimacy to privacy, it is necessary to treat not only the extension of the concept as used in this context but also the reasons that courts have offered, especially when the concept was extended to new areas of the law. In this way, we might isolate, at least from the core cases that make up the general law of privacy, the element(s) that underlie all of them and that will give us the full range of possible privacy cases.

What is at issue is the conceptual content of privacy, or what in the alternative H. L. A. Hart calls the clear instances of the application of the concept.[10] Presumably, once the clear instances are found, we will be in a better position to judge whether the courts justifiably applied the concept to the penumbral hard cases. The reason for looking to case law rather than consulting a legal treatise for a definition is that in this area (unlike statutory law) there are no preexisting definitions. One discovers what the law is primarily by reading the cases that have interpreted it.

What we discover, however, and what makes this inquiry interesting is that the legal concept of privacy (as determined from case law) has no obvious content that might link a single set of so-called clear instances. As will be made clear shortly, privacy appears on the surface to be a set of seemingly independent objects when viewed from within the developing case law. But then the question arises, On what basis are the courts justified in holding that these objects fall under the rubric privacy? Certainly, some justification is necessary if the law in this area is not to be viewed as the arbitrary and capricious whims of judges. But exactly what sort of justification will work is not apparent. Indeed, that the courts have failed to offer adequate justification becomes clear from a historical analysis of the development of the law in this area.

Before attempting such an analysis, we should note that the legal concept of privacy differs from the adjectival use of the word *private*. While the latter term is used to qualify certain definite objects, conditions, or circumstances (such as private persons and private property), the former (as will be shown below) captures a portion of the state of liberty or freedom, only one of which the law happens to create. Consequently, any overlapping of the two uses is not the result of a necessary relationship between the two. Instead, in the expression of a judicial or (less common) legislative policy, the former may take account of the latter.

Historical Antecedents

The modern term *privacy* has its roots in *privatus*,[11] the Latin word meaning "apart from the state; peculiar to one's self; of or belonging to an individual; private."[12] More recent derivations of the term seem no more precise. Indeed, one of the problems in tracing the history of the legal concept of privacy is determining exactly what is being sought. This becomes clear in contemporary parlance, where the word *privacy* appears to have a wider extension with no single definition that connects the various uses. As a consequence, tracing the history of the legal concept of privacy means tracing the history of the various modern uses of the word, with no obvious connection between the two.

Take, for instance, one of the specific constitutional provisions the Supreme Court has referred to as a "privacy" provision, namely, the Fourth Amendment restriction on governmental searches and seizures.[13] Adopted in 1791, this provision of the Bill of Rights states:

The right of the people to be secure in their persons, houses, papers, and effects, against unreasonable searches and seizures, shall not be violated, and no warrants shall issue, but upon probable cause, supported by oath or affidavit and particularly describing the place to be searched, and the persons or things to be seized.[14]

The amendment has its roots in two areas of the common law: Magna Carta and the 1604 *Semayne* case.[15] Chapter thirty-nine of Magna Carta provides: "No freeman shall be taken or (and) imprisoned or disseized or exiled or in any way destroyed, nor will we go upon him nor send upon him, except by the lawful judgment of his peers or (and) by the law of the land."[16] On its face, the chapter appears to be more protective of individual liberty than privacy, at least in its common meaning. Nevertheless, it does seem to be asserting the existence of a right somewhat analogous to that found in the Fourth Amendment. For by guaranteeing to every freeman security from being arrested or imprisoned without due process of law, the chapter is essentially recognizing the independence (i.e., privacy) of every freeman from the state.

In a related manner, the 1604 *Semayne* case is also a privacy case. That case involved an attempted execution by the sheriff on the personal property of a decedent judgment-debtor. The joint-tenant survivor of the house in which the property was located refused to let the sheriff inside. The court, per Lord Coke, held that the sheriff's failure to afford prior notice of his arrival to the joint tenant made the refusal of admission lawful. From the privacy standpoint, what is significant is that the court reached its decision by relying on the principle

that the house of everyone is to him his castle and fortress, as well as his defense against injury and violence, as for his repose; and although the life of a man is a thing precious and favoured in the law so that, although a man kills another in his defense, or kills one per infortunium [by misfortune] without any intent, yet it is a felony, and in such case he shall forfeit his goods and chattels for the great regard the law has to a man's life, but if thieves come to a man's house to rob him, or murder, and the owner or his servants kill any of the thieves in defense of himself and his house it is not a felony, and he shall lose nothing.[17]

Thus, the *Semayne* case recognized in *dicta* the extension of individual independence from the state to the house in which one resides.

In addition to justifying the criminal punishments of burglary, arson, nuisance, and eavesdropping, William Blackstone lends credence to the rule that the state could not have the doors to a person's house broken down in order to execute any civil process. In the *Commentaries on the Laws of England*,[18] published between 1765 and 1767, Blackstone writes:

And the law of England has so particular and tender a regard to the immunity of a man's house, that it stiles it his castle, and will never suffer it to be violated with impunity; agreeing herein with the sentiments of ancient Rome, as expressed in the words of Tully: "*quid enim sanctius, quid anni religione munitius, quam domus uniuscujusque civium.*"[19]

The key language, "never suffer it to be violated with impunity," suggests that the law of England, at least as Blackstone understood it, regarded a person's house as so deserving of deference that even the state could not violate it without justification. Since presumably this notion of a limitation on the authority of the state arose at a time when the state was regarded as having a great deal more authority than is generally accepted today, the idea was significant for future development of the legal relationship of the individual to the state.

In like manner, various nineteenth-century American courts, echoing Blackstone's sentiments, held that there is no authority to break down the doors of a house in the execution of civil process,[20] and that the dwelling house is "the place of family repose."[21] Thus, by the end of the seventeenth century in England, and the end of the nineteenth century in the United States, a legal definition of privacy had begun to take hold in both criminal and civil laws. What was less recognized in the United States, at least until the end of the last decade of the nineteenth century, was that significantly different cases in the area of tort law were also becoming thought of as privacy cases.

Although this may have represented a broadening of what the courts would be willing to consider privacy cases, it was not until 1890 that, in the area of torts, any attention was paid in the United States to the idea that there might exist a general right to privacy. In that year Samuel D. Warren and Louis D. Brandeis published the seminal article that was to provide the foundation for recognizing a torts right to privacy.[22] In fact, what concerned Warren and Brandeis were technological inventions (like instantaneous photography) that made it possible for newspapers and similar media "to invade the sacred precincts of private and domestic life."[23] Previously, some members of the legal community had felt that the law ought to provide protection against the unauthorized circulation of portraits of private persons. The necessity for protection became more evident with the rise in the number of reported instances in which the press seemed to act beyond the bounds of propriety and decency. Warren and Brandeis argue in the article that a right to privacy is implicit in the common law; indeed, these men recognized that individual thoughts, sentiments, and emotions should be judged not in terms of private property rights (as was often claimed in prior common law cases) but in terms of a right that protected an "inviolate personality."[24]

A man records in a letter to his son, or in his diary, that he did not dine with his wife on a certain day. No one into whose hands those papers fell could publish them to the world, even if possession of those documents had been obtained rightfully; and the prohibition would not be confined to the publication of a copy of the letter itself, or of the diary entry; the restraint extends also to the publication of the contents.[25]

Once this new right was unpacked, the rest was obvious. After going on to show that any narrower grounds for explaining the court decisions in this area are faulty, Warren and Brandeis stated:

these considerations lead to the conclusion that the protection afforded to thoughts, sentiments, and emotions, expressed through the medium of writing or of the arts, so far as it consists in preventing publication, is merely an instance of the enforcement of the more general right of the individual to be let alone.[26]

The key phrase here is "the more general right of the individual to be let alone." The phrase is significant because if this is the current legal definition of privacy, as seems to be true from the article, then two important issues are raised. First, if a general right to be let alone is now to replace the specific right against the state previously recognized, then there must be someone or something in addition to the state against whom this right can be asserted. In other words, there must exist a correlative duty on some respondent or respondents other than the state to leave the claimant alone. Indeed, because what is being talked about here is a general right to privacy, the new set of respondents includes all other persons, including the state. In other words, the concept of privacy, which when first recognized from the Latin had the meaning "apart from the state," has since been broadened to mean also "apart from all other persons." But the second issue now arises of specifying exactly what the objects are about which a person can legitimately claim a right to be left alone.

Consequently, with the development of even this much of a definition, the courts began to specify those things to which the right legitimately attached. For example, the courts began to place restraints on how far the press could intrude into the private lives or affairs of individuals. They also began to consider prohibiting the commercial exploitation of someone's likeness without authorization.[27] What is of more significance is that this right, which came to be recognized after the Warren and Brandeis article, had its root in an extension of the common-law tradition that proclaimed one's house to be one's castle[28] and prohibited prying into another's unopened mail[29] or obtaining individual census data.[30]

Just as the Fourth Amendment view of privacy appears to differ from that of tort law, recent Supreme Court decisions recognizing a right to privacy in a woman's decision to have an abortion[31] and a married person's decision to obtain contraceptives[32] appear to differ from both of the others. There is no obvious connection between these cases and those the courts have previously described as privacy cases with respect to either their subject matter or the provisions of the law relied upon to justify the decisions. Although one important similarity with the Fourth Amendment cases is that each of these new cases also represents a claim by an individual or couple against the state, the differences warrant the view that the right to privacy was again extended. Even so, this right, which has been recognized only in the last two decades, was implied as early as 1928 in a Supreme Court dissenting opinion. In that year the Supreme Court decided *Omstead v. United States*,[33] in which Brandeis (now Justice) dissented by pointing out that yet another version of the privacy right was inherent in the law.

The case involved an alleged conspiracy to violate the National Prohibition Act by unlawfully importing, possessing, transporting, and selling intoxicating liquors. The evidence that led to the discovery of the conspiracy was obtained by the interception of telephone messages. One question on appeal was whether the method by which the evidence was obtained constituted a search or seizure within the meaning of the Fourth Amendment. The Court, per Justice Taft, held that it did not, stating, among other things: "The [Fourth] Amendment does not prohibit what was done here. There was no searching. There was no seizure. The evidence was secured by the sense of hearing and that only. There was no entry of the houses or offices of the defendant."[34] In dissent, Justice Brandeis countered with a view, for which historical evidence was scanty at best, that foreshadowed the development of this area of privacy law.

The protection guaranteed by the [Fourth and Fifth] Amendments is much broader in scope. The makers of our Constitution undertook to secure conditions favorable to the pursuit of happiness. They recognized the significance of man's spiritual nature, of his feelings and of his intellect. They knew that only a part of the pain, pleasure and satisfactions of life are to be found in material things. They sought to protect Americans in their beliefs, their thoughts, their emotions and their sensations. They conferred as against the Government, the right to be let alone—the most comprehensive of rights and the right most valued by civilized men.[35]

The argument presented by Justice Brandeis in 1928 was to have a long incubation period before it emerged as the law of the land. Granted that other cases eventually picked up the idea that the Fourth Amendment should be extended to cover wiretaps and similar sorts of privacy invasions, but these cases all dealt with the regulation of searches and seizures.[36] Although these cases did delimit the realm of illicit governmental intrusion as at least in part what one could reasonably expect to keep private,[37] certainly no more general concept of privacy emerged until in 1965 the Court decided *Griswold v. Connecticut*.[38]

In *Griswold* the Court considered whether the state of Connecticut could by statute prohibit married couples from obtaining contraceptives and licensed physicians from giving information on their use. The Court, per Justice Douglas, held that the provision was violative of the Constitution.

Various [Bill of Rights] guarantees create zones of privacy. The right of association contained in the penumbra of the First Amendment is one, as we have seen. The Third Amendment in its prohibition against the quartering of soldiers "in any house" in time of peace without the consent of the owner is another facet of that privacy. The Fourth Amendment explicitly affirms the "right of the people to be secure in their persons, papers, and effects, against unreasonable searches and seizures." The Fifth Amendment in its Self-Incrimination Clause enables the citizen to create a zone of privacy which government may not force him to surrender to his detriment. The Ninth Amendment provides: "The enumeration in the Constitution, of certain rights, shall not be construed to deny or disparage others retained by the people."[39]

The decision was controversial even among some of the justices who voted with Douglas, in part because grounding the decision reminded the justices of the difficult and embarrassing time the Court had had in developing the law of substantive due process.[40] Certainly, one of the motives that Douglas must have had for grounding the constitutional right to privacy in the penumbra of certain of the Bill of Rights was to avoid having to ground it in substantive due process.

Even so, some justices thought that Douglas's idea of zones of privacy could not justify the right to privacy that was being recognized. These justices suggested alternative groundings either in the Ninth Amendment[41] or in a concept of ordered liberty implicit in the Fourteenth Amendment due process clause.[42] The differences in how the right should be grounded were accompanied by differences over what the right should mean, the significance of which will be explained more fully in the next section.

For instance, Justice Goldberg, citing an earlier case in his argument to ground the right to privacy in the Ninth Amendment, stated:

Adultery, homosexuality and the like are sexual intimacies which the State forbids . . . but the intimacies of husband and wife are necessarily an essential and accepted part of the institution of marriage, an institution which the state not only must allow, but which always and in every age it has fostered and protected.[43]

Despite the problematic use of the word *must*, Goldberg's claim appears compatible with Douglas's further statement:

We deal with a right of privacy older than the Bill of Rights—older than our political parties, older than our school system. Marriage is the coming together for better or worse, hopefully enduring, and intimate to the degree of being sacred. It is an association that promotes a way of life, not political faiths; a bilateral loyalty, not commercial or social projects. Yet, it is an association for as noble a purpose as any involved in our prior decisions.[44]

In contrast, Justice Harlan's concurring opinion grounded the right to privacy in the Fourteenth Amendment due process clause. It is arguable whether his view of the Fourteenth Amendment, which is based at least in part on an earlier case that sought to protect the "basic values 'implicit in the concept of ordered liberty,'"[45] provides the same limitations on extending the right beyond the marriage relationship that Goldberg discusses.

The point of raising this controversy is to show that the Supreme Court, at the time it first recognized a constitutional dimension of this right, did not have a consensus (beyond the case at hand) as to which objects the right should protect. What is even more significant is that the cases since *Griswold* still do not indicate a clear consensus about the objects to which the newly recognized constitutional right to privacy applies. Is there only one object at stake or are there two or more objects involved? Of this, more will be said below.

Privacy in the Law Today

It has been assumed that the field of law relevant to discussions about privacy can be divided along traditional lines into three distinct areas, namely, Fourth Amendment, torts, and constitutional. While clear distinctions between the Fourth Amendment and constitutional areas are not easy to draw, in general the following seems apparent: The Fourth Amendment area (which, strictly speaking, is part of constitutional law) concerns certain procedural restrictions on the state's gathering of evidence, whereas constitutional law is more concerned with the correct interpretation of the original constitutional text, as well as the cases that have interpreted it. Both areas differ from torts in that they are concerned with rights claims against any of the various governmental entities, whereas torts law is concerned with rights claims against one or more persons. In light of the historical development discussed in the previous section and the possibility of a tripartite division of the law relative to privacy, the claim that the right to privacy recognized by the law in the United States today manifests itself uniquely in at least three different areas of the law (namely, Fourth Amendment, torts, and constitutional) should not be surprising. Indeed, that the right is separately grounded in each of these three areas can be made explicit by considering only the principal or most typical cases in each area.

FOURTH AMENDMENT PRIVACY
Two 1967 cases essentially set the direction for how the Fourth Amendment area of the law was to develop. These cases under-

mined the objective approach taken by Justice Taft in *Omstead v. United States*[46] for determining when a breach of privacy existed. In its place they substituted a subjective approach that relied upon what the persons involved expected would remain private, as long as the expectations were reasonable relative to the surrounding circumstances. Thus, in *Berger v. New York*,[47] the Court struck down a state statute that allowed an *ex parte* order for eavesdropping, even though the statute required that there first be a reasonable belief that evidence of a crime might be obtained.

The case arose out of an investigation by the New York City district attorney's office into allegations, especially those of Ralph Pansini, that agents of the New York State Liquor Authority accepted bribes before issuing liquor licenses. At the direction of the district attorney's office, Pansini was equipped with a miniature transmitting device and told to interview an employee of the authority. Based on the information obtained from that interview, the district attorney obtained a bugging order. Thirty days later, a second order, similar to the first, was issued based on evidence obtained as a result of the first order. There was no question that the evidence gathered at each stage supported a reasonable belief that further evidence of a crime would be gathered at a later stage. What seemed questionable was whether the statute permitted "a trespassory [i.e., an unexpected and unwanted] invasion of the home or office, by general warrant contrary to the command of the fourth amendment."[48]

The Court, per Justice Clark, held that it did and thus brought within the zone of sanctuary those telephone wires that Chief Justice Taft had earlier excluded in *Omstead*. But the point was not that henceforth telephone wires should always be included along with "persons, houses, papers and effects." The point was, as one commentator has pointed out, that the Court took note of the increase in the "number of telephones in the country, and the convenient change in status from luxurious business equipment to necessity of modern life."[49] In other words, the Court had shown a willingness to consider expectations or privacy, as implied by the phrase *trespassory invasion*, in determining the scope of Fourth Amendment sanctuary.

That this notion would be the foundation for this area of the law in the future was made clear in the landmark decision *Katz v. United States.*[50] In *Katz*, the petitioner had been convicted under an eight-count indictment for "transmitting wagering information by telephone from Los Angeles to Miami and Boston, in violation of federal statute."[51] The evidence on which the conviction was based had been obtained by FBI agents by attaching an electronic eavesdropping device to the outside of a public telephone booth. In holding that the FBI had violated the petitioner's Fourth Amendment rights, the Court, per Justice Stewart, stated: "What a person knowingly exposes to the public, even in his own home or office, is not a subject of Fourth Amendment protection. But what he seeks to preserve as private, even in an area accessible to the public, may be constitutionally protected."[52] Thus, *Katz* established that the zone of Fourth Amendment sanctuary extends as far as a court would consider a reasonable person to expect.

Since *Katz*, other cases have determined how far one could actually expect this zone of privacy to extend. In *United States v. White,*[53] for example, the Court held that the zone does not extend to an individual voluntarily confided in who is in league with the state. Nor does it extend to conversations an individual might have with his or her brother while in jail, as in *Lanz v. New York.*[54] The point of this chapter, however, is not to address subtle questions about the scope of the right but to note that the object of privacy in this area is tied to the idea of expectation, as in what a court might think is a reasonable expectation of privacy. With one important exception, the same is not true in the torts area.

THE TORT AREA OF PRIVACY
In the torts area, William Prosser has categorized privacy decisions as falling under four headings, "without any attempt to exact definition."[55] Most of the cases under these headings arise because of an action by one person against another. Some cases, however, arise because a state or the federal government acts to either promote or restrain what otherwise would be common-law privacy protections. Where this happens, the privacy issue may take on constitutional significance if the complaining party can also show a violation of a constitutional guarantee, such as freedom of speech or the press. The headings are:

1. Intrusion upon the plaintiff's seclusion or solitude, or into his private affairs.
2. Public disclosure of embarrassing facts about the plaintiff.
3. Publicity which places the plaintiff in a false light in the public eye.
4. Appropriation, for the defendant's advantage, of plaintiff's name or likeness.[56]

The first heading is an example of the use of the word *private* independent of the word *privacy*, which reflects a policy decision to protect only certain kinds of affairs. Of this, more will be said below as we discuss significant cases under each of the four headings.

Under the first heading—intrusion upon the plaintiff's seclusion or solitude, or into his private affairs—three cases stand out as typical of where the Court has drawn the line between permissible state action and constitutional infringement. The first case, *Martin v. Struthers*,[57] involved an industrial community, the city of Struthers, where many inhabitants worked at night and slept during the day. The city of Struthers had passed an ordinance banning knocking on doors or ringing doorbells for the purpose of delivering handbills. The appellant delivered a leaflet inviting the recipient to a religious meeting. For this, she was convicted of criminal trespass and fined ten dollars. On appeal, the Supreme Court held, per Justice Black, that because a less drastic ordinance, such as one requiring the homeowner to hang out a DO NOT DISTURB sign before a leaflet carrier could be convicted of criminal trespass, would have accomplished the legislative purpose, the city's action in promoting the wider ban placed too much of a restriction on the exercise of First Amendment rights.

The situation is different, however, where a municipality passes an ordinance banning solicitation only at private residences (as opposed to commercial establishments) of orders for the purchase of goods. *Breard v. Alexandria*[58] differed from *Martin v. Struthers* in that now the Court saw "the living right of [people] to privacy [in the sense of being left alone] and repose"[59] as more important than the financial gain of commercial vendors. Thus, the Court showed a willingness to allow a municipality to protect a right to repose even if doing so meant narrowing the range of the First Amendment.

On a related point, the Court also held that the privacy one is entitled to in the home does not accompany one on public buses. Therefore, the Court in *Public Utilities Commission v. Pollack*[60] rejected the claim by some passengers on a District of Columbia bus that their right to privacy under the First and Fifth Amendments was violated because the buses carried FM receivers that broadcast music, news, and occasional commercial advertising, which the passengers did not want to hear.[61] Since the majority assumed that the Public Utilities Commission, a governmental agency, had permitted the Capital Transit's practice of operating the radio service, it felt that sufficient federal government action had been involved for it to consider whether the company had overstepped constitutional restraints.

Under the second category—public disclosure of embarrassing facts about the plaintiff—two cases are especially enlightening. The first, *Melvin v. Reid*,[62] involved Gabrielle Darley, a former prostitute who had been involved as a defendant in a murder trial. After her acquittal, Darley gave up prostitution and married. Seven years later, a motion picture entitled *The Red Kimono*, which portrayed Darley's life, was made and distributed. The California Appellate Court held that Darley had a cause of action for invasion of her privacy under California's constitution. That constitution guaranteed to each person an inalienable right to pursue and obtain happiness, and the Court, considering the necessity to protect against prejudice and irrationality, held privacy to be a part of that inalienable right. Since *Melvin*, other cases in California and elsewhere have recognized this invasion of privacy as a tort and have to some extent set its limits.

Perhaps the most famous of these cases is *Sidis v. F-R Publishing Co.*[63] In that case, plaintiff was an infant prodigy who had graduated from Harvard at age sixteen and at age eleven had lectured to eminent mathematicians on the fourth dimension. After suffering a psychological breakdown, he disappeared from the public eye and began collecting streetcar transfers and studying the lore of the Okamakammessett Indians. Some years later, *New Yorker* magazine sought him out and featured an article detailing his career and present whereabouts. The feature had devastating consequences; it was alleged that the story may have contributed to Sidis's early death. Still, the court held that there was no cause of action since the case involved the privilege of reporting on matters of public interest, and there was nothing in the story that would have been objectionable to a "normal" person.

How are these two cases related? Prosser suggests that what emerges is something like a "mores" test. That is, the courts will recognize a cause of action only where the publicity involved concerns "those things which the customs and ordinary views of the community will not tolerate."[64]

Concerning Prosser's third category—publicity that places the plaintiff in a false light in the public eye—it seems less obvious exactly how this is a privacy doctrine. Nor have the courts been particularly helpful in making clear exactly what the privacy concern is in these cases. Still, if we are not to conclude that Prosser and the courts were misguided in considering this a privacy doctrine, we can assume they considered the doctrine to be one of "being let alone" from the effects of a false reputation or false publicity. In this light, two points should be noted. The first is that the wrong done must involve a falsification either negligent or intentional, and the second is that it must place an identifiable individual before the public eye.[65]

Perhaps the best-known case in which this tort was recognized was *Lord Byron v. Johnston*,[66] which involved the affixing of Byron's name to a poem that he did not write. (It has been said that even in a stupor he could not have written it.) The English court held that the case was actionable and enjoined circulation of the poem. Since *Byron*, similar conclusions have been drawn in other cases. A limit is found where the courts, acting in light of their own understanding of the customs and practices of society, determine that it is no longer reasonable to expect that one's privacy in regard to what one says or does (or even in terms of who one is) is secure. This is the exception in the torts area mentioned earlier.

This exception was recognized in the case of *Time, Inc. v. Hill*.[67] In that case, a family had the misfortune of being held hostage in their own home by three escaped convicts. The incident inspired a novel and a play. *Life* magazine printed a story about the play, depicting the infliction of violence on the hostages. In fact, no such violence had been inflicted. On these facts,

Hill won a judgment against the magazine under a New York statute that allows such actions whenever the article lacks newsworthiness or is materially and substantially false.[68] The Supreme Court, per Justice Brennan, reversed, holding that the test to be applied in cases where the constitutional freedoms of speech and press are concerned is whether the report was published "with knowledge of [its] falsity or in reckless disregard of the truth."[69] Justice Douglas, in his concurring opinion, also pointed out that "such privacy as a person normally has ceases when his life has ceased to be private."[70] The clear implication of Douglas's remark seems to be that the right to privacy is attached to the expectations one has in living life when outside the public eye. Or to put the point in a different way, it is a right whose object is now defined in terms of being let alone to pursue life as one sees fit.

The last of Prosser's headings—appropriation, for the defendant's advantage, of plaintiff's name or likeness—has to some extent already been dealt with. Although it is not a hard and fast rule, commercial exploitation of some aspect of a person's identity (where there is no mitigating public interest) is less likely to be protected by the courts than other forms of privacy. The *Roberson* case,[71] for example, involved a woman whose likeness had been taken against her will to adorn advertising for a certain "Flour of the Family." The New York Court of Appeals ruled in favor of the defendant on the ground that there was no precedent that allowed the plaintiff to recover. The case caused such a controversy that shortly after the decision the New York legislature passed a privacy statute that afforded protection against commercial exploitation. Many other states have since followed suit.

This brief review of the torts area suggests that the right to privacy, as used here, is, or at least should be, thought of as the right to be let alone to pursue one's life as one sees fit. Moreover, it seems that the right ranges over the four distinct categories of cases or objects that Prosser identifies (namely, repose, selective disclosure, false light, and commercial exploitation). Perhaps more than four objects can be distinguished. Even so, since the point of this analysis is to show that among the different areas of the law, privacy ranges over different objects, the subtle divisions of objects within any particular area need not be discussed in full.

CONSTITUTIONAL PRIVACY

A very different object is found in the line of constitutional cases beginning with *Griswold v. Connecticut*.[72] Earlier, it was noted that in *Griswold* the Court recognized a right to privacy attaching to a married couple's decision to use and secure information on how to use contraceptives. Seven years later, the Court decided *Eisenstadt v. Baird*.[73] That case involved the question of whether the state could prohibit distribution of contraceptives to unmarried persons. A lecture on contraception had been given to a group of students at Boston University, after which a young unmarried woman was given a package of Emko vaginal foam. The State of Massachusetts alleged that the transfer of contraceptives violated a state law prohibiting such transfers to unmarried persons. The Court, per Justice Brennan, held that the statute violated the rights of single persons under the Fourteenth Amendment's equal protection clause. In reaching its decision, the Court, citing an earlier case, noted: "A classification 'must be reasonable, not arbitrary, and must rest upon some ground of difference having a fair and substantial relation to the object of the legislation, so that all persons similarly circumstanced shall be treated alike.' "[74] It also notes that "if under *Griswold* the distribution of contraceptives to married persons cannot be prohibited, a ban on distribution to unmarried persons would be equally impermissible."[75] While the Court acknowledged that *Griswold* did involve a right to privacy inherent in the marital relationship, it went on to say:

The married couple is not an independent entity with a mind and heart of its own, but an association of two individuals each with a separate intellectual and emotional makeup. If the right of privacy means anything, it is the right of the *individual*, married or single, to be free from unwarranted governmental intrusion into matters so fundamentally affecting a person as the decision whether to bear or beget a child.[76]

The quoted passage suggests that privacy is a kind of negative freedom, that those who hold that freedom encompass a wider class than married persons, and that the kinds of interferences that are prohibited are those that would affect the choice of whether to bear or beget a child.

In essence, what *Eisenstadt* did was to further clarify the meaning of privacy in the area of intimate decisions. It also set the stage for one of the Court's most controversial decisions. In the next term, the Court was to decide whether or not a woman's right to privacy included the decision to obtain an abortion.

In *Roe v. Wade*,[77] a single woman sought a declaratory judgment that certain Texas statutes prohibiting abortions, except when necessary to save the life of the mother, violated her right to privacy. The State of Texas argued that the statutes were justified by the state's legitimate interest to (1) discourage illicit sexual conduct, (2) protect the life and health of the mother, and (3) protect prenatal life. But the Court, per Justice Blackmun, disagreed, holding that

> this right to privacy, whether it be founded in the Fourteenth Amendment's concept of ordered liberty and restrictions upon action, as we feel it is, or, as the District Court determined, in the Ninth Amendment's reservation of rights to the people, is broad enough to encompass a woman's decision whether or not to terminate her pregnancy.[78]

The right is not absolute, however. The Court made it clear that the state, in order to safeguard the health of the mother, could prescribe procedures to be followed in the second trimester of pregnancy, and in order to protect prenatal life could prohibit any abortion in the last trimester.

The rationale the Court claimed to rely on in arriving at its decision rested heavily on earlier privacy cases, which, in the opinion of the Court, "make it clear that only personal rights that can be deemed 'fundamental' or 'implicit' in the concept of ordered liberty are included in the guarantee of personal privacy. [These cases] also make it clear that the right has some extension to activities relating to marriage."[79] What exactly that relationship is was never specified by the Court. Still, the manner of the remark and the limited discussion that followed suggest that the Court viewed the marital relationship as merely one area in which personal privacy was recognized.

Indeed, reading *Roe*, especially in the light of *Eisenstadt*, one wonders whether the Court viewed privacy as autonomy or as selective disclosure. In both cases the plaintiff was unmarried, which suggests that privacy does not mean the right to selectively disclose information related to a privileged status such as marriage. More important, *Roe* involved an action (namely, having an abortion), rather than a question of who would be allowed to learn of the action (selective disclosure). Additionally, *Roe* and *Eisenstadt*, when read together, suggest that the Court saw the marital relationship as just one of the due process liberties to which the right to privacy attaches, rather than the only one. Moreover, both cases involve personal decisions related to performing an act. Expectations of what others might learn were never discussed, and repose was noted in *Roe* only to the extent that some of the cases cited were taken from torts.

In *Carey v. Population Services International*,[80] the Court struck down a New York statute that made it a crime to distribute contraceptives to minors. The case had involved a number of different issues, and the justices were unable to agree on an opinion concerning distribution. However, seven of them were agreed that the prohibition did violate a right to privacy afforded by the due process clause of the Fourteenth Amendment. Is this further evidence that the Supreme Court had come to think of privacy as an aspect of autonomy and not as a condition confined to certain preferred states, like marriage? This issue cannot be resolved without an opinion or a definitive subsequent case on the matter. Thus far, the Court has been indecisive on this issue.

Nevertheless, the idea that the Court is moving toward treating the right to privacy as a right to individual autonomy, and not merely as a right to selectively disclose information within certain societally preferred groups, got a boost in three 1983 Supreme Court decisions[81] and one 1986 decision[82] relating to a woman's right to obtain an abortion. The 1983 decisions essentially upheld a woman's "constitutional right to obtain an abortion and struck down an array of local legislative restrictions on access to abortions."[83] In the most sweeping of the three decisions, *Akron v. Akron Center for Reproductive Health*, the Court, per Justice Powell, held, citing two earlier cases, that

although the Constitution does not specifically identify [the right to privacy], the history of this Court's Constitutional adjudication leaves no doubt that "the full scope of the liberty guaranteed by the Due Process Clause cannot be found in or limited by the precise terms of the specific guarantees elsewhere provided in the Constitution." Central among these protected liberties is an individual's "freedom of personal choice in matters of marriage and family life."[84]

Similarly, in its 1986 decision, *Thornburgh v. American College of Obstetricians and Gynecologists,* the Supreme Court, per Justice Blackmun, struck down as unconstitutional several state statutes that would have had the effect of intimidating women into continuing their pregnancies. In holding such statutes unconstitutional, the Court states:

The constitutional principles that led this Court to its decisions in 1973 still provide the compelling reason for recognizing the constitutional dimensions of a woman's right to decide whether to end her pregnancy.... The states are not free, under the guise of protecting maternal health or potential life to intimidate women into continuing pregnancies. Appellants claim that the statutory provisions before us today further legitimate compelling interests of the Commonwealth. Close analysis of those provisions, however, shows that they wholly subordinate constitutional privacy interests and concerns with maternal health in an effort to deter a woman from making a decision that, with her physician, is hers to make.[85]

The rationale for saying that privacy construed as individual autonomy received a boost from these cases is that the focus of the decisions seems to be the freedom of the individual qua individual and not qua member of a select group. This seems to be indicated, for example in *Akron,* where "liberties" includes but is not limited to "matters of marriage and family life."

Still, several subsequent Supreme Court decisions, beginning with *Bowers v. Hardwick,*[86] are inconsistent with treating privacy as autonomy. *Hardwick* involved the question of whether Georgia's sodomy statute violated a gay man's constitutional right to privacy when it prohibited him from engaging in adult consensual homosexual activity in his home. Up to this time the position of the Supreme Court on the issue had been unclear. On the one hand, the Court had previously affirmed without opinion a Virginia case[87] holding such actions to be outside constitutional protection, while, on the other hand, it had refused to grant certiorari in a New York case[88] in which the Court of Appeals had held unconstitutional that state's sodomy statute.

In *Hardwick,* the Court, per Justice White, states: "We first register our disagreement with the Court of Appeals and with respondent that the Court's prior cases have construed the Constitution to confer a right of privacy that extends to homosexual sodomy and for all intents and purposes have decided this case."[89] The Court then interpreted three cases construing the due process clause of the Fourteenth Amendment to confer a fundamental individual right to decide whether or not to bear or beget a child.

> Accepting the decisions in these cases and the above description of them, we think it evident that none of the rights announced in these cases bears any resemblance to the claimed constitutional right of homosexuals to engage in acts of sodomy that is asserted in this case. No connection between family, marriage, or procreation on the one hand and homosexual activity on the other has been demonstrated, either by the Court of Appeals or by the respondent. Moreover, any claim that these cases stand for the proposition that any kind of private sexual conduct between consenting adults is constitutionally insulated from state proscription is unsupportable.[90]

The decision has caused much confusion, especially in light of previous privacy cases. In the same year that *Hardwick* was decided, the Supreme Court refused to grant certiorari in an Oklahoma criminal appeals case that held that state's sodomy statute unconstitutional when applied to opposite-sex, but not to same-sex, sodomy.[91] More recently, Minnesota has begun enforcing its criminal statute prohibiting adultery, citing the Supreme Court's unwillingness to extend the privacy doctrine, and other states may soon follow suit.[92] Parenthetically, there has been some movement in striking down state sodomy statutes under state constitutions that have explicit privacy protections.[93]

Perhaps the Supreme Court's decision in *Hardwick* can be made consistent with a view of treating privacy as an aspect of autonomy by limiting the autonomy at stake to states of affairs in which society already recognizes a certain degree of privacy. In this view, autonomy is protected only if there is a preexisting state of affairs (such as a marriage) in which the autonomy is expressed.

The argument begs the question, however, in that it assumes without explanation that certain states of affairs are worthy of privacy protection while others are not.

However, even this more limited view that autonomy will be protected as long as it attaches to a socially recognized state like marriage was dealt a severe blow by the Supreme Court in *Webster v. Reproductive Health Services*.[94] In *Webster*, the Supreme Court held that a Missouri statute prohibiting the use of public facilities, public employees, or public funds in performing abortions was constitutional. The Court narrowed *Roe* and its progeny and gave the states a great deal more control in regulating abortions than they had after *Akron*. One of the issues the Court considered was whether the state could require physicians to perform viability tests prior to performing abortions on women thought to be at least twenty weeks pregnant. *Roe* had stated that the state had a compelling interest to protect potential human life only after viability, that is, in the third trimester. In holding that doctors could be required to determine whether a twenty-week fetus was viable, a plurality of those justices deciding the case interpreted the Missouri statute to create a presumption in favor of viability at twenty weeks, which the physician would have to rebut with tests indicating that the fetus was not viable prior to performing the abortion. As to the statute's requirement that the physician's determination of viability be based on gestational age, fetal weight, and lung capacity, Chief Justice Rehnquist, in his plurality opinion, speaking on behalf of two other justices, states that the doubt cast on the statute was not a flaw of the statute but the result of a rigid trimester analysis of the course of a pregnancy.

The key elements of the *Roe* framework—trimester and viability—are not found in the text of the Constitution or in any place else one would expect to find a constitutional principle. Since the bounds of the inquiry are essentially indeterminate, the result has been a web of legal rules that have become increasingly intricate, resembling a code of regulations rather than a body of constitutional doctrine.[95]

In his dissent, Justice Blackmun pointed out that without the trimester system or something like it, *Roe* could not survive.[96] Instead of explicitly overruling *Roe*, as Justice Scalia would have preferred, the plurality's reasoning, if eventually adopted, will have the effect of discarding *Roe sub silentio*.[97] Finally, with respect to the tests themselves, the plurality opinion also stated:

The tests that Section 188.029 requires the physician to perform are designed to determine viability. The State here has chosen viability as the point at which its interests in potential human life must be safeguarded. . . . It is true that the tests in question increase the expense of abortion and regulate the discretion of the physician in determining the viability of the fetus. Since the tests will undoubtedly show in many cases that the fetus was not viable, the tests will in fact have been performed for what were second-trimester abortions. But we are satisfied that the requirement of these tests permissibly furthers the State's interest in potential human life, and we therefore believe Section 188.029 to be constitutional.[98]

Since *Webster*, the Supreme Court has decided two other abortion restriction cases. In *Hodgson v. Minnesota*,[99] the Court held (five to four) that a state could require a pregnant girl to inform both her parents (regardless of their custodial relationship to her) before having an abortion, as long as the law provides the alternative of a judicial hearing. In *Ohio v. Akron Center for Reproductive Health*,[100] the Court upheld (six to three) a state law requiring notification of one parent, with the alternative of a judicial hearing. The Court did not address the question of whether the judicial hearing was necessary where only one parent was involved.

An apparent recognition of the right to die but with a limit on its degree of protection (by classifying it as other than a privacy right) occurred in the Supreme Court's seminal decision in *Cruzan v. Director, Missouri, Department of Health*.[101] That case involved the question of whether a guardian may order that all nutrition and hydration be withdrawn from an incompetent ward who is in a persistent vegetative state but is neither legally dead nor terminally ill. While holding that Missouri may set a high standard of clear and convincing evidence before it will recognize an incompetent's wishes for withdrawal of life-sustaining treatment, the Court did for the first time assume that under appropriate evidence a right to die is encompassed by the Constitution. That right, however, was not found to be a part of a general right to privacy. Instead, it exists as a liberty interest under the due process clause of the Fourteenth Amendment. This is made clear in Chief Justice Rehnquist's majority opinion, where he states in a footnote: "Although many state courts have held that a right to refuse treatment is encompassed by a generalized right of privacy, we have never so held. We believe that this issue is more properly analyzed by a 14th Amendment liberty interest."[102] The chief justice continues in the text of the opinion: "For purposes of this case, we assume that the United States Constitution would grant a competent person a constitutionally protected right to refuse life-saving hydration and nutrition."[103]

Of significance is the effect of the Court classification of this case. Surely, the Court was avoiding the compelling state interest test that would attach to placing this case under privacy. By recognizing the right without stating that it was fundamental, the Court left to the states a great deal of room to decide how and under what circumstances the right should be protected.

Whether or not Missouri's clear and convincing evidence requirement comports with the United States Constitution depends in part on what interests the state may properly seek to protect in this situation. Missouri relies on its interests in the protection and preservation of human life, and there can be no gainsaying this interest—indeed, all civilized nations—demonstrate their commitment to life by treating homicide as a serious crime.[104]

This effect of the Court's reliance on the weaker standard is also made clear by the dissenters. Justice Brennan, in dissent, states: "If a fundamental right is at issue, Missouri's rule of decision must be scrutinized under the standards this Court has always applied in such circumstances."[105] Similarly, Justice Stevens writes: "The Court's willingness to find a waiver of this constitutional right reveals a distressing misunderstanding of the importance of individual liberty."[106]

At one level the classification may appear to make sense, since an aspect of this decision is to determine whether persons can make life-sustaining choices. However, at another level, the Court readily admits that the decision is the individual's; that is, that no other interest is involved. If, as many have thought, the concept of privacy encompasses autonomy (when the interests of another are not affected), then the two may not be as distinguishable as the Court majority might like to think. Moreover, if the protection of autonomy is a fundamental end of democratic government, then similarly there would be no justification for applying less than a compelling interest standard to the right to die.

A few additional constitutional cases should be mentioned. Even though they are generally recognized to fall within the same area, these cases were not discussed above because they seem to be concerned more with the idea that privacy bars intrusion upon a person's seclusion or solitude, and they resemble some of the torts cases cited earlier.

In *Stanley v. Georgia*[107] a search warrant was issued for the appellant's home to locate evidence of bookmaking. What was found instead were reels of film containing obscene matter. The appellant was then arrested and convicted for possession of obscene matter in violation of a Georgia statute. The Supreme Court, per Justice Marshall, reversed, noting that

the right to receive information and ideas, regardless of their social worth is fundamental to our free society. Moreover, in the context of this case— a prosecution for mere possession of printed or filmed matter in the privacy of a person's own home—that right takes on an added dimension. For also fundamental is the right to be free, except in very limited circumstances, from unwarranted governmental intrusions into one's privacy.[108]

The Court then referred to Brandeis's dissent in *Omstead* and concluded with the statement:

whatever may be the justifications of other statutes regulating obscenity, we do not think they reach into the privacy of one's home. If the First Amendment means anything, it means that a State has no business telling a man, sitting alone in his own house, what books he may read or what films he may watch. Our whole constitutional heritage rebels at the thought of giving government the power to control men's minds.[109]

The phrase "free . . . from unwarranted governmental intrusions into one's privacy" is consistent with the view of privacy as negative freedom mentioned earlier with respect to the *Griswold* case. Moreover, it suggests a difference between the legal use of the word *privacy*, referring here to a right to a degree of seclusion (like in the torts area), and common use of the term, which refers to matters that are not set out before the public eye.

Unfortunately, despite the proprivacy language in *Stanley*, a recent Supreme Court decision has cut back the protection when the evidence sought concerns child pornography. In *Osborne v. Ohio*,[101] the Supreme Court upheld an Ohio law that makes it a crime to possess pornographic photographs of children. In a six-to-three ruling, the Court, per Justice White, distinguished *Stanley* on the ground that there the state "sought to proscribe the private possession of obscenity because it was concerned that obscenity would poison the minds of its viewers."[111] A state may not adopt such a paternalistic motive under the First Amendment. By contrast, the goal of the Ohio statute was to "protect the victims of child pornography."[112] Moreover, it was "reasonable for the state to conclude that it will decrease the production of child pornography if it penalizes those who possess and view the product, thereby decreasing demand."[113]

In dissent, Justice Brennan argued that the majority's refusal to follow *Stanley* does not withstand scrutiny. "Although the states 'retain broad power to regulate obscenity'—and child pornography as well—'that power simply does not extend to mere possession in the privacy of his own home.' "[114]

In a separate decision, *Minnesota v. Olson*,[115] the Court held that an overnight guest has a legitimate expectation of privacy in the host's home, and, therefore, an arrest without a warrant constitutes an unreasonable search and seizure under the Fourth Amendment. The decision did not reach the issue of a visiting guest who does not stay overnight.

Still, however strong the right to privacy may be inside one's home, the situation is very different outside. There, the right to privacy may not exist, at least not in the same way. In *United States v. Orita*,[116] for example, the Court held that a state may prohibit an individual from transporting obscene material for private use. In *United States v. Reidel*,[117] and in *United States v. 12 200-Ft. Reels of Film*,[118] the Court respectively held that a state may prohibit an individual from receiving obscene materials through the mail and from importing them from foreign countries. Finally, in *Paris Adult Theatre I v. Slaton*,[119] state officials

filed civil complaints for a declaration that certain movies shown
by the defendant to adult patrons were obscene within the meaning of a Georgia criminal statute and for an injunction of those
movies. The trial court refused to issue the declaration on the
ground that since the movies were being shown to adults only,
they were constitutionally protected. The Supreme Court, per
Chief Justice Burger, disagreed:

> Our prior decisions recognizing a right to privacy guaranteed by the
> Fourteenth Amendment include "only personal rights that can be
> deemed fundamental or 'implicit' in the concept of ordered liberty." . . .
> Nothing, however, in this Court's decisions intimates that there is any
> "fundamental" privacy right "implicit in the concept of ordered liberty"
> to watch obscene movies in places of public accommodation.
>   . . . If obscene material unprotected by the First Amendment itself
> carried with it a "penumbra" of constitutionally protected privacy, this
> Court would not have found it necessary to decide *Stanley* on the narrow
> basis of the "privacy of the home," which was hardly more than a reaffir-
> mation that "a man's home is his castle."[120]

How Courts Justify Decisions

Anglo-American courts often claim to justify present decisions by
reference to past decisions. The United States Supreme Court in
particular claims to justify its decisions by referring to the written
Constitution and past-case precedent. Some scholars dispute
whether the Court always acts on this basis, especially in the
Fourth Amendment area.[121] They offer other explanations for
Court decisions, including political sentiments that arise with
new appointments.[122] Even so, for our purposes in evaluating the
development of privacy law, it is valuable to take the Court at its
word. If it turns out that some of the Court's decisions are inconsistent, then we have a strong reason to believe that some cases
may have been wrongly decided. In any event, before we reach
this issue, we must understand exactly how courts claim to decide cases.

Except where a statute directly applies or there is no prior
case law, most court decisions take the form of interpretations of
prior cases. An interpretation is thought to be correct if it essen-

tially captures the intention of the prior case(s); that is, if it captures what the courts in the prior case(s) understood the law to be. However, if courts misinterpret prior cases (intentionally or through inadvertent misunderstanding), then the justification for their present decision collapses. That the courts have offered so many different justifications to account for the many objects to which the right to privacy has been extended over the past century suggests that such misinterpretations of prior cases have been likely.

However, it might be expected that the different purposes courts act upon explain the wide divergence of cases falling under the legal term *privacy*. But this raises questions: What is the mechanism that produces so varied a set of results? How is it that this mechanism has been relatively secure from attack by those who must consider its use a form of judicial anarchy?

With respect to the first question, Edward Levi, in his book *An Introduction to Legal Reasoning*,[123] argues that the mechanism relied on by the courts is simply their own ability to emphasize different facts in a case for the purpose of achieving different results.[124] By this mechanism, seemingly unrelated cases can be made to appear related. In the hands of an activist court, it can be used for social change. This mechanism is often obscured by the tendency to presuppose that courts, when they interpret the law, apply the law as it presently exists to new cases. As for the second question, Levi argues that what has kept the courts relatively secure when they treat unlike cases as like is that their doing so is seen less as a means for social change than as a reflection of changes in society's values.[125]

That this mechanism may be obscured is not solely the fault of the courts, which often present their decisions as if they were applications of prior law to present cases. At least some of the obscurity is the result of a change in social norms, which often color the way court actions are seen and the way courts understand what they are doing. The change in social norms itself frequently goes unnoticed, at least by the general populace. Indeed, courts use this mechanism most effectively to sign a social change by producing changes in the law that are already desired by a majority of the public. Arguably, this occurred in the *Roe* case, although it later became evident (if it was not evident at the time of the decision) that the minority would prove to be very vocal.

These considerations are consistent with Levi's discussion of the development of legal concepts. Levi indicates that what are often firmly established legal principles will give way to exceptions. The line of cases beginning with *Winterbottom v. Wright*[126] illustrates this point.

In that case, the plaintiff, a coachman, was thrown from a wagon under contract to the postmaster general and permanently lamed. The plaintiff sought to recover from the manufacturer for defects in the wagon, but the English court refused to allow recovery on the ground that the manufacturer's contract was with the postmaster general and not the coachman. In the court's words, any other result would lead to "absurd and outrageous consequences."[127] Ten years later in a New York case, *Thomas v. Winchester*,[128] a husband purchased a bottle of belladonna (a deadly poison), erroneously marked "Extract of Dandelion" (a medicine), for his ill wife. The wife nearly died. When she recovered, she sued and was allowed to recover against the manufacturer on the ground that its negligence in labeling the bottle "put human life in imminent danger."[129] In other words, in this case there emerged an exception to the old principle requiring privity of contract (i.e., a contractual relationship) between the manufacturer and the consumer-plaintiff where the item in question was inherently dangerous.

Sixty-four years and several cases later, in another New York case, *MacPherson v. Buick*,[130] a plaintiff was severely injured when his car suddenly collapsed because of a defective wheel. The New York Court of Appeals, per Judge Cardozo, allowed recovery on the ground that the automobile was an inherently dangerous device. Because of these and subsequent cases in the area of products liability, the principle of privity of contract is now almost never enforced.

First, there was the privity rule. Then came the exception. Finally, the exception became the rule and privity the exception. Cardozo explained it by saying that "the principle that the danger must be imminent does not change, but the things subject to the principle do change."[131] What were exceptional circumstances at one time are commonplace today. This is simply reflected in the changed climate of social norms. Automobiles are more subject to hidden defects than wagons. Consequently, what society (as the retailer or consumer) expects by way of inspection in regard to automobiles is different from what it expected in regard to wagons.

Even so, courts would not have been able to account for changing circumstances and norms were it not for their ability to fashion exceptions to the general rule. But this ability is a result of emphasizing different facts for different purposes and thereby creating application gaps where the rule no longer applies. When the emphasis is shifted, a principle that was previously recognized may not appear to fit the case at hand. Once the old principle does not fit, a new principle can be fashioned—initially as an exception. But over time as more cases arise that accord with the basic purpose for adopting the exception, the old principle is pushed to the side and the new principle becomes the rule.

We have good reasons to think that emphasizing different facts for different purposes accounts for the variety of cases categorized under privacy. In the constitutional area in particular, the line of cases beginning with *Griswold* and developing through *Roe* seems to bear this out. In *Griswold*, the right to privacy was arguably confined to a married couple's right to use and to obtain information on the use of contraceptives. But the question of whether the Court was protecting the individual's right to decide (assuming privacy is to be interpreted as autonomy) or the married couple's right to be free from governmental interference (if it is interpreted as protecting the marital relationship) remains.

John Ely has argued that the guarantees the Court cited in *Griswold* to justify their use of privacy "all limit the ways in which, and circumstances under which, the government can go about gathering information about a person he would rather it did not have."[132] Another commentator goes even further, noting:

In addition, the Court contrasted the intrusive Connecticut criminal statute to other measures, such as the regulation of the sale and manufacture of contraceptives, that would also have achieved the state's goal of discouraging their use. Arguably implicit in this contrast was the suggestion that such alternative measures would survive constitutional scrutiny. On this reading, the holding is more consistent with a desire to eliminate certain types of "governmental snooping" than with a desire to protect married couples' autonomy to use contraceptives.[133]

If autonomy is the issue, presumably any regulation designed to discourage the product's use would not survive constitutional muster. Whereas, if the issue is only that some means of regulation are improper (because they involve intrusions on a privileged status), then presumably a governmental entity could seek to discourage, if not prevent, all use of contraceptives by unmarried persons, at least where the potential user is not acting under doctor's orders. In short, the real issue is one of interpretation of the word *privacy* in this area of the law.

Certainly, if it is true that *Griswold* is just another selective disclosure case raised to the constitutional level because the state was involved and, in general, the state cannot be sued in tort, then this would certainly bring it much closer to the tort line of cases previously discussed. It would also, at least as to its object, place it much further from the *Roe* decision, which clearly was not oriented to the gathering of information but to the actual obtaining of an abortion.

Perhaps selective disclosure is the correct interpretation of the *Griswold* decision, but if so, it seems rather curious that the *Roe* decision would have relied for at least part of its justification on *Griswold.* In *Roe,* the Court specifically cites the *Griswold* decision as a case where the justices "found at least the roots of [the right to privacy] . . . in the penumbras of the Bill of Rights."[134] Moreover, the Court in *Roe* cites other cases, like *Eisenstadt,*[135] for the extension of the right to privacy, which also have relied on *Griswold* for both the interpretation and justification of this new right.

It seems, then, that it is better to interpret *Griswold* as a pivotal case—the case in which tort privacy was to change to constitutional privacy—and that for reasons of judicial prudence certain matters had to be left intentionally vague. First, the Court needed to lay a foundation in the old law for the existence of the new right. That could only be done if the Court recognized the importance of the old law as providing a trend to fulfill the gap it had created. Second, the Court did not want to close off future options in setting the direction of the new right by giving it a broader construal than was necessary to decide *Griswold*. Indeed, it is a well-recognized rule of constitutional interpretation that a court will generally not decide a case more broadly than is necessary to obtain the "correct" result.

Still, if this is true or even only partially true, why choose privacy as the grounding for these new cases? Perhaps doing so was the Court's way of insuring that it had a case to ground the existence of this newly recognized right. The Court might have reasoned that privacy, being a sufficiently vague and ambiguous term, would be better suited for providing the foundation for a broad new right than a more precisely defined term. Alternatively, it may have been that society had come to think of privacy differently than it had in the past, and the justices, as members of society, to a certain extent shared this view.[136] Certainly the latter interpretation would conform to Levi's explanation of how legal concepts, such as privity and now privacy, change.

The liability of a seller of a previously innocuous article was not enlarged because some economic theory said this would be appropriate. Rather the growth of inventions made it hard to distinguish, when reasoning by example was used, between steam engines thought unusual and dangerous in an early day, and engines that move and were commonplace. A change in the method of selling and social life made it hard to distinguish between what had once been the small known group around the seller and the vast outside world. Since the difference could no longer be felt, it fell away. And similarly in the development of a constitution, increased transactions and communications made activities previously remote and local now a matter of national concern.[137]

Finally, there is the view offered by feminist writers such as Catharine MacKinnon, who argues that in a society where women do not control access to their own sexuality because of a pervasive male ideology, giving to women the promise of sex with men on the same terms as it is given to men (namely, without consequence) is to facilitate women's heterosexual availability and to free male sexual aggression.[138]

When the law of privacy restricts intrusions into intimacy, it bars change in control over that intimacy. The existing distribution of powers and re-sources within the private sphere will be precisely what the law of privacy expects to protect. Just as pornography is legally protected as individual freedom of expression—without questioning whose freedom and whose expression and at whose expense—abstract privacy protects abstract autonomy, without inquiring into whose freedom of action is being sanctioned, at whose expense. It is probably not coincidence that the very things feminists regard as central to the subjection of women—the very place, the body; the very activities, intercourse and reproduction; and the very feelings, intimate—form the core of privacy doctrine's coverage. From this perspective, the legal concept of privacy can and has shielded the place of battery, marital rape, and women's exploitive labor; has preserved the central institutions whereby women are *deprived* of iden-tity, autonomy, control and self-definition; and has protected the primary activity through which male supremacy is expressed and enforced.[139]

Whatever the reason for choosing privacy, courts are not thought of as acting legitimately if they make, as opposed to merely interpret, the law. Consequently, the justices' view of pri-vacy, whatever the cause, had to appear to be grounded in preex-istent legal doctrine, and indeed they may have even thought of it as having such a grounding.

Does this mean that the Court was not justified when it pro-claimed a constitutional right to privacy? Not necessarily so. In-deed, the present debate between interpretivists and noninter-pretivists should provide valuable insights into the bases on which the Court relies for the grounding of constitutional rights in general.[140] Certainly, providing a definitive basis for grounding the right to privacy requires an understanding of the concept of legal privacy and a conception of how courts should decide pri-vacy cases. These will be the goals of Chapters 2 and 3 respec-tively. This chapter leaves off with a single implication about the legitimacy of constitutional decision making in the area of pri-vacy: If one views constitutional decision making as being con-fined solely to the accurate selection and application of estab-lished constitutional precedent (the view that courts should only interpret the law), then not only is the Supreme Court, when it treats privacy cases, not properly interpreting precedents, it is not interpreting precedents at all.

THE CONCEPT OF
LEGAL PRIVACY

2

In Chapter 1, we noted that three distinct objects seem to have been subsumed under the concept of privacy. These objects correspond to three areas of United States law: Fourth Amendment, torts, and constitutional. In the Fourth Amendment area, the object is what one can reasonably expect to keep private. In the torts area, it is one's seclusion or solitude, not having embarrassing facts published, not being placed in a false light, and not having one's likeness taken for commercial purposes without permission. In the constitutional area, it is being free to make certain kinds of intimate decisions about whether to bear or beget a child. The differences between these objects has led several scholars to ask whether the law recognizes three distinct concepts of privacy or a unique concept subsumes all three privacy-objects.[1]

The use of the word *concept* here is meant to imply that the controversy concerns the search for a single intensional definition capable of classifying all the privacy-objects. If such a definition is possible, it will provide a way to account for controversial privacy issues such as abortion. Of course, if any definition is to work for this purpose, it must be nontrivial. That is, it must not merely list the types of cases that are privacy-objects but must be able to aid a critique of existing court decisions as well as provide a direction for future decisions.

Since American law operates at least in part by precedent (past cases are thought to be sources of current law) and since very little about privacy has turned on statutory enactments (except in a few states), one benefit of resolving this controversy will be to identify the issues that need to be resolved in light of the Supreme Court's relatively recent extension of the privacy right into the constitutional area. In other words, if there is a single concept of privacy, then a constitutional grounding will justify the recognition of a right to privacy in the constitutional area. Whereas, if there are three distinct concepts of privacy, then to the extent that the constitutional concept of privacy differs from the other two, it is necessary to identify the concept as well as ground the right in constitutional law. Indeed, the same point should be made for each of the other areas of the law in which a right to privacy has been recognized. This may explain why much of the recent literature on the law of privacy has focused more on definition than on justification.

Problems with Current Definitions

For some time now the standard approach of those trying to understand the law of privacy has been to propose a suitable definition. This is because of a long-standing assumption that courts act rationally when deciding cases. By rationally what is meant is that the judges or justices know what the law is and that they decide a case as an instance of that law because they see a connection between the case and a preceding case or statute. The courts' rationale amounts to the application of a taxonomy for cases, based on conceptual links between statutes, principles of law, or precedent cases and the salient features of the case before the court. Definitions provide the conceptual links that judges rely on. Thus, setting forth a definition is an important part of explaining court decisions in a particular area.

Since the assumption that courts act rationally when deciding cases is not implausible, let us begin by accepting this assumption. This will allow us to review the literature on privacy to determine whether anyone has arrived at a definition capable of providing a coherent and judicially usable account of the three privacy areas mentioned above. Our task is made easier by the fact that a recent article by W. A. Parent offers a critical review of the literature following the definitional approach.[2]

Not all the authors Parent cites attempt simply to define the concept of privacy. At least some offer normative arguments in support of a particular definition. Even so, it is fair to say that all emphasize definitions as the key to understanding the concept of privacy. Therefore, a critical analysis of their definitions is in order.

In Parent's summary, the definitions of privacy offered in the literature are the following: being let alone, sexual autonomy, control of information about oneself, control of access to oneself, and limitation of access to oneself.

Parent notes that the definition of being let alone, otherwise known as the Brandeis definition (Warren and Brandeis implied that privacy was a special case of this definition in their seminal law review article of 1890[3]) has been recently advocated by several well-known legal scholars.[4] Nevertheless, Parent argues that the definition is unsatisfactory because it does not allow for what he terms the conceptual integrity of the various concepts.[5] The following example illustrates the point. When Mary is assaulted by Robert, there is a sense in which Mary has not been let alone. Still, treating this situation as an infringement of the right to privacy does not, according to Parent, afford the concept much in the way of descriptive clarity or justificatory power. We have other concepts, like assault, that already describe—and indeed are better suited to describing—this situation.[6] Parent's point is that the Brandeis definition confuses what we mean by privacy by overlapping it with other concepts.

It might be thought that the concept of autonomy that is inherent in the idea of being let alone could serve as the genus of a definition that fits both assault and privacy cases. The difference between the two might then be brought out by a further criterion. In fact, such an approach will be taken later in this chapter and will show that legal privacy is a species of negative freedom. For now, however, it should be noted that Parent does not limit autonomy to only the genus of a definition.

Parent offers the same objection to the concept of privacy as condemning unwarranted boundary crossings or intrusions upon personal space.[7] In that instance, what could we say about the deaf and blind person who accidentally stumbles into the room where Jane is giving birth? Clearly, there would be a sense in which Jane's seclusion was intruded upon. Nevertheless, Parent claims, it would require a strained interpretation to say that Jane's privacy was invaded. Parent seems to be concerned with the idea that privacy is often associated with the ability to selectively disclose information about oneself. In the illustration, no information has been obtained, nor has there been an attempt to obtain information. Consequently, Parent asks, what could privacy amount to in such a case? Parent's point is that this interpretation of privacy fails to capture what we usually mean by privacy.

A better objection to both of these definitions is that they are too broad. Neither defines the types of actions or states of affairs that fall only under the rubric "privacy." The significance of this point is not that we have better concepts to describe what we usually mean by privacy, but that an action like assault could very well be treated as a privacy concern, even though we would not normally think about assault as a private matter. The point is that whether or not a matter is private depends not on the action but on whose interests are involved. Of this, more will be said below. For now it suffices to point out that on the face of these definitions, there is no action in the world that could not be described as a private action. This difficulty might have been alleviated by the use of *unwarranted* in the second definition, but insofar as no explanation is given for this word, the problem remains.

Sexual autonomy, Parent argues, is more appropriately a definition of a liberty than of privacy,[8] for it seems to designate a species of self-determination or individual autonomy. Moreover, to the extent that the definition takes the body as the first and most basic reference for control over personal identity and, therefore, as the conceptual core of privacy, it "has the unfortunate effect of blurring the vital distinction between the public and the private. The body is, after all, a very public entity."[9]

The criticism confuses the entity affected by certain privacy considerations and the considerations themselves. The question is not whether the body is public or private, which seems only to mean that it can be viewed by others. Instead, the question is: Are there some situations in which the body can properly be said to be outside the public view?

A better objection Parent raises concerns the comatose patient counterexample. In that example, one is inclined to say that Richard's privacy is being protected by his doctors and family, even though his condition prevents him from being able to act on his own behalf. Thus, if autonomy refers to the ability to engage in voluntary acts, then here is a case where the privacy of the patient is protected despite the patient's inability to engage in voluntary acts. In contrast, consider the case of the prisoner who may be able to exercise control over his sex life and yet has no privacy from the guards. While privacy and sexual autonomy may be overlapping concepts, they are nevertheless different, since they do not share the same extension.

The definition of privacy as control over information about oneself could be termed an information management theory of privacy.[10] The difficulty with this sort of theory, as Parent notes, is that it is too broad: "It is not any kind of information about a person where acquisitions violate his privacy."[11] Usually, although not always, when people speak of violations of privacy it is in reference to particular information they do not want others to have.[12] We may not mind, for example, if someone knows that we are sick yet mind very much if he or she knows the nature of our illness.

Neither can we avoid this problem, as Parent notes, by construing the scope of the term *information* to encompass only personal information. The comatose patient counterexample illustrates the fact that control over personal information is not a necessary condition of privacy. Similarly, if someone invented an X-ray device capable of seeing into the home (henceforth referred to as the threatened loss counterexample), there would be a real sense in which our privacy was threatened because we could no longer control access to personal information. Still, unless the device were actually used, there would be no invasion of privacy. While such a lack of control would undoubtedly threaten our privacy, it would not, without further action, involve its loss. Thus, control of information (personal or otherwise) is not even a necessary, let alone sufficient, condition for determining when privacy has been invaded. For this reason, the definition fails.

As for the definition of controlling access to oneself,[13] Parent points out two problems. First, it would be impossible to control access to oneself without *eo ipso* depriving others of their privacy. Such a situation would entail a type of sovereignty in which one person could unilaterally define at any time his or her relationships with other persons. The second objection is that the definition succumbs to both the comatose patient and the threatened loss counterexamples discussed above. Again, control is not a necessary element of privacy.

To put the point more generally, the difficulty with all the control-related definitions is that "they force the core meaning of freedom, namely the absence of coercion or restraint on choice, onto the concept of privacy."[14] As was shown above, the absence of coercion or restraint (which is correlative to the ability to exercise control) is not a necessary part of the concept of privacy. Consequently, any definition that treats control as essential to privacy will be inadequate.

Pertaining to the definition of privacy as the limitation of access to myself,[15] a distinction has been drawn in the literature between two types of personal access; causal and interpretative. "The former involves physical contact or physical proximity while the latter has to do with acquiring knowledge about someone."[16]

According to Parent, serious difficulties arise with conceiving privacy as a limitation on causal access. For one thing, the definition falls prey to the threatened loss counterexample. For example, A could have unlimited causal access to B and yet never take advantage of it.

On the other hand, if the definition is conceived to mean a limitation on interpretative access, it may still be vulnerable to the threatened loss counterexample. One author to whom Parent refers contends that privacy "is a condition of human life in which acquaintance with a person or the affairs of his life which are personal to him are limited."[17] Under this interpretation, B retains privacy even when his or her phones are tapped, as long as the tapes are subject to the restrictions of a warrant; that is, the *definiens* of the definition are served. Of course, the obvious problem with this definition is that it confuses a ground for separating legitimate from illegitimate invasions of privacy with an elucidation of the definition of privacy. Presumably, there will be times when privacy, however defined, should be overridden.

Having thus criticized the previous definitions of legal privacy, Parent offers his own definition, which he claims is optimal.[18] Parent says that "privacy is the condition of a person's not having undocumented personal information about himself known by others."[19] Parent's "personal information" refers either

to facts that most persons in a given society choose not to reveal about themselves (except to friends, family, advisors, etc.) or to facts about which a particular person is extremely sensitive and which therefore he does not choose to reveal about himself (even though most other persons don't care whether these same facts about themselves are widely known).[20]

Parent's definition of privacy excludes much of the law of privacy. Indeed, Parent admits as much when in defense of his definition he states that the only area in the law that raises a bona fide privacy issue is Prosser's "public disclosure of embarrassing facts about the plaintiff."[21] Intrusions upon the plaintiff's seclusion or solitude, or into his private affairs"[22] may implicate privacy if the intrusion is deliberate and pertains to undocumented personal knowledge. Otherwise, the remainder of the law of torts and the whole of the constitutional area are excluded.

Parent's justification for his definition of privacy (and thus for his exclusion of much of what the law has traditionally recognized as privacy-objects) is based on what he terms an awareness and respect for the different meanings and uses of our concepts. Thus, Parent would distinguish privacy as far as possible from such concepts as liberty, autonomy, peace (or repose), health, property, solitude, seclusion, secrecy, and anonymity. He claims that we must guard against encroachments that are antithetical to conceptual integrity, despite the fact that adjustments to the definitions of some of these concepts will admittedly affect adjoining concepts.

The personal knowledge definition results from a careful application of this methodological ideal of conceptual discrimination. It isolates the distinctive meaning of privacy without appropriating ideas which properly belong to the definitional core of other concepts. Consequently, its application will minimize the chance of confused, distorted reasoning.[23]

What is problematic with Parent's approach is that he gives us no independent criteria for determining where the delineation of our concepts should end. Every case decided by a court is in some sense factually distinguishable from the cases relied upon to decide it. Consequently, the analogies drawn or not drawn must presumably be based on legally recognized and relevant criteria if the decision-making procedure is not to be regarded as ad hoc. Parent lists several concepts that he claims must be kept distinct without stating the criteria that would explain why we should accept this conceptual map. Indeed, the process of delineation of concepts could go on until we got to the absurd result of having each case represented by a single concept. This would violate our assumption that courts operate rationally—that is, by discovering conceptual links between cases. Parent's difficulty is thus one of justification. Without grounding, his conceptual map appears to be ad hoc.

Finally, a brief word of criticism should be addressed to the personhood discussion of privacy that Lawrence Tribe presents in *American Constitutional Law*,[24] which has recently aroused the attention of some legal scholars. Tribe objects to taxonomies on privacy that "leave essentially unspecified the substance of what is being protected, telling us neither the character of the choices or the information we are to classify as special, nor the contexts of decision in which classification is to be employed."[25]

Moreover, Tribe also objects to the emphasis by most writers on what he terms "the inward-looking face of privacy."[26] "By focusing on the inward-looking face of privacy, the taxonomies slight those equally central outward-looking aspects of the self that are expressed less through demanding secrecy, sanctuary, or seclusion than through seeking to project one identity rather than another upon the public world."[27] The difference is just the difference between "a person's desire *not* to be known as a user of drug X and that person's desire to be known as someone who does *not* use the drug."[28]

Where Tribe seems to err is not with respect to the first objection, which certainly represents a powerful criticism of much of the current literature on privacy. Rather, his error arises in the second objection, which masks a confusion between the value one associates with privacy and the reasons privacy is regarded as a value in the law.

Certainly, no one would deny that many people value their privacy because it allows them to project an image they want the public to believe. Indeed, this is even sometimes done in the interest of the public, as, for example, when we expect judges to conduct themselves in ways that avoid even the appearance of impropriety.[29] But that is not to say that privacy is always valued by society because it allows people to project the image they wish others to believe. For example, a criminal might want his or her privacy protected in order to project the image of a law-abiding citizen. But surely the public does not want to protect privacy for this reason, since it would be in the public's interest to discover the person as a criminal. To the extent that the public interest is served by having the criminal's privacy protected, it must be for reasons not related to the criminal's own motivation. Indeed, the reason may be strategic—to avoid certain kinds of police actions that could not be controlled on a case-by-case basis. Thus, it is important to distinguish between a person's motivation for seeking to protect his or her privacy and society's justification (which can be thought of as a kind of motivation) for affording such protection. A judicially useful definition of privacy must take into account the effect one's actions may have on society so that the concept is not broader than the ultimate value under which action will be allowed. To the extent, then, that Tribe has not been sensitive to this distinction, his approach is unsatisfactory.

A Conceptual Methodology

Even granting that a useful definition of privacy must be tied to a justification of privacy as a value, the question still remains whether definition alone can classify the objects to which the concept has been extended. For the remainder of this chapter, the term *legal privacy* will be used in place of the term *privacy* to refer to a single concept that will have as its extension those objects previously discussed.

Earlier, I pointed out that the courts have failed to give a

unique definition of legal privacy that would coherently account
for its extension to the Fourth Amendment, torts, and constitutional areas. To account for this failure, the hypothesis was offered that judicial opinions that extend the concept, drafted by
judges who are members of society, reflect the changes in society's views on privacy. In this respect, the concept of legal
privacy stands in a causally dependent relationship to the standard English usage of the term at any given time.

An alternative explanation for the courts' failure to provide a
univocal definition is that the courts rely on several different
concepts, all of which coincidentally have been labeled "privacy"
but are otherwise unrelated or related by a Wittgensteinian family
resemblance.[30] If the latter, this means that each of the privacy
concepts overlaps some other privacy concept(s), but there is no
single conceptual core that all the concepts share. Of course, if
we adopt this explanation, then our task will have grown from
searching for a single definition of privacy to searching for three
distinct definitions. Even so, this could be an advantage if the
three definitions were easier to derive than a single unifying
definition. Nevertheless, because there is value in the conceptual
simplicity and elegance that would result if the same concept
were involved in all three areas of the law where privacy has been
an issue, we should look at the usage of the term *legal privacy* to
see if there exists a unifying conceptual core.

It is important to note that we seek to clarify a univocal concept based on the usage reflected in case law. Or, to put it differently, we seek to understand how the concept works in order
to understand how the various uses may be connected. Nothing
valuative is at stake at this point. We are interested in an illumination of the concept as it functions in the three areas wherein it has
been recognized. Consequently, we need not stipulate that our
definition encompass every case in which the courts have found
privacy to be an issue. It is sufficient to start with the standard (or
clear instance) uses which derived from settled cases before considering the hard cases.

This clarification is intended to offset an objection raised by
Ruth Gavison and others.[31] Gavison argues that any attempt to
derive a definition of privacy from existing case law is doomed to

be misleading.[32] There is no way of ensuring that the cases will be coherent,[33] and surely one could not derive anything toward critiquing the cases. Consequently, one is forced to reduce the concept of privacy to the extension of cases wherein the courts have found privacy.[34] The objection, however, presupposes a naïve lexicographical ordering. When we want to know what a word means, we search out a collection of instances in which the word is used. We do not count every use, only correct uses, determined by the standard and settled cases in which the word is applied in a regular way. For privacy, the correct use of the word is determined from the settled cases in the three areas in which privacy has been recognized. Note that in the constitutional area much less is settled than in the tort and Fourth Amendment areas. More important, the very object at which privacy is aiming (autonomy, selective disclosure, or autonomy only in preferred states) is itself in doubt. As a result, I am free to choose whichever use of the word I prefer provided that what I ultimately offer as an elaboration of the concept coherently unites the various privacy objects in the areas where the law is settled.

An objection might be raised that the cases on which I focus in the constitutional area reflect a hidden value judgment. This objection is premature. The only thing at stake here is coherence, which means that the concept eventually arrived at will be able to unite the various privacy-objects. Later, in Chapter 3, an argument will be offered to justify a duty to protect privacy along lines specified below.

In this section, we will assume for the sake of argument that a univocal definition of legal privacy is both possible and judicially desirable. We do this to look for a judicially useful intensional definition for legal privacy—that is, one based on the invariant characteristics or properties with which courts should be concerned when classifying cases. The judicial value of such a definition is that courts will be able to rely on it when deciding which legal principles should govern a particular case. The principles will then provide the basis for deciding the case by determining the rights and duties of the parties involved.

Indeed, the significance of this point should not be understated. For in every case a court is confronted with two questions.

First, which legal concept best classifies the case? Second, what are the principles (including constitutional principles), rules, and statutes that need to be relied upon in order to decide the case? The remainder of this chapter will discuss the first of these two questions, using the method of definition. I hope thereby to provide a useful way to classify future cases as falling within or outside the privacy area.

The Definition of Legal Privacy

Earlier, I pointed out that a statement about the right to privacy can be cast in the following form:

A has a (Fourth Amendment, tort, or constitutional) claim-right to privacy against B by virtue of Y.

Casting a rights statement in this form allows one to clearly specify the complete range of objects to which the right extends. Moreover, it allows for this even where the range of objects is further divided, as in the torts area, where four subclasses of objects were specified. Of course, what does not appear in the syntax of the statement, because it is not a syntactical object, is the intensional definition that classifies the objects involved. Still, that such a definition exists is implied by the fact that the right claim being asserted occurs within the context of a legal tradition that assumes courts to act rationally (in the sense we have discussed). In other words, each extension of the right to privacy should be connected in some way (if the courts are acting rationally) to prior privacy cases.

In the last chapter, several preliminary definitions of privacy were offered. A pre-Fourth Amendment definition describes privacy as being apart from the state. An interesting aspect of this definition is that it also helps us identify private property as property the state does not possess, whereas a torts definition defines it as being apart from all other persons. In the Fourth Amendment area today, privacy is the courts' reading of society's reasonable expectation that certain matters will not become public knowledge. In the torts area, it is also more precisely defined as being able to pursue one's life as one sees fit: having one's seclusion or solitude protected, not having embarrassing facts published about oneself, not being placed in a false light, and not having one's likeness taken for commercial purposes without permission. In the constitutional area, one view of privacy assigned it the meaning of being free to make certain sorts of intimate decisions (such as whether to bear or beget a child) without governmental interference.

Each of these definitions is either too narrow or too broad to account for the myriad cases the courts have subsumed under legal privacy. "Being apart from the state" is too broad in that the term *apart* is not clearly defined. Similarly, "reasonable expectation" is too narrow to account for the court decisions involving false light and commercial exploitation. Whereas, "being able to pursue one's life as one sees fit" is so broad as to be virtually meaningless. The alternative torts definitions are too narrow to account for a woman's right to an abortion. "Being free to make certain sorts of intimate decisions" is too narrow to account for either the Fourth Amendment cases or the seclusion, false light, and commercial likeness cases.

Obviously, it would be preferable to have a definition that on its own terms could precisely determine if a privacy-object was at stake in each case wherein privacy was alleged to be an issue. Unfortunately, none of the above definitions is capable of this, for each is confined to the narrow sphere of privacy concerns that identifies the area from which the definition is taken. Still, each represents a view of privacy used by the courts when deciding cases in that area. Moreover, taken together, the definitions do exhaust the present law of privacy. Consequently, it should be possible to arrive at a definition for legal privacy from the elements these preliminary definitions have in common.

Let us begin by constructing typical right claims to privacy in each of the three areas of the law in which privacy has been recognized. Next, let us see where the three different statements overlap. At the point of overlap, we should have at least as inclusive a part of our definition of privacy as could be afforded by the statements. In other words, at the point of overlap we should have the genus part, if not the whole, of our sought-after definition of legal privacy.

Three typical formulations of claims to the right to privacy in the areas of Fourth Amendment, torts, and constitutional law, respectively, are:

(1) A has a right to be secure in his or her person, house, papers, and effects from unwarranted governmental searches and seizures.

(2) A has a right to pursue life as he or she sees fit without interference from any other person.

(3) A has a right to make certain sorts of intimate decisions, such as whether to bear or beget a child, without interference from the government.[35]

Clearly, these three formulations differ in regard to the objects to which the right claims are attached: (1) attaches to persons, houses, papers, effects, and such other objects as might fall under a reasonable expectation of privacy; (2) attaches to Prosser's four categories (seclusion, false light, embarrassing facts, and not having one's likeness taken for commercial purposes without permission); and (3) attaches to such intimate decisions as whether to bear or beget a child. Additionally, the respondent for (1) and (3) is the state, while for (2) it is all other persons.

On the other hand, one fact that unites these formulations is that they each ignore certain definite interests. In (1), the interests of the victims of crime are not accounted for; in (2), the interest of gossip columnists is not considered; and in (3), in the application to abortions, the interest of the father (assuming fetuses are not persons) is being ignored. The association that is suggested is that when one makes a privacy claim one is in effect saying that certain other interests ought not to be taken into account. What is the relevant criterion for determining which interests should be taken into account and which should not?

Obviously, the answer will depend on the relationship of the person asserting the privacy claim to the respondent(s). For example, while the amount of one's income may be private with respect to certain members of one's family, the law provides that it is not private with respect to the IRS. On the other hand, whether or not one wears a toupee may not be private with respect to these same family members, but it is not the business of the IRS. Similarly, certain acts (such as having an abortion) are private with respect to the state (so long as the fetus is not considered to be a person and there is no jeopardy to the mother's health).

None of this is to suggest, however, that a claim under a different right by one person could not end up in conflict with a privacy claim of another. Indeed, one might imagine Ted admitting that both he and Jane have plausible rights claims while declaring that only his should be considered valid. Then it becomes a matter of determining the relative strengths of the conflicting rights. However, in the present context, the problem is not about resolving conflict of rights situations, where one of the rights happens to be the right to privacy, but about the plausibility of making a rights claim to privacy.

Moreover, as each of the three formulations indicates, privacy is a species of negative freedom because the claim being made in each instance is to a right of the actor to be free from outside interference where no other relevant interests are involved.

While this observation is necessary (in the sense that without it we would be unable to explain the cases courts have subsumed under privacy), it is insufficient as a definition of legal privacy because the extension of the self-to-be-let-alone concept is broader than the extension of legal privacy. A satisfactory definition must also include the insight that claims about privacy are by their nature subject regarding, or to use John Stuart Mill's expression, self-regarding. This follows from the fact that constitutional privacy claims separate out a sphere of autonomous activity that the government should leave alone. It also follows from the fact that torts and Fourth Amendment privacy claims delineate a set of conventions that keep information about a person's actions out of the public domain. Parenthetically, as this chapter is concerned with the concept of privacy, and not with its justification, I have avoided any reference to a commitment to privacy. Looking ahead, however, I hope it is obvious from the way privacy relates to both negative freedom and self-regarding actions that I will ultimately rely on a justification of privacy based on autonomy. In this way, I hope to distinguish myself from the purely Millian formulation of a self-regarding act that has its ground in maximizing pleasure over pain.[36]

Still, if actions are to be protected, certain interests of relevant others are not taken into account. But, because there is a sense in which any action affects the interest of another, even if only by the fact that the other knows such actions are permitted, we must ask: Which interests and why? The problem is both conceptual and normative.

At the conceptual level, the concern is to establish the possibility of a private action. This means being able to distinguish actions that affect the interests of relevant others from actions that do not. Mill is attempting to draw just this distinction when he says:

There is a sphere of action in which society, as distinguished from the individual, has, if any, only an indirect interest; comprehending all that portion of a person's life and conduct which affects only himself, or if it also affects others, only with their free, voluntary, and undeceived consent and participation. When I say only himself, I mean directly, and in the first instance: for whatever affects himself may affect others through himself.[37]

Nevertheless, Mill's effort was unsuccessful and has been the brunt of much philosophical criticism.[38] Even so, Mill was on the right track in talking about self-regarding actions. It is clear that when we describe such actions, we do not normally think of them as affecting all other persons. In fact, we do not usually think of them as affecting any other persons whose interests are not part of the description of the action. Granted, we may eventually become convinced of a causal connection between the type of action being described and the alleged interest affected, but that comes later. This suggests that in our description of actions we are logically bound only to what the description entails. Mill seems to have realized this point, although only vaguely. That is why he used the phrase "in the first instance." But Mill failed to set forth precisely how an action in the first instance could be viewed as not affecting the interests of relevant others.

Of crucial importance to a definition of legal privacy, then, is the idea that the consequences of a private action can impinge in the first instance only on the interests of the actor and not on the basic interests of any other person in the relevant group of comparisons. To understand this idea, let us consider what it means to have an interest and what it means for an interest to be infringed.

In essence, we can say that Karen has an interest in an object if the object is something Karen claims, has title to, sees a benefit in, shares in, has concern for, or has a right to. Karen's interest in the object is impinged if Karen's claim is ignored, title is not recognized, benefit is restricted, share is limited, concern is overlooked, or right is denied. Karen's interest in the object is impinged upon by Steve when Steve performs an action that consequently impinges Karen's interest in the object. Finally, we can say that Karen's interest in the object is impinged by Steve in the first instance if Steve performs an action, the mere description of which entails consequences that would impinge Karen's interest in the object. Specific examples of this will follow. For now it suffices to say that by mere description I mean a description without the inclusion of any additional facts or causal theories. In other words, one need know nothing more than what the action is to see that it conflicts with Karen's interest. In this sense one might say the action logically presupposes a conflict with Karen's interest.

Even with the restriction implied by "in the first instance," there is a problem with the breadth of meaning often associated with the term *interest.* We would, after all, not want to undo what we will achieve (through restricting the consequences of actions to only those that impinge in the first instance) by an overbroad concept of interest. Consequently, we must limit the meaning of *interest.* This will have the positive effect of precisely defining an area of action within which acts are plausibly private.

Certain interests (basic interests) differ from other interests (derivative interests) in that basic interests are independent of conceptions about facts and social conventions, while derivative interests are dependent on the combination of basic interests with conceptions about facts and social conventions.

There are two general categories of basic interests: freedom and well-being.[39] The category of freedom includes interests in freedom of expression, privacy, freedom of thought, worship, and so on. The category of well-being includes interests in preserving one's life, health, physical integrity (as in not being assaulted), and mental equilibrium (as in not being subject to mental harassment). In neither of these two categories are particular conceptions about facts or social conventions presupposed.

With respect to derivative interests, however, conceptions about facts and social conventions are presupposed. Consequently, an actor can misunderstand his or her derivative interests by misunderstanding the facts or the social convention. Such mistakes are not possible with basic interests.[40] An example of a derivative interest is to receive a good education. The interest is derivative of the basic interest in well-being combined with the factual conception that one's well-being will be benefited by education. Similarly, the interest in being allowed to marry is derivative of the basic interest in freedom combined with the social convention of marriage.

From these observations, the following definition of a private act emerges:

> *An action is self-regarding (private) with respect to a group of other actors if and only if the consequences of the act impinge in the first instance on the basic interests of the actor and not on the interests of the specified class of actors.*

The definition has *direct* applicability in the constitutional area where the privacy-object (such as the subject's intimate decision whether to bear or beget a child) is the very action to be carried out. In this sense, the constitutional privacy-object differs from the privacy-objects recognized in both the Fourth Amendment area and the tort area, which involve noninterference with the selective disclosure of information or intrusion upon a given state of affairs. Here, the action is what is to be protected directly.

For example, suppose Jim, a public school teacher, announces in a public forum in the community or school district where he teaches that he is gay. Suppose also that Roger, a parent, has an interest in not having his child taught by a gay or lesbian teacher, perhaps because Roger believes that being taught by a gay or lesbian teacher would influence his child's sexual orientation. In this case, it cannot be said that Jim's action conflicts with Roger's interest in the first instance. For the consequence Roger is worried about (namely, the influence on his child's sexual orientation) can be made out only by appealing to a certain type of causal theory about how sexual orientation is acquired. In other words, one needs to consider the causal explanation as part of the description of the action in order to make out the conflict. But this is to go beyond the restriction implied by the phrase *in the first instance*, which concerns consequences that would impinge on Roger's interest only under a description of the action itself. Consequently, in this case the gay orientation of the teacher, as revealed in the public announcement, is nevertheless private with respect to the interest of the parent.[41]

This is not to suggest that if Roger could prove the causal connection, Jim's privacy claim would still control. In that instance, Jim's privacy claim might be defeated, assuming the state has a compelling interest to protect Roger's interest. (The rationale for this will be examined below.) The example here, however, concerns only whether or not Jim could make a plausible claim to privacy, not whether the claim ultimately succeeds.

In another example, Cynthia seeks to terminate her pregnancy, by means of an abortion, in a district where the courts have determined that the fetus is a person. In this example, the fetus can be thought to have a prospective interest in being allowed to continue to term. Therefore, Cynthia's action would not be private with respect to the fetus because nothing needs to be specified once the action is described in order to see that the interests conflict. Of course, treating the fetus as a person may seem implausible, and herein lies the principal difficulty with the position that would seek to prevent Cynthia's action.

A different example, which shows the connection between legal privacy and private property, is the following: Suppose Richard has a 100 percent ownership right without condition in Blackacre. Suppose also that Sam, a neighbor, begins to construct a driveway that oversteps his property line onto Blackacre. In that case the consequences of Sam's action impinges on Richard's claim in the first instance and Sam's action is not private with respect to Richard. In other words, Richard could seek a legal remedy to Sam's action without showing anything more than the nature of his interest and what Sam has done. In contrast, suppose Rita and Debbie each have a 50 percent divided interest in Whiteacre and Rita begins to build a house on Whiteacre. In this case, the court could determine only whether Rita's action with respect to the property impinged on Debbie's interest in the property from a site plan of Whiteacre. Rita would have a plausible claim to privacy (which in this instance would manifest itself as a prima facie claim to enjoy the property without disturbance), which would give way only to an evidentiary determination that Debbie's interest has been impinged upon.

Here an objection may be raised as follows: Let us assume there is concrete evidence that Debbie's interest is infringed. What basis would the court have to disturb Rita's claim to privacy, since the mere description of the act does not entail an impingement of any basic interest of Debbie's? Here the point is that protecting only basic interests may not encompass all the actions the state has a legitimate right to prohibit; whereas, protecting all derivative interests would be overinclusive. The situation is best understood in the context of a compelling state interest (only where the state is not formally a party to the action) to protect legitimate property rights. Precisely why a compelling state interest analysis should be looked to will be set forth in the next chapter. For now, we need only show how the analysis would apply.

In determining whether the impingement of any derivative interest raises a compelling state interest, one must ask the question at a second order of generality in order to ensure that a fundamental right is not being sidestepped for an idiosyncratic reason. Is the action one that could be empirically verified to affect adversely another's capacity for autonomous action? Impingements upon one's interests are to be considered harmful and an object for state limitation only if they would adversely affect anyone's capacity for autonomous action. Actions claimed to cause such harm must be ascertainable by the usual empirical methods that courts follow in determining questions of evidence. Mere adverse effect on one's personal moral or religious beliefs, the validity of which cannot be ascertained, is not enough. Whereas, verifiable evidence of a threat to a democratic or other fundamental end of government would be sufficient. Otherwise, a court loses its neutral ability to balance different interests within a pluralistic society and becomes a spokesperson and champion for a particular set of narrower interests. In the case of developing legislation, where a specific case is not at issue, it is sufficient that the type of action to be guarded against is one whose tendency would be to adversely affect anyone's capacity for autonomous activity.

How would this analysis bear on a case similar to the first example but where Roger's interest is *merely* in not having his child taught by a lesbian or gay teacher? In that situation, it would appear that the consequences of Jim's public announcement conflict with Roger's interest in the first instance. However, there is an underlying assumption here that all interests are the same, when, in fact, they are different.

Having earlier set forth basic and derivative interests, we can now resolve the situation in which Roger claims an interest merely in not having his child taught by a gay or lesbian teacher. In this case, Roger's interest is derivative, probably of his basic interest that his child have the freedom to develop his or her own sexual orientation combined with the idea that exposure to a lesbian or gay teacher would limit that freedom. But it was Roger's derivative interest, not basic interest, that was in conflict with the consequences of Jim's announcement. The analysis concluded that a true conflict existed only because the situation had not, as yet, been sufficiently analyzed to distinguish the difference in the interests that were being opposed. Indeed, the problem with the preliminary analysis was that it kept hidden the very thing that it was supposed to make explicit, namely, the underlying factual conception. Thus, a conflict appeared where in fact none existed.

One objection to this analysis is that it is overinclusive. It looks like any infringement on one's freedom to act is an invasion of privacy if the act can be described as self-regarding. For example, suppose one for no apparent reason is prevented by a city ban from roller-skating down the street. While such a restriction is not normally thought to invade privacy, it does under the proposed definition. Similar, and more controversial, would be the use of illegal drugs on the street. To construe these situations as private, the theory would have to show that self-regarding behavior is properly legally innocent and that paternalism and legal moralism is out of place. This would be difficult given that the Supreme Court has permitted states to operate in this area.

The problem with this objection is that it misunderstands the level at which questions of privacy arise. Privacy is, in its primary form, activity that is self-regarding. To understand activity, one needs to understand the rules that govern the activity. Once one understands these rules, one realizes that the rules themselves entail limits. To participate in certain activities is to accept rules on one's behavior. To play chess, for example, is to accept the rules of chess. To participate in street traffic is to accept the rules governing the use of the streets, which in the case of public drug use may be designed to insure protection to passersby. Since all activities are understood as rule-governed behaviors, privacy must therefore be understood in the context of rule-governed activities.

The question of whether the enforcement of the rules themselves limit privacy is at a higher level. Here one is not addressing privacy that arises in the context of the rules. Rather, one appeals directly to autonomy. Consequently, the objection that privacy is overinclusive fails because it conflates questions about privacy with questions about autonomy.

Nor does this response expose me to the objection that privacy has become so limited that it is no longer able to resolve controversial questions. For example, some states prohibit by statute adult consensual homosexual acts. Is privacy no longer an issue in such states because the rules governing the activity in question prohibit it? The answer is that privacy remains an issue, although now we are concerned with the scope of the right.

The objection fails to notice that at the higher level the government must show a compelling interest in order to limit the range of privacy protection. (Or, in a conflict of rights issue, the right opposing privacy must better foster maximal autonomy.) Consequently, unless the government can show a compelling interest, it is not justified in passing a sodomy statute to limit individual private activity. By the same token, since the government is clearly justified when it seeks to insure safe commerce, it can regulate the use of streets and the public use of drugs and alcohol. The difference between these compelling interest situations and the pure privacy situation is that now the question is about autonomy.

The value of our definition of private acts is fourfold. First, the definition makes clear that privacy concerns arise where the consequences of one's action affect only one's own interests.[42] In this sense, the definition conforms to how we usually think about privacy. Second, the definition shows that the concept of privacy is not relative, even though the privacy status of the act in question is always related to the group under consideration. Third, the definition is applicable to the kinds of cases with which the law of privacy is concerned. This is evident from the way the definition emerged, namely, from observations of three typical privacy claims and a comparison and contrast of the objects to which the right to privacy has been extended. Finally, from the definition of a private act, we can specify a definition of a private state of affairs, as that term would apply to the Fourth Amendment and torts areas:

> *A state of affairs is private with respect to a group of other actors if and only if there is a convention, recognized by the members of the group, that defines, protects, preserves, or guards that state of affairs for the performance of private acts.*

Cases involving states of affairs that we normally think of as private are usually subsumed under the Fourth Amendment or tort categories of repose, sanctuary, private places, or private persons.

Certain forms of selective disclosure, such as those that relate to sexual intimacy, are often treated as private, although not always to the same degree in every culture.[43] Other forms of selective disclosure, such as veiling one's face, may be profoundly private in some cultures[44] but only stylistic in others. Which information is taken as private, then, is determined by the conventions or states of affairs the given culture adopts to insure the possibility of performing private acts.[45] In some cultures, sexual acts may need to be private in order to ensure that the individuals involved will not be too embarrassed to perform them.[46] In others, this may not be necessary.[47] The value of selective disclosure is its ability to avoid a possible chilling effect on the performance of private acts. Nor need all such selective disclosure relate to sexual activities. Some information may be private because of its relation to private business transactions in a capitalistic system. The businessman who wants information about a deal not to fall into the hands of the opposition will take steps to protect that information, such as placing it under lock and key. There is also the possibility of information that is private because it is too difficult to separate from information that actually supports the performance of private acts. For example, what one wears to bed at night may not bear on any private act. Still, to try to discover that information may open the door to finding out information that would have a chilling effect on privacy. In the United States, how one raises one's children is so closely related to information that would be private that except for gross abuses, it is generally taken as private. Note that the extension of applicability of what is private via selective disclosure and states of affairs is beyond Mill's notion of a self-regarding act.

In the Fourth Amendment area, the privacy-object includes but is not limited to the subject's person, house, papers, and effects, but only to the extent that the subject has acted in some way or taken advantage of some condition (like shutting the door to the house), which in our culture is recognized as conferring on the subject a reasonable expectation of privacy. Indeed, such a precedent action or condition is how we recognize a claim to privacy in this area. Similarly, in the torts area, one type of privacy-object involves the value of the subject's reputation, but, again, only to the extent that the subject has either performed an act or taken advantage of a condition (such as not storing personal papers where the public will likely have access) to protect against the publication of false or embarrassing facts. Other types of tort privacy-objects, including the commercial value of the subject's likeness and the value of her or his solitude, follow a similar pattern. Thus, in both the Fourth Amendment and torts areas, the subject has to perform an action or take advantage of a socially recognizable condition before a claim to privacy can even arise.[48]

One advantage of the definition of a private state of affairs is that it is dependent on our definition of a private act—thus making it unnecessary to have to provide an independent analysis of the concept of a private state of affairs. Cases involving a house as a private place, for example, are now easily explained, for such a place is established in part so one can perform private acts. Similar arguments can be made to explain the selective disclosure afforded private papers and effects under both Fourth Amendment and tort law. In these cases, the concern is with information. Still, the reason the information is protected is that it facilitates private action. Exactly why private action should be valued will be discussed in the next chapter.

A second advantage of this definition is that conventions determine whether a state of affairs is private. It might be worth examining whether closing the door to one's room in a traditional Japanese home would be understood to mean that whatever is spoken inside the room is private. Certainly in the United States, closing the door to one's apartment would not be understood as conferring privacy on what is said inside unless the voice level is low enough that the words do not precipitate naturally through the apartment walls. The rationale behind these conventions is the society's determination to set aside certain situations as situations in which private acts can be performed outside the public's scrutiny. For example, the convention of being able to step behind closed doors (both literally and figuratively) is at the heart of Fourth Amendment privacy. Similarly, the conventions associated with being able to seclude oneself or being able to selectively disclose information about oneself are fundamental to tort privacy.

Finally, we should note the value of both the definitions of a private act and of a private state of affairs in critiquing the law of privacy. The definition of a private act provides a basis for criticizing a court's determination about whether an act is private by whether the consequences of the action impinge in the first instance only on the basic interests of the actor. The definition of a private state of affairs provides a basis for criticizing court decisions that do not take into account how persons within social groups develop reasonable expectations of privacy.

Still, none of what has been said so far is sufficient basis for determining whether privacy should be protected as a right. Even less is it a basis for deciding in a conflict of rights situation (where privacy is one of the rights involved) how a court should decide the case. Neither has anything been said about whether the same or a different standard applies to deciding a conflict situation in the tort area from one raised in the constitutional or Fourth Amendment areas. And what about the situation where privacy seems to conflict with a compelling interest of the state? Obviously, answers to these questions are critical to a complete analysis of the law of privacy. But, inasmuch as they are not part of our analysis of the concept of privacy, it is important to first specify the context in which these questions are raised.

The Coverage-Protection Distinction

It is in the nature of a law case that the parties involved have different and conflicting interests they wish to see protected. The function of the legal system is to try to resolve disputes that are cognizable before a court. Legal concepts are means courts use to characterize cases in order to decide under which legal rules or principles (the distinction need not concern us here) the case should be decided. For this reason, attorneys, whose job it is to represent their client's interests, are understandably concerned to interpret the facts of their cases so as to bring them under those legal concepts that will produce the most favorable results in light of their clients' interests. This activity is known in contemporary legal parlance as setting forth the theory of the case.

The only factual interpretation that finally counts is that of the court deciding the case. It is important to note that courts sometimes have difficulty deciding a case because an honest interpretation of the facts brings the case within the scope of two or more concepts. When this happens, the bodies of law referenced by the different concepts may produce inconsistent results. This is particularly a problem in constitutional cases, where the issue of what constitutes the correct factual interpretation of the case is often controversial. Here, the policies underlying different interpretations are thought to have more serious political, social, and moral consequences and are thus more prone to conflict. Witness the U.S./Iraqi war. Does the public's right to know outweigh the need to protect national and military security? To avoid the possibility of constitutional cases becoming unresolvable, the Supreme Court has developed various tests to reveal the salient underlying rights involved.

In essence, the tests provide a means for determining which rights should prevail in a given case. Such tests, Frederick Schauer states, coincide with the protection of the right, which differs from coverage of the right in that protection is a determination of the relative strength of the right when measured against competing rights; whereas, coverage of the right is the domain or class of acts to which the right extends.

If I'm wearing a suit of armour [Schauer explains], I am *covered* by the armour. This will *protect* me against rocks, but *not* against artillery fire. I can be wounded by artillery fire despite the fact that I am covered by the armour. But this does not make the armour useless. The armour does not protect against everything; but it serves a purpose because with it only a greater force will injure me.[49]

The combined extensions of our two definitions of a private act and a private state of affairs constitutes the extension of legal privacy. The extension of legal privacy is broader than the coverage of the individual rights to privacy that have arisen in the three areas of the law where privacy has been recognized. But this was to be expected since the elaboration of our concept of legal privacy grew out of our analysis of the similarities of right claims in these three areas.

Perhaps a more interesting question is why these three distinct areas developed in the American legal system. Obviously, the answer has to do with history and the purposes the Constitution and common law were intended to serve. For instance, one of the purposes of the First, Fourth, Fifth, and Ninth Amendments is to manage the relationship of the federal government to its citizens (including resident and visiting aliens), which was extended to management of the relationship of state government to its citizens with the adoption of the Fourteenth Amendment. It seems only natural that issues of privacy concerning the state or federal government and their citizens would develop as part of constitutional law (including constitutional procedure). In contrast, tort law developed in response to a need to regulate relations among individual members of society. In tort law, the emphasis is not on citizen-state or citizen-federal government relations but on interpersonal relations. It is therefore understandable that privacy concerns between individual (including corporate) members of society (that are not provided for by statute) would develop in this area of the law.

In sum, we can specify the coverage of the right to privacy in the three areas of the law where privacy has been recognized as follows: In the tort area, coverage of the right is the extension of our definition of a private state of affairs, qualified by the limitation that the issue arises between individual members of society.[50] In the Fourth Amendment area, coverage of the right is the extension of our definition of a private state of affairs, qualified by the limitation that the issue arises in regard to the state's gathering of evidence. In the constitutional area, coverage of the right is the extension of our definition of a private act, qualified by the limitation that the issue arises in respect to an interpretation of a statute or executive decree. (The emphasis on interpretation reflects the original reason for distinguishing the Fourth Amendment and constitutional areas of privacy law.) The question that should thus concern us now is whether we can specify the protection of the right in a way that will assist courts in deciding conflict of rights situations and situations wherein the state has a compelling interest.

Conflict of rights situations arise in privacy law where a valid privacy claim is in conflict with another constitutional right. The classic example of a rights conflict is the reporter who refuses to reveal sources despite their potential value to a defendant's defense in a criminal case.[51] Here the conflict is between the First Amendment right to a free press and the Sixth Amendment right to a fair trial. One could imagine similar conflicts in a case involving privacy.

In *Roe v. Wade*,[52] the Supreme Court specified the protection of the right to privacy where the state asserts a countervailing interest to be as follows: "Where certain 'fundamental rights' are involved, the Court has held that regulation limiting these rights may be justified only by a 'compelling state interest,' . . . and that legislative enactments must be narrowly drawn to express only the legitimate state interests at stake."[53]

A compelling state interest is the basis for a test of strength applied by the Supreme Court only to those cases where the interest at stake is deemed to be among the most constitutionally important. The idea conveys the notion that the state must show more than a rational relationship between a limitation of the privacy right and the promotion of a social good. In addition, the state must demonstrate that but for the limitation of the right an important social good cannot be realized. The significance of the Supreme Court decision to apply this test in *Roe* is that the Court must have considered the object of legal privacy in that case (namely, the ability to decide whether or not to bear or beget a child) to be a fundamental right.

One might ask, Exactly how precise is the compelling state interest test? Can it determine in every privacy case what the court's decision ought to be? The fact is that where the test was applied, in every case but one the right protected by the test prevailed. The only exception was the now infamous *Korematsu v. United States*,[54] but that case is distinguishable on the ground that it involved an issue of national security during wartime, and it has since been subject to sharp criticism. Still, a careful analysis of this test would not rely solely on the fact that the Supreme Court has in every case but one treated it as dispositive of the issue. For this certainly is no guarantee that the Court will continue to treat the test as dispositive in the future. More important, leaving the analysis at this point would not provide us with an understanding of why certain rights are afforded greater protection than others. The question of how to decide a conflict of rights situation, where one of the rights is to privacy, warrants a deeper analysis. This will be supplied in the next chapter, where the degree of protection will be specified as a normative consequence of the justification of the right.

So far, the discussion regarding the protection of the right to privacy has emphasized the constitutional area. Implicit in both the Fourth Amendment and tort areas is a similar protection. However, because of the way these two areas of the law are described, one does not usually refer to them in terms of protection.

In the Fourth Amendment area, protection of privacy is taken into account in two ways. First, there is the requirement that a search be conducted pursuant to a valid warrant issued by a judge or magistrate on the basis that there is probable cause to believe such a search will reveal evidence of a particular criminal activity.[55] Second, there are exigencies in which a warrant need not be issued because the warrant requirement has been effectively nullified by the circumstances. An example of such an exigency is the search incident to a lawful arrest.[56] In that instance, the probable cause necessary for the arrest is construed to allow a search of the person arrested in order to protect the lives of police officers from hidden weapons. Additional exigencies include a search incident to a stop and frisk, to knowing consent, to an unwitting invitation, to an abandonment, to hot pursuit of a criminal, to an urgent necessity, and to a custodial prerogative.[57]

Without examining the details of specific legal implications assigned to each of these exigencies (which may at the moment be in flux),[59] it suffices to say that each of the exceptions involves a type of situation where the Supreme Court has determined either that the protection of the right is outweighed by a greater policy interest on the part of the state (as with an arrest, stop and frisk, hot pursuit, urgent necessity, or custodial prerogative) or that no policy purpose of the Fourth Amendment is served by extending coverage of the right to the situation in question (knowing consent, unwitting invitation, abandonment). In the former situation, no specific test for protection of the right is mentioned, although it is obvious that the Court must have had a balancing test in mind when it recognized the exigencies.

In the torts area, a prima facie case exists for an invasion of privacy when the facts conform to elements of the common law tort or a statute. Conflicting interests enter in only if they serve to point out other relevant legal principles that might provide a defense to the prima facie case. For example, it would clearly be an invasion of privacy, under Prosser's first category, for one to barge into the private residence of another uninvited. Nevertheless, the law recognizes the Good Samaritan doctrine and grants an exception to the person who comes to the rescue of one innocently endangered. It is, therefore, a defense for intrusion into another's residence that the intruder entered for the purpose of rescuing a person trapped in a fire.

Again, in the torts area, as in the Fourth Amendment area, protection of the right of privacy is not made explicit. Here it is implied in the recognized defenses to a privacy claim. Thus, the Good Samaritan doctrine is one defense that applies in this area because the understanding is that the policy interest underlying the doctrine is more compelling than the interest supporting the privacy claim.

In cases where the invasion of privacy addresses embarrassing facts about a public official or public figure or holds the same up to a false light, the Supreme Court has recognized another relevant test of protection: A publication about a public official or a public figure is not an invasion of privacy where the statements contained therein were published without knowledge of their falsity or reckless disregard of their truth.[59] In effect, the test recognizes that a greater public interest is served by the constitutional right to freedom of the press than by the tort right to privacy. The rationale for the public official exception is that society should not be stifled by fear of liability in its legitimate interest to scrutinize those who hold public office.[60] A similar rationale for the public figure exception is that those who hold themselves out to the public, presumably for the purpose of influencing what the public does or believes, should be subject to a stricter form of public scrutiny than is the average citizen.[61] Otherwise, the law of torts governs intrusions on the seclusion or solitude of, publication of false or embarrassing facts about, or commercial exploitation of the citizen. The only other exception governed by constitutional law is the private citizen who is part of a current news story.

Based on the idea that rights have both coverage and protection, we can now distinguish privacy cases involving true conflicts of rights from those in which there is not even a prima facie claim for privacy protection. In *Bowers v. Hardwick*,[62] the Supreme Court held the State of Georgia's adult consensual sodomy statute constitutional when applied to homosexual activities in the home. The Court's rationale was that such activities do not fall within the coverage of the privacy right. The majority's opinion in *Bowers* implies that the constitutional right to privacy extends only to cases, like those involving the marital relationship, where privacy has traditionally been recognized. Given the above definition of a private act, however, the constitutional right to privacy does indeed cover adult consensual homosexual activities in the home. The only questions left, then, are whether or not privacy in the sense described is to be valued, and, if so, whether or not the state in *Hardwick* had a compelling enough interest to avoid the protection of the right. Since these questions go beyond the scope of the definition of privacy to its normative grounds, we have, as yet, to develop the machinery to fully answer them. For the present, given our definition of a private act and the fact that the Court mentioned only coverage in *Hardwick*, we can state that the decision is inconsistent with prior privacy cases.

In sum, the protection of the right to privacy is not an analytical object in the way that coverage of the right is. That is, it is not a consequence of conceptual analysis of the objects subsumed under *legal privacy*. Instead, the protection of the right is a normative object, based on a normative analysis of a proper conception of legal privacy. This means that if we are to provide a coherent and judicially useful explanation of the case law, we must be willing to address the normative issues. We must first provide a justification for legal privacy on a normative ground and then specify, in light of our justification, the protection of the right. Failing this, we will be unable to significantly advance the analysis of the law of privacy.

A JUSTIFICATION FOR LEGAL PRIVACY

3

A Normative Methodology

To say something is a norm is to say, first, that it is a standard, model, or pattern for a group and, second, that it is valued by the group as such a standard, model, or pattern for some concrete or abstract reason. The reason is concrete when it relates to fulfilling the immediate purpose of a person, as when one claims that some object, information, or action is private in order to prevent a particular interference. The reason is abstract when it relates to promoting a broader social value, as when one claims that privacy is an essential element of liberty or the democratic end of autonomy.[1] The point in bringing out this distinction between the concrete and the abstract is to avoid confusion about how the norm must be justified if it is to play an important role in the law.

Surely one who has a motive to assert a privacy claim and thinks a norm exists to protect that claim would feel justified (in the sense of believing that the norm applies to the type of situation they are confronting) in asserting the claim. That is, in light of a recognized societal value and the person's knowledge of how that value is applied in certain situations, the person would judge the given situation to be an appropriate one for the application of the value. A very different situation results where there is a question about whether something is (or, perhaps, more to the point, should be) a value or not. Here a strategy to justify the value's existence is to show that, within the context of an institution created to achieve certain goals, the value in question is necessary to achieving a goal of the institution.

Since one of the problems in the law of privacy has been to formulate the prescriptive force associated with a claim to privacy, this chapter will focus on the latter sort of justification. The reasons for taking up this question at this point are twofold. First, the existence of a norm falling under the concept of privacy with the meaning specified above has still to be demonstrated. Earlier, I said that protection of the privacy right differs from coverage in that protection is related to justification of the right; whereas coverage is related only to its definition. This implies that it is no longer satisfactory to consider only the objects that courts have found to involve a privacy interest. It is essential to also consider why the courts were right or wrong in affording protection to these objects and not to others. Since, taken together, these objects signal the coverage of privacy, what is at stake in this question is why privacy warrants legal protection.[2] Here justification means not that the courts have recognized the extension by which the concept was elaborated but that the courts were correct in recognizing the existence of a right to privacy to begin with.

Second, the weight of the norm associated with the concept of privacy has yet to be specified. Earlier, I gave another reason for why it was not enough to define legal privacy in order to explain how courts should decide cases: the method of definition does not provide crucial insight into the degree of protection (i.e., the weight) of the right, which determines when, and under what circumstances, a given interest in a case should take priority over competing interests. A good definition is capable of setting forth criteria that determine the extension or the coverage of the concept. While this is essential for deciding whether a case comes within the scope of a particular right, it is insufficient to decide the case in which there are other rights or interests present. In such cases, there may be conflict if these rights or interests overlap. When this happens, it is necessary to decide under which right or interest the case ought to be decided. Protection, then, provides a means for deciding how the case ought to be decided.

What a Privacy Justification Is

A privacy right is a valid claim falling under a particular norm I will call the "privacy principle." By this I refer to a norm that is subsumed under the concept of legal privacy and whose value is determined by the end to which the norm is related. (Exactly how this determination is made will be set forth below.) The value of the separation between right and principle is that, in this context, it provides us with an equivalent expression for the term *privacy right* that is more suggestive or productive of insight into the normative nature of the right. In other words, if the right of legal privacy, at least in its constitutional manifestation, is related to an end of democratic institutions (because the principle upon which it is based is thought to promote the end), then the value of that right to those institutions will be its value in promoting democratic ends. In this narrow sense of falling within institutional designs to effect particular ends, value becomes transitive. Essentially, we are specifying Y in the Gewirthian paradigm

A has a right to X against B by virtue of Y.[3]

Separating the idea of a privacy right from the idea of a privacy principle in this way implies that the justification of the right is dependent on the existence of a principle. A principle is properly described not as a goal to be reached (such as an economic, political, or social feature of the community) but as a standard that is observed because it is a requirement of justice or fairness or some other dimension of morality.[4] Rights, on the other hand, are valid claims based on standards.[5] The separation has the benefit of directing our attention to more fundamental ends that would set the basis for this and other standards (such as, in the case of constitutional law, those inherent in the kind of government under which we live). It also has the benefit of providing us a measure for deciding, when competing rights claims promote a common end, which claim should dominate.

Thus, the idea that a privacy right can be justified, based on the end for which the principle exists, assumes the existence of an institution with certain definite ends. The plausibility of this assumption is practical since institutions are created to achieve certain ends, such as the establishment of democratic government. Consequently, in the context of an institution with a defined set of ends, to will the ends is to will the means necessary to achieve them. In other words, not to recognize those principles by which desired institutional ends can be achieved is (within the context of those institutions) to erode the importance of the ends.

It might be objected that the ends do not justify the means where the means violate other values. But this objection misses the point, for what is at stake here is the justification of a right, not the justification of a particular application of the right. Particular applications may indeed be unjustified even though under some right they would seem completely justified. But the difference here is that there may be conflicting rights or other interests that have to be taken into account. Whereas, when justifying a right, there is only one principle to be taken into account—and it only to the extent of the value associated with the end to which it relates. Thus, principles are of a much more general order than rights, and this accounts for their application in the justification of rights.

The significance of this point is in what must be shown if the law of privacy is to be set on a firm foundation. For in drawing the connection between a privacy right and a privacy principle, the framework has been laid for showing the centrality of privacy to an end valued in all Western democracies.

Privacy and Autonomy

The justification of the right to privacy under a democratic government is its role in fostering individual autonomy. Here I assume that individual autonomy is justified as providing an ethical foundation for constitutional decision making. The basis of this assumption will be described briefly in the Epilogue.

By individual autonomy, I mean that the conditions that govern a person's participation in a rule-governed activity are only those conditions that are set by the activity itself. In this sense, individual autonomy is to be understood always in relation to an activity, as opposed to the more traditional method of trying to define it independent of context.

Traditionally, an action is said to be autonomous to the degree to which the actor manifests competence (in learning how actually to realize the changes he or she intends), independence (from the control of others), and self-control (over his or her own impulses).[6] While this definition presents valuable insights into the psychology of an autonomous person, it fails to distinguish situations in which, no matter what the state of mind, individual autonomy is limited. Such situations arise frequently in legal and moral discourse because there the actions of others, including the state, can affect the autonomy of the individual. For example, a person playing the stock market can be said to be acting autonomously with respect to the market only when the conditions under which he or she is acting are imposed by the market itself. Similarly, a couple's choice to beget a child may be autonomous if the government has not sought to interfere with their choice.

Additionally, my departure from the traditional approach alleviates the problem (except where the individual's mental state is in question) of determining where to draw the line on the kinds of influences that affect whether one is acting autonomously or not. For under this analysis one looks to the activity rather than the individual in order to make this judgment.

Finally, viewing autonomy in this way makes sense of the concept normally associated with autonomy in the context of democratic theory, namely, acting independently, by one's own law, as opposed to being subject to coercion or force by other persons or government. Furthermore, it opens the door to what we take to be the role of privacy in regard to autonomous activities.

In contrast to autonomy, which concerns the context in which one acts, I understand privacy to involve the nature of one's actions, because privacy is concerned with the effects one's actions have on other persons in the specified group. Thus, an autonomous action may not always be a private action (e.g., the President signing a bill into law). Moreover, a private action may not always be performed autonomously (e.g., a soldier, taking a shower under orders of his sergeant, is acting privately with respect to the press corp). In a culture that emphasizes conformity and stereotypical forms of behavior, there may be few truly autonomous people. Nevertheless, to the extent that people are autonomous at all, privacy helps to insure that autonomy. In this formulation, I deviate from the position of scholars who believe that privacy attaches only to information and states of affairs in favor of a position that includes self-regarding acts.

An objection to this approach is that the concept of autonomy as involving rule-governed activity is not able to distinguish situations that we normally consider to be autonomous from those we do not. For example, it might be argued that a slave whose qualifications for participation in the practice of slavery are only those set by the activity of keeping slaves is an autonomous individual.

However, this objection fails to distinguish between questions of privacy, which arise in the context of rules, from questions of autonomy, which ask what the rules should be. Under the former set of questions, a slave who is intruded upon by another slave might have a claim to privacy, depending on the rules that govern the master's household, even though the slave would not have a claim against an intrusion by the master. Whereas, under the latter set of questions, the institution of slavery would itself be called into question. In other words, since autonomy is being limited, privacy is to be understood in the context of the rules, not in comparison to what it should be in the nonslave (free person) situation. An argument for maximizing autonomy and thus maximizing privacy will be presented below. Its application to slavery will be seen once we recognize that the slave possesses the same basic voluntary and purposive traits that describe most human agents.

The justification of the right to privacy depends on a peculiar relationship of the four concepts of privacy, individual autonomy, democratic government, and other fundamental ends. The feature that distinguishes democratic government from other forms of government is that individual autonomy is one of its fundamental ends. Therefore, under a democratic government, the protection of certain acts is justified in order to foster individual autonomy.

Perhaps it will be objected that although autonomy might be a hoped for result from democracy, since democracy may be justified in many other ways (as productive of happiness or peace or as an application of sovereignty), it is by no means necessary that autonomy be produced. Consequently, it may very well be that democracy does not produce autonomy.

This objection assumes, however, that autonomy (like privacy) is necessarily a form of negative freedom or freedom from certain kinds of interferences. But this is not true. As will be made clear below, autonomy in the context of Western democratic institutions has elements of both positive and negative freedom. The positive side of autonomy is related to the very quality Western democracy is supposed to promote, namely, self-rule. In contrast, the negative side is related to self-rule by making the conditions for it possible. The difference between the two is that while the positive freedom is logically connected to self-rule, the negative freedom operates by a causal connection.[7] Hence, it cannot be said on either score that democracy does not produce autonomy.

Still, the protection afforded autonomy is not absolute, because democratic government is a species of government in general, which means that it has to fulfill all other fundamental ends of government, such as providing an economic system for the exchange of goods and services. Consequently, the permissible extent to which protection will be afforded autonomous acts is the maximum consistent with the promotion of other fundamental ends of government. Privacy is the criterion to determine which autonomous acts government can or can not proscribe. In this sense, privacy is not the same as autonomy because there are many acts that people can perform autonomously that are not private and that government can, therefore, proscribe. Privacy does reduce to autonomy, however, in the sense that those acts that government will protect are private acts with respect to the citizens at large.

Under this analysis, certain autonomous acts (such as using contraceptives) are to be protected a priori. For these are just the sort of acts that a government bent on fostering individual autonomy should want to protect. Similarly, certain states of affairs, which are less directly related to autonomy, but which, nevertheless, set out the conditions necessary for the performance of autonomous actions (either by guaranteeing selective disclosure or by protecting certain environments for the performance of private acts), should be protected a posteriori. In neither case does the protection extend to acts or states of affairs that are inconsistent with the other fundamental ends of government.

From this analysis, we have a basis for distinguishing between constitutional and Fourth Amendment privacy on the one hand and tort privacy on the other. In constitutional or Fourth Amendment privacy, a truly democratic government will proscribe only those acts that are inconsistent with other fundamental interests the government is obliged to protect. Whereas, in the case of tort privacy, government should rely on privacy as a means for the peaceful resolution of certain kinds of disputes.

PRIVACY AND WESTERN DEMOCRACY

Privacy should be valued in Western democracies because of its kindred relationship to the value of personal autonomy. Indeed, it will be argued below that protecting privacy (in the sense of the definition of a private act specified above) is, within the context of a democratic institution, a necessary precondition for guaranteeing personal autonomy. Conceived in this way, privacy should take on, relative to the institution in which it is set, the same prescriptive force as personal autonomy. In other words, if personal autonomy is a fundamental value to be fostered by democratic institutions, then privacy should be valued by those institutions to the same extent.[8] For the value of privacy is riding piggyback on the value of personal autonomy. This raises three questions. First, what is meant by personal autonomy in the Western sense? Second, what is the precise connection between privacy and personal autonomy, and in what sense is this a necessary connection? Third, to what degree is privacy valued by a democratic society?

Here we limit the focus of the answers to democratic institutions that are participatory, even if only in a representative sense.[9] By representative sense I mean that the members of these societies do not directly decide most of the substantial issues that affect them but rather elect representatives to decide such issues on their behalf.[10] Such institutions are thus distinguishable from those designed to foster what is substantially beneficial to society treated as an organic whole,[11] that is, to society treated as having a uniquely (or at least limitedly) defined set of interests. For such institutions are by their nature inclined to recognize individual self-interest, at least within certain constraints (concerning the very possibility of effective coordinate political action), as a legitimate basis for political action. Autonomy (with respect to the above description of Western democratic institutions) is an end for which such institutions exist. For this reason, democratic institutions provide for the election of a government by free citizens acting on their own interests.[12] The idea is that this arrangement is more likely than any other to foster individual autonomy. (Even though one could conceive of a benevolent despot who allowed his subjects more autonomy than are allowed citizens in certain democracies, there would be no guarantee that future leaders would be so generous.) The guarantee under a democratic form of government is that citizens can turn to the ballot box when concerned that too much individual autonomy is being given up.

This has two implications, only one of which is relevant to privacy. First, autonomy, in the sense used above, presupposes that the individual is free to vote; that is, that it is possible for the individual to meet citizenship requirements for voting. I call this freedom procedural, since it relates to how citizens participate within representative democracies. Second, autonomy presupposes that the individual is free to discover his or her interests, compatible with a like freedom for all. This qualification recognizes that the autonomy that is the end of democratic institutions is the autonomy of all citizens. I call this freedom substantive, since it gives significance to citizen participation in the electoral process. Because of the nature of the two freedoms, only the second of the two implications is relevant to privacy.

The procedural freedom might be thought of as the threshold condition for participation in a democratic institution. After all, voting is the most basic method by which citizens can influence governmental decisions. Moreover, while different societies will have different threshold conditions, obviously if the requirements for meeting those conditions are too stringent, the conclusion will be drawn that such institutions are less democratic than those that foster a more expansive participation. In this sense, then, procedural freedom should be considered positive, for it concerns the citizen's right to participate in the process of deciding Who governs me?[13] It does not deal with the negative aspect of freedom involved in How far does government interfere with me?[14] The latter, as will be more fully argued below, is important to questions of privacy.

The substantive freedom component of autonomy should be thought of as the condition that makes electoral participation in democratic institutions meaningful. For such institutions (as I have described them) have as their end the election of a government in which individual autonomy will be fostered to the maximum extent consistent with other ends of government. But the election of such a government would not occur were those who participate in the electoral process prevented from obtaining knowledge of what is in their self-interest. Realistically, I can rule out the case where the individual's actions in participating in the electoral process without knowledge of his or her own interests just happen to coincide with those interests.

Thus, from the standpoint of Western democratic institutions, individuals should be given the maximum amount of freedom to discover their own interests, compatible with a like freedom for all. In other words, the grant of freedom should not be limited to what individuals may presently perceive to be in their interests, for often human beings misperceive their true interests. Indeed, sometimes the only way human beings learn their true interests is to discover them as a consequence of actions based on perceived interests. The point is that at no time in the discovery process is there any guarantee that individuals have it right. This is because what is in one's interest is usually a matter of experience, and it is only in the context of experience that human beings identify their interests. But, this is no threat to democratic institutions as long as people vote, based on their perceived interests, against a background of opportunity to discover their true interests. As the perception of one's interest changes, how one chooses to vote can likewise change in order to reflect the new perception. Consequently, the most important factor for people to vote meaningfully is that they continually be allowed to discover their true interests.

In the United States, the Ninth Amendment provides some valuable assistance in guaranteeing to people the liberty to discover what is in their own interests. The amendment states, "The enumeration in the Constitution, of certain rights, shall not be construed to deny or disparage others retained by the people."[15] John Hart Ely has interpreted this clause to signal the existence of federal constitutional rights beyond those specifically enumerated in the Constitution.[16] This differs from the traditional position that the Ninth Amendment was brought into the Bill of Rights only to assure the ratifiers that the bill would not extend the federal powers beyond those specified in article 1, section 8. The argument was originally made by James Madison as a reason for adding the Ninth Amendment.[17] Ely argues that since the Tenth Amendment also serves to assure the ratifiers of the limit on federal powers, the Ninth Amendment must serve the function of bringing in additional rights beyond those specifically enumerated in the Constitution. We know from historical analysis, states Ely, that the Ninth Amendment was not meant to give either Congress or the states the authority to create new rights.[18] Consequently, Ely concludes, it must have been intended to incorporate other federal constitutional rights than what the first eight amendments set out in the Bill of Rights.[19]

In *Griswold v. Connecticut*,[20] Justice Goldberg argued, in his concurring opinion, for grounding the right to privacy in the Ninth Amendment. If Ely is correct, then perhaps the link to Goldberg's claim is what I identify as the substantive freedom component of autonomy. In other words, at the time *Griswold* was decided, it may have been too large a claim to say along with Goldberg that the Ninth Amendment protects "the 'traditions and [collective] conscience of our people.' "[21] This was Justice Black's point in his dissent when he stated, "The scientific miracles of this age have not yet produced a gadget which the Court can use to determine what traditions are rooted in the '[collective] conscience of our people.' "[22] However, if this chapter is able to show a clear connection between the protection of autonomy as a fundamental end of democratic government and the protection of privacy, then it would not be too large a claim for the Ninth Amendment to protect privacy as we have construed it. Moreover, insofar as fostering privacy promotes this goal of democratic government, there is all the more reason for Ninth Amendment protection. The legal basis for recognizing this justification of privacy in relation to the law will be detailed in Chapter 4.

Perhaps it will be objected that under the above conception of democratic institutions there is no guarantee that persons will in fact vote based on their interests. (From here on I shall use *interests* to mean *perceived interests.*) Indeed, it is not uncommon for people to vote against what they perceive as their interests. This objection, however, treats too narrowly what it means to vote on one's own interests. Presumably, if a person chooses to vote against his or her perceived interests, it is because he or she values another interest as more important. But this means the voter has adopted this other interest as his or her own. In other words, because of the circumstances in which the decision is made, an interest the voter would normally not treat as his or her own is now treated thus. From the standpoint of democratic institutions, however, this is of no consequence as long as the circumstance is not the state coercing or allowing someone else to coerce the voter. An exception to the aforesaid limitation allows for the provision of an honest education to aid the voter in determining his or her interests. The rationale behind the exception is an end of democratic institutions to promote autonomy in general.

The reason substantive freedom is valued at all is what gives rise to the view that an end of democratic institutions is not just to protect autonomy but to overtly foster it. The ideal is that knowing what is in one's own interests makes one a better voter. ("Better" being understood here to mean more aware of the impact the vote will have on one's own interests.) This comes about only if people have the training and resources to discover what is in their own interests. Where they do not have such training or resources, the ideal is just as much sacrificed as where government affirmatively interferes with the right to vote. In other words, where the ideal is not achieved, the end of democratic institutions is not served.

Consequently, in order to fulfill its institutional end, a democratic institution must not merely allow for the protection of autonomy in general but must overtly seek to foster it.

Another type of objection would be that if everyone were to vote based on their interests, this could have a negative effect on democratic institutions. Probably it would have little effect, since by and large most people already do vote based on their interests. But, even if it does have an effect, it will do so only if there are significant common interests or a strong consensus on who the representatives should be. In that case, however, a constraint is placed on just how far the institution can go in fostering the interests of the majority. The constraint follows from an end of democratic institutions to encourage all individuals to vote based on their interests. In other words, the concept of democracy specified above would be lost were a majority able to limit the right of a minority to vote based on their interests.

Given this end of autonomy, it should now be evident that we have democratic institutions because the way to insure autonomy is to ensure that each citizen votes according to his or her interests. And the way to insure that each citizens vote thus is to grant them the maximum amount of freedom to discover their interests, compatible with a like freedom for all. Consequently, one can evaluate the institutional structures of Western democracies according to their ability to foster the autonomy of their individual members.

The connection between privacy and autonomy is made in the following way. To be autonomous in the relevant sense presupposes being free to discover one's own interests, compatible with a like freedom for all. But, in order to discover one's own interests, it is often necessary to act based on one's perceived interests. Therefore, autonomy presupposes being free to act on one's perceived interests as long as one's actions do not constrain the possibility of a like freedom for all. Here freedom to act involves the negative sense of freedom, where the respondent is all other persons including government. This is to avoid alternative uses of autonomy, as when a disease or some other similarly uncontrollable force is said to affect one's autonomy. Moreover, it is to focus on the exact usage when one speaks about privacy, namely, that involving one's relationship to government or other human beings.[23]

Since being free to act so as to discover one's interests includes being free to act on one's interests, a fundamental end of democratic institutions must be the maximization of possibilities for all citizens to act on their interests. This occurs by insuring that every citizen is given the maximum opportunity to develop his or her potentials (via health, welfare, and educational programs) to compete for society's resources. Moreover, the state must not favor a particular subgroup of citizens (vis-à-vis special programs) so as to provide them with greater advantages not provided to others, except that the state may offset unjust advantages that exist because of past favoritism.[24] Otherwise, treating persons differently with respect to the basic distribution of goods of the state enhances the autonomy only of those favorably treated over those unfavorably treated. It does not maximize autonomy in general.

The objection that what is at stake is not the number of choices but the quality of the choices misses the distinction between Marxists and Western democracy. In Western democracies, the state has no business determining which scarce resources are worth competing for. Such judgments vary with the interests of the citizen making the choice. Of course, this does not mean that the state cannot enact educational programs that might affect the judgments one makes, perhaps by providing previously unknown information about the resources in question or about other alternatives that might be available. Nor does it prohibit the state from enacting laws that proscribe certain actions from being performed either because they are not compatible with a like possibility for others (as, for example, when the state does not allow as a criterion for voting that a person be of a certain race) or they directly infringe on another's basic freedom of action (as in the enactment of most criminal statutes). But it does mean that the decision as to the quality of available choices should (within the above exceptions) be left to the individual.

Privacy appears as a necessary precondition for maximal autonomy. That is to say, privacy defines an area in which a person can act without the actions being deemed incompatible with a like freedom for all. The point is that the consequences of one's action or one's potential to act can always be seen to interfere with the freedom of another person if for no other reason than that the other person may have knowledge that the act is permitted. Thus, if autonomy is to have any meaning it must be the case that certain consequences of one's actions are not deemed to be incompatible with a like freedom for all. In other words, because Marge is a private person, she can act as she wants to, do as she wants to, and think as she wants to, unlike the slave, who must act according to the master's wishes, or even the public official or the professional person who in certain contexts must act according to the interests of his or her constituency or the recognized canons of his or her profession.

It is now possible to make explicit the reason for the restrictions that were built into the definition of a private act, namely, that the act should not impinge in the first instance on a basic interest of another in the relevant group. Obviously, if an act can be described so as to meet these two requirements, this suggests that performance of the act is not incompatible with a like liberty for all. Hence, the act should be prima facie protected for all in the group.

Any looser restrictions that might incorporate derivative interests (without a compelling reason) would open the door to the possibility that no act is ever private. For example, to include derivative interests (which take into account social conventions and causal theories), would open the door to the possibility that offensiveness might become the measure of whether an act impinged on the interest of another. Obviously, offensiveness cannot be the measure, for then no one's actions would ever be safe. Even to limit the measure to what a substantial majority would find offensive could drastically limit the minority's participation in society. For example, a part of the gay and lesbian political agenda may be to obtain social, political, and legal acceptance for persons of nontypical sexual orientations. If offensiveness were the measure by which lesbians and gays were allowed to participate in society, the agenda certainly would be inhibited.

Still, it may become apparent that a given act (warranting prima facie privacy protection) is not actually worthy of protection because the state has a compelling interest to protect the derivative interests on which it impinges. What precisely is a compelling interest will be made clear below. For now it suffices to state that it cannot be any derivative interest that the state should protect, or no act would ever be private. Nevertheless, there may be some interests worthy of protection because they are essential to the possibility of autonomous action (for example, rules governing the possession of explosive materials in populated areas). Consequently, in deciding whether or not a claim to impingement of a derivative interest offsets privacy protection, a court must pass from an analysis of the self-regarding character of the act (which I call a level one claim) to an analysis of rules for determining autonomous behavior (which I call a level two claim).

Now the use of the phrase *necessary precondition* in describing the relation of privacy to autonomy is not meant to suggest that the connection between all forms of privacy and autonomy is logical. Instead, the connection that joins private information and private states of affairs to autonomy is a natural one. Human beings have conscious interests that can be impinged upon by other human beings. One way an individual's interests can be impinged on is for another human being to obtain certain kinds of information. For example, suppose Sally wants to be perceived as an honest person. Information that twenty years ago Sally cheated on a college admissions examination will run contrary to the perception Sally wants to create should it become known. Similarly, suppose Bill has an interest to live in a certain apartment building in Peoria. Suppose further that Bill knows that Gail, the landlord, will not rent Bill an apartment if she discovers that he is gay and that there is no law that prevents such discrimination. In this instance, Bill's freedom to live where he wants is directly contingent on certain information not becoming known to Gail.

A different situation occurs if what is at stake is a self-regarding act, for here the connection between privacy and autonomy is logical. That is to say, privacy in this instance merely delimits the boundary of autonomous actions democratic institutions will protect from those they will proscribe. For example, assume Bruce and Carol (both unmarried adults) want to have sex with each other but do not want to have children. Assume further that the legislature in the state where the two reside has passed a statute prohibiting the availability of contraceptives to unmarried adults. In this instance, Bruce and Carol's freedom to act may have been illegitimately proscribed by the action of the state legislature, since the act in question is by our definition a private act.

Related to private acts is the idea of a private state of affairs. The connection to autonomy, which again is causal, is made by providing a place or situation where private acts can occur. For instance, the privacy of one's home is protected because the home is recognized as a place where private acts should be able to occur.

From the above discussion, it follows that privacy is valued by democratic institutions for two reasons. First, it is a sort of boundary marker setting out the area wherein an individual's actions are thought (at least in the first instance) to affect only that individual. Second, it is a means for making possible private actions. In these ways, privacy allows for the possibility of autonomy by delimiting those human actions, information, and states of affairs that prima facie should not be interfered with. In this sense, then, privacy is connected to democratic institutions, namely, in making the object for which the institutions are valued (i.e., autonomy of the individual) possible. Thus, the importance of privacy as a value is tied to the importance of autonomy as a fundamental end of democratic legal institutions. Just how important a value privacy is will be made clear below.

Here it might be questioned whether one needs to protect private information or private states of affairs at all. It might be argued that autonomy can be protected merely by prohibiting interferences (that is, physical attacks or invasions or obstructions) of one's self or one's actions. Privacy, in the sense that it applies to information, does not limit interference only with one's self or one's actions. It also, and one is tempted to say, most characteristically, limits observation of one's self or one's actions. While it is clear how interference limits privacy, it is not so clear how observation or the possession of personal information does. For example, is one's autonomy limited by a Peeping Tom who watches one in the shower? Well, one might, because of shyness, stop taking showers, and that would be a limit to autonomy. But what would be the cause of this limit? Arguably, the cause is shyness (not the observer); one would be more autonomous by overcoming the shyness and concern about being watched. From this, it follows that a government that wants to foster maximal autonomy might best proceed by not catering to shyness with a privacy right, and the same would hold true to unpopular (but legal) actions one might shy away from doing because of fear of adverse public opinion. Indeed, the point becomes stronger if we assume there are laws prohibiting the physical invasion of body or property that directly block people's autonomous actions.

Recall, however, previous arguments. First, to maximize autonomy, we need to protect private acts. This is logically required once we treat autonomy as a value. Second, to protect private acts, we need to protect certain information and states of affairs. This is causally required depending on the society in which one lives. The question is, does protecting certain information and states of affairs contradict maximizing autonomy? Not necessarily, depending on the way people actually view themselves in society. If people will in fact be inhibited if certain information becomes known or certain states of affairs are not protected, then not to protect these things would be to inhibit autonomy. However, the challenge goes deeper than this to explore what the government should do with respect not only to what it protects, but also what it promotes—education, for example. Here the response may be put in two alternative lights.

Should the government try to change people's basic attitudes so as to make unnecessary in the long run protection of information or states of affairs? Or, are such protections necessary because of the inherent nature of human beings? Jeffrey Reiman argues that the right to privacy "is a right which protects my capacity to enter into intimate relations, not because it protects my reserve of generally withheld information, but because it enables me to make the commitment that underlies caring as *my* commitment uniquely conveyed by *my* thoughts and witnessed by my actions."[25] On somewhat different footing, Stanley Benn argues that "it was not that allowing men privacy would give them a better chance to be autonomous. It was rather that a person—anyone potentially autonomous—was worthy of respect on that

account; and that if such a person wanted to pursue his enter-
prise unobserved, he was entitled, unless there were overriding
reasons against it, to do as he wished."[26] Obviously, the matter is
by no means clear and is deeply psychological. What is clear,
however, is that in a society where knowledge can be gained
about the actions of another, there is the possibility of that knowledge having a chilling effect on the autonomous actions of others.
Therefore, in such a society privacy of information and states of
affairs has a prima facie claim to protection.

One might ask whether privacy exhausts the whole of liberty
that a democratic system would want to protect. Put in different
terms, privacy protects self-regarding acts. But are there any
other-regarding acts that government should protect?

Privacy does not exhaust the whole of democratic liberty. The
right to vote, for example, is an other-regarding act in the sense
that it affects both who is elected and what policies the government will maintain. Yet, this right is protected in a democratic
society. Beyond voting, at least in Western democratic countries,
certain property relations that are clearly other-regarding are
protected. For example, if I try to outbid my competitors by
making a bid to buy a company at a price lower than theirs, then I
am engaged in an other-regarding act. Capitalism is replete with
such actions, most of which are perfectly legal. What is their
justification?

It is not that the acts in question are self-regarding. They
are not. Instead, the justification is based on broader questions
of political theory. In voting, for example, the justification may
rely on the moral principle that no one be held to an obligation
to which he or she has not consented.[27] In the type of economy
the state adopts (capitalism or socialism), the justification may
be moral[28] or amoral,[29] depending on what human rights or
considerations of efficiency are taken to be the operant conditions.

Here we are concerned only with the limited area of liberty
that involves self-regarding acts. Consequently, we need not deal
with the broader questions of liberty. It suffices to say that the
concept of liberty, regardless of its ultimate justification, is a
broader concept than that of privacy.

Perhaps it is troubling to think of so close a connection between the value of privacy and the value of autonomy. If there are other bases, like freedom of expression, upon which the value of individual autonomy could be guaranteed, why elevate privacy to so high a level? The answer is that Western democratic legal institutions should value privacy, as they should value freedom of expression and certain other fundamental rights-principles, as necessary conditions for the possibility of autonomy. Were they not to value privacy, even if they were to value freedom of expression, how could it be said that autonomy was a fundamental end of these institutions? There is a difference between valuing privacy and valuing freedom of expression in regard to possible ends to be achieved. For freedom of expression could be valued on the ground that it is most likely to get at truth without having any concern for autonomy per se. The same would not be the case for valuing privacy.

Within the context of democratic institutions, valuing privacy is a necessary condition for valuing autonomy. In other words, although it might be possible to have autonomy based on other values, such as the principle of freedom of expression, with no consideration given to valuing privacy (indeed, one might imagine a legal institution that recognized a fair amount of individual freedom based on principles other than privacy), it would not be proper to say that individual autonomy is really a fundamental end of this institution. It is not the fact of autonomy that is at issue here. That may exist by mere circumstance. What is at issue is whether autonomy is valued as a fundamental end to be achieved by the institution.

Despite the specific freedoms that a seemingly democratic institution might afford, it may not be that autonomy is valued as a fundamental end. After all, one can value an autonomous person's possession of many specific freedoms (such as freedom of expression) without valuing their autonomy. The point is that valuing autonomy within the context of democratic institutions involves valuing the freedom to act for the purpose of discovering one's interests; whereas, valuing other freedoms usually means valuing them because they serve a goal, which may be, but is not necessarily, autonomy.

Nor is it possible to narrow our concept of Western democratic institutions to conform to a nonindividualistic point of view, because a central value of Western democracy is the sovereignty of the individual to discover his or her interests, compatible with a like freedom for all. So central, indeed, is this value to Western democracy that one could not claim that a democratic society in this sense existed if there were no institutions that valued autonomy as a fundamental end. Consequently, since autonomy is a fundamental value in such democracies and since valuing privacy is a necessary condition for autonomy (as has already been shown), it follows that for democratic institutions to fulfill their purposes, privacy must be similarly valued.

THE VALUE OF PRIVACY
Now that we have established the connection between the value of privacy and autonomy, the question arises: What is the degree of protection of the privacy norm? Here it is important to recall that privacy is valued because autonomy is valued, and privacy is conceived either as part of autonomy or (at least in this world) as a necessary precondition for autonomy. Furthermore, given that democratic institutions are established to effect certain ends, to the extent that autonomy is valued as an end of such institutions, privacy must be similarly valued.

Indeed, this is the key to answering the question, namely, that there are only two circumstances in which privacy must be sacrificed in a democracy. The first occurs when a competing right is in conflict with the right to privacy and the circumstances are such that autonomy is better served by protecting the competing right. The second occurs when the government seeks to protect an interest that is more compelling than privacy to the preservation of autonomy in general. Still, privacy provides the default position if the government is unable to establish its compelling interest. Otherwise, privacy regulates the degree of the state's intrusion to the minimum necessary to satisfy the state's compelling interest.

Here someone might make the following objection. The theory holds that the test of whether the state has an interest that justifies limiting privacy is whether that interest is necessary to promote autonomy in general. But if the state must limit one's freedom to act in order to promote autonomy, then that limitation determines the area of one's privacy and thus it cannot be a limitation of one's privacy.

This objection, however, does not pay close attention to the different levels of analysis being compared. The objection seems plausible only when one is dealing with a compelling state interest question, where one is no longer at the level of privacy in the context of rule-governed activities but at the second level, where the rules themselves are seen as limiting privacy. The objection fails because at the second level, autonomy itself is brought into question. What should the rules governing autonomous activities be? The answer will have the effect of defining the area in which questions of privacy at the first level will be decided. But it also has the effect of limiting that area of privacy at level one, if the government is able to establish its compelling interest. Consequently, actions at level two can also limit privacy, although in a different sense from actions at level one.

Conflicts of Rights

All conflicts of rights involving privacy can be resolved by an appeal to maximal autonomy. In other words, privacy conflicts with no rights where the conflict could not be resolved by asking which right best fosters autonomy in general. That is because privacy and all other rights with which it may conflict are necessary conditions for the very possibility of autonomy.

Essentially, every right is one of two types: active or passive. Active rights are those that permit the holder of the right to perform an action, such as making a speech, publishing a news report, or practicing a particular religious belief. Active rights involve negative freedom in the sense that the respondent of the right has a duty not to interfere with the holder in the performance of the right. In contrast, passive rights are those that afford the subject a benefit, such as a trial by his or her peers, a speedy and public trial, the right to compulsory process to obtain the testimony of witnesses, and the right to the assistance of counsel. Passive rights involve positive freedom in the sense that the respondent of the right has the duty to afford the holder certain benefits. The relevant difference between active and passive rights is that while in the former case the holder of the right is free to perform certain actions, in the latter case the holder of the right merely has a valid claim against the respondent to afford the holder certain benefits.

Privacy sets out the boundary within which the holder of the right is free to act. Other active rights also set out boundaries within which the holder is free to act. The boundaries of these different rights can overlap as, for example, when the press reports on the private lives of public officials. Consequently, the right to privacy can conflict with the active rights of others, as in the example, which is interpersonal. This is not true of passive rights because, from the standpoint of the holder, passive rights are more of an interest than are active rights. In other words, passive rights are intrapersonal in the sense that they represent specific benefits due the holder, rather than an unspecified freedom to act. Consequently, if the effect of an individual's act is to impinge on another's passive right, the conclusion has to be (at least where the interest is a basic interest) that between the two parties involved there is no valid claim to privacy. This follows from the definition of a private act, once it is recognized that a passive right can be treated as an interest of the right holder.[30]

Even where privacy is seen as protecting information, as in the selective disclosure cases, the result would be the same. For if the information could be shown to be relevant to the protection of a basic interest of another person, then between that person and the privacy right holder no privacy claim would be valid. Such cases are likely to arise in either the Fourth Amendment area or the torts area.

In the Fourth Amendment area, the problem is to balance the state's gathering information (usually as part of a criminal investigation) against its obligation to foster autonomy. To generally allow such gathering of information would probably have a chilling effect on persons in the exercise of their autonomy. Consequently, the state must be held to a high standard to show in advance of its gathering of evidence the relevance of the information sought.

One method is for the state to be required to obtain a warrant from a neutral magistrate based on a showing that it has probable cause to believe that such information exists and that it is relevant to the crime under investigation. What constitutes probable cause is always a matter of how much evidence the state must present in order to be allowed to obtain the additional information it seeks. Certainly, a minimum requirement, if autonomy is to be protected, is that the state give a coherent explanation for its belief that such information exists and that it is relevant to the matter under investigation. Furthermore, the state's explanation should be backed up by a source whose credibility is not substantially in doubt or by a source that has been independently corroborated. The only exceptions to obtaining a warrant should be where the state can show that it is not necessary to protecting autonomy or that it would lead to hiding or destruction of evidence.

In the tort area, the state is not usually a party. Even so, the same considerations concerning autonomy apply. The only difference is that now they apply in terms of how the law recognizes that one can be liable for another being damaged. In particular, damage occurs when an individual's autonomy is limited because of an intrusion upon his or her seclusion or solitude or into his or her private affairs; there is a public disclosure of embarrassing facts about the individual; he or she is brought into a false light in the public eye; or the individual's name or likeness has been taken for commercial purposes without permission or compensation.[31] In any of these situations, the individual's autonomy (in the sense of freedom to be let alone to act without interference) is limited.

For example, assume a person's solitude or seclusion was not protected or that any kind of information could be published about that person. Normally, individuals develop a reasonable expectation that they are free to perform certain actions within their own homes because of a general societal convention, which the law will recognize, that what goes on in a person's house is in most instances beyond public scrutiny. The assumption that the law will cease to protect such a state of affairs could have a chilling effect on such actions. This could have the effect of limiting a person in the discovery of his or her own interests. Similarly, with respect to the publication of private facts or facts that show a person in a false light, there is a chilling effect on a person's ability to act or to interact with others because what that person does or how he or she is known might be exposed (either honestly or in a distorted manner) to a public with whom the person does not wish to share that information.

Even the taking of one's likeness without compensation is a limitation on one's choice to appear as one wants or to contract to appear as others want. Consequently, unless there is an overriding reason to excuse liability, the law should provide civil protection for the person whose privacy has been invaded.

One such overriding reason is consent. If the party whose privacy is invaded consents, and if the invasion falls within the scope of the consent, no liability results.[32] In such a situation it can be construed that one's autonomy is not threatened since one has freely chosen to allow the invasion. Along this same line, cases allowing reasonable investigations into a person's credit status can be explained in terms of an explicit consent that is rendered on applying for credit. However, the situation becomes more troublesome when companies that receive these reports sell or give them to others without permission.[33]

Other cases where a defense to the privacy tort is recognized include the absolute privilege of a witness to testify in court or of an executive officer (such as a governor) to perform his or her duty, or the qualified privilege of the news media to report on public events.[34] In these instances, any breach of the recipient's autonomy is balanced against the greater protection to everyone's autonomy by allowing these practices to continue. Indeed, such an explanation would account for the high degree of protection afforded newspapers when publishing stories about public officials and public figures in contrast to their more limited protection to publish stories on a private person involved in a public activity.[35] In all these instances, it can be construed that the end of autonomy is better served by allowing the practices to continue.

This analysis suggests that since autonomy is geared to the actions one should be able to perform within the context of democratic institutions, any conflict between two or more active rights should be resolvable on the basis of which right better promotes autonomy in general. In other words, since the promotion of autonomy is an end of democratic institutions, any time one party's freedom to act conflicts with another's, a determination must be made as to which action will be allowed. That determination should be based on which action is most likely to promote the autonomy of all persons who stand in the same relation (namely, that of being a citizen) to the institution. This, then, should be the test for resolving conflict of rights situations involving privacy. Its basis is that autonomy is both a formal and a material principle concerned with fostering the freedom of all persons to discover what is in their own interest.

The point of limiting the determination to only those who stand in the same relationship to the institution is to recognize an important feature about political institutions: namely, that political institutions are designed to achieve certain goals for a certain set of persons and that for all members of that set the goals will be the same. In a democracy, the criterion for membership in the set is citizenship. More particularly, it is having met the requirements for the right to vote. The criterion may also be extended in a limited way to aliens to encourage them to become citizens or because it is believed on broader moral or political grounds to be the right thing to do. Consequently, for persons who have met the requirements, at least the fundamental ends of the institution must be the same. Moreover, inasmuch as there is no other legitimate basis in a democracy upon which to differentiate between persons who have not been found guilty of a crime (other than whether or not they have met the criteria for voting), at least no citizen's relation to the institution can be given a more preferred status than another's. Consequently, should a citizen, by some fault of the institution, be given a preferred status (say because the institution's protection of their privacy impinges the autonomy of others), the institution must correct that situation by bringing into balance its relationship to all its members. This is a moral claim to consistency that is implicit in the idea of an institution acting for a purpose.

Furthermore, it should be noted that the end of autonomy is not satisfied where the institution seeks only to maintain the same degree of autonomy for all. For if there were a way to increase for all citizens the range of possible choices for acting on their interests without loss or conflict, it would be contrary to the institution's end (to guarantee that all citizens be given the right to vote based on their interests) not to maximize the available choices. There is, after all, no reason for circumscribing rights, unless they are incompatible or so numerous as to overburden the practice defining them. Thus, no serious distortion of the conception of privacy is likely to follow from including within it the concept of maximal autonomy.

By way of illustration, consider two examples in which the test for resolving conflict of rights might be applied. In the first situation, the press publishes very personal information about a private citizen. In this situation, there is a conflict between freedom of the press and the citizen's right to privacy. The conflict is resolved by asking which right under these circumstances best promotes maximal autonomy. That is, which right better promotes the greatest amount of freedom for individuals to discover their interests? Clearly, a general practice of the press publishing personal information about individual citizens will hamper the actions of many citizens who might fear they will become the subject of an unwanted news story. Moreover, personal facts will not be a source of valuable information to readers. Consequently, here the consideration of promoting autonomy clearly favors the right to privacy over freedom of the press.

In contrast, for the press to report on a public official could serve the public interest since the official's actions can affect the interests of members of the public. Consequently, the information may be very important to voters' interests if it allows voters to determine whether the character or politics of the official will tend to advance their interests. Here it should be noted that the public would not have a legitimate interest in obtaining information that did not bear on the character or politics of the official. However, if such information cannot be separated from what the public does have a right to know, then the press should be protected unless it acts with actual malice or reckless disregard of the truth. Thus, in this instance, the promotion of autonomy would favor freedom of the press over privacy. The argument is not relying on the view that the real justification for the press in this example is that the public official qua public official has waived his or her right to privacy, for the point is not that the public official has waived the right but that the information is useful to the voters in being able to understand their own interests.

A somewhat different situation occurs where the press is reporting on a public figure such as a well-known entertainer, athlete, or former high public official. In this instance, the public's interest resides in the degree of influence these people can have by virtue of their access to media. Consequently, depending on what the press is reporting, the information may be very important to voters, whose attitudes are often shaped by the qualities these personalities represent. However, not all information should be discoverable, but only information that bears on the figures' credibility or the attitudes they are overtly promoting. Covert promotion of attitudes is not sufficient, as these could be too easily construed to justify any intrusion on privacy. Again, the malice test applies regarding the impossibility to distinguish private information that cannot be separated out from what the public has a right to know.

Two important exceptions are: first, where the public figure is no longer involved in mass communications or theatrical media and, second, where the medium has a limited audience. In the first instance, it is reasonable to determine a period of time after which these people will no longer represent a significant influence on the public. This would have to be based on an empirical analysis and would vary from personality to personality (former presidents perhaps having the longest-term affect).[36] Regarding the second exception, public figure status should apply only within the range of the audience that is likely to be affected. Beyond that, such figures should be treated as private citizens.

Finally, a word should be said about the private citizen who inadvertently falls within the public eye by unexpectedly becoming embroiled in a newsworthy event. In this instance, public status is not in their own right but is determined by the event about which the public has a right to know. Therefore, it would not be appropriate for the press to report any information beyond what is either connected with the event or arises out of it. Moreover, even this level of reporting should cease when the event ceases to be newsworthy.

This brings up the recent issue of "outings" that has arisen within the gay and lesbian communities. Should progay or proslesbian newspapers or magazines publish the names of closeted public officials and figures? The issue is one over which many people disagree.[37] One reason given for such outings is that they afford young lesbians and gay men role models and lift the "curse of secrecy" from gay life.[38] Another reason given is that those who remain in the closet unfairly benefit from the progress made by those who have come out. Some, however, would limit outings only to those persons who try to hide their sexual orientation by supporting homophobic (i.e., irrational antigay or antilesbian) legislation.[39] My own analysis would focus on whether the information such outings provides is relevant to making a citizen a better voter. Here the issue is one of fact. If the reason for the outing is to expose hypocritical officials or figures who overtly use their positions to support a homophobic agenda, then such outings may be justified provided that other less intrusive efforts have first been applied to convince these persons on rational grounds to change their positions. The point of the proviso is to guarantee that the action taken maximizes autonomy. Consequently, someone who makes an unwarranted attack on the autonomy of others in order to hide his or her sexual orientation or someone who promotes irrational legislation against lesbian or gay people cannot rely on the promotion of autonomy for protection. If the reason for such outings, however, is to provide role models, then (even if such role models may promote autonomy) the reason does not warrant the intrusion, because the precedent that would be set could more easily have a chilling effect on people's discovering what is in their own interests. Regarding the issue of fairness, the problem is that some may have chosen other alternatives to the freedom now available had they known that the cost would be coming out of the closet. For private persons, outings are almost never justified, since such persons usually do not command the kind of public attention that warrants an invasion of their privacy.

A second illustration involves freedom of religion and privacy. Assume a religious group felt that it would be damned to hell unless it attempted to prevent other persons from entering places of "ill repute." Here, the right to privacy of the patrons would be in conflict with the right to free exercise of religion by the group members. Again, the promotion of autonomy would provide the deciding criterion. However, the promotion of autonomy must take into account that the truth of the religious view probably cannot be assessed. Consequently, since it is likely that the promotion of a particular religious view, rather than allow individuals to decide in what religious practices they want to engage, will inhibit persons in discovering their own interests, the promotion of autonomy in this case would favor protecting the right to privacy over freedom of religion. Indeed, in this case, privacy is autonomy.

Compelling State Interest

The protection of autonomy is relevant to deciding whether an interest the state seeks to protect is truly more compelling than privacy. In such a situation, a court must decide whether the state's interest is indeed more compelling. Of course, this means there must be a criterion for making that determination. Since justification for the right to privacy is protection of autonomy in general (by making possible the discovery of individual interests), the state's interest is more compelling than privacy when it is more fundamental to fostering autonomy than is protecting privacy. For instance, the protection of the health and well-being of the general public is more compelling to fostering autonomy than is allowing a person to keep explosives or wild animals in the home. Only where the state's compelling interest would in fact better protect autonomy in general than would protecting an individual's or a group's privacy can privacy be restricted.

The basis for this claim is similar to that of the conflict of rights situations, but *interests* replaces *rights*. First, fostering autonomy in general is a fundamental end of democratic institutions, and privacy (in the two senses argued above) is a necessary condition to the possibility of autonomy. Second, it is at least plausible when considering autonomy against individual privacy claims that certain interests may better promote autonomy than privacy. Consequently, in democratic institutions whatever best promotes the end of autonomy in general (be it an individual privacy claim or some other interest) must be protected.

From this analysis follows a test for determining whether the state's interest is sufficiently compelling to warrant intrusion on an individual's privacy. The test is whether promoting the individual's privacy would in fact inhibit autonomy in general. If it would, then the institution is duty bound, if it is to fulfill its purpose of fostering autonomy, to intrude on the individual's privacy.

Here, the following question may be raised. Can one sensibly argue that autonomy matters most, no matter what the consequences? What if the interest at stake is related to another end of government (not necessarily democratic, but government in general)? For example, if the government raises taxes in order to provide for the common defense, health care, and so on, does this not impinge on the autonomy of the taxpayer to determine how to spend his or her money? One does not have to advocate a utilitarian theory in order to point out that any maximizing or unifocal outlook is doomed to be insensitive to moral and social nuance.

However, we must be sensitive to the level at which the dispute arises. The example concerns the government's compelling interest to provide certain kinds of needed services. This is a level two issue. It is resolved by appealing to autonomy. True, where the government can prove its compelling interest (as for most of the examples cited in the objection), the area of private actions, at level one, will be limited. In this situation, the maximum the government can intrude on private action is the minimum necessary to satisfy its compelling interest. In other words, protecting autonomy is not incongruent with the government's fulfilling its other fundamental ends. Rather, it is the measure of how far the government can go in fulfilling these other ends.

Still, it may be objected that some interests of government have nothing to do with autonomy. In that case, how should a court decide whether the state's interest is sufficiently compelling that privacy can be overridden? Obviously, if promoting another end of government truly would have no effect on autonomy, there would be no conflict with privacy at level one. Under the more likely interpretation of the question, however, providing for another end does limit autonomy. Therefore, the real issue is: How do we characterize the interest government is seeking to protect?

Any end of government can be expressed in terms of the interests of the person or persons on whose behalf the government is acting. If the proper characterization of this interest is a basic (as opposed to derivative) interest, then, again, no conflict arises. The reason is that, by definition, the right to privacy circumscribes an area of seemingly clear instances in which only self-regarding actions are at stake. Privacy concerns only actions the consequences of which do not impinge in the first instance on the basic interests of any other person in the specified group. Where the interest is basic, any action that impinged on it in the first instance would by definition not involve privacy. As for the case of a derivative interest, if promoting the interest would conflict with privacy, the matter would need to be disposed of according to the usual method of deciding whether the government could show that the interest it sought to protect was more likely (than protecting privacy) to protect autonomy in general.

Finally, it may be objected that in a certain very narrow set of circumstances, the interests government needs to protect may be so strong that although they may affect autonomy, they should not be subject to being measured in terms of autonomy. Take, for example, Abraham Lincoln's suspension of the writ of habeas corpus during the Civil War. A modern analogy might occur in the aftermath of a nuclear war. In either of these situations, the problem is not that the analysis has failed, however. Democratic institutions cannot operate at the point where the very stability of the system is at stake and where there is a real and imminent threat of war or revolution by force and violence. As soon as the democratic institutions are restored to operation, the above analysis becomes applicable, and any action taken during the intervening time has to be justified as meeting a compelling state interest.

A variation on the above objection is: Should we view democratic government as directed toward promoting (and where possible maximizing) autonomy in general, or might democratic government merely allow autonomy after other fundamental ends of government are met? The question presupposes that other fundamental ends might not be met in certain circumstances were autonomy to be promoted. Here one has to wonder what the appeal of democratic government would be if the only time it was given deference was when little else was at stake. Otherwise, a threat to the very survival of democratic government may necessitate a limit on the promotion of autonomy. However, the state then would not be justified in extending the limitation to any period longer than the period of threat.

The existence of a compelling interest does not mean, however, that the state can intrude to any degree it likes on the individual's privacy. The limit is drawn where the state can achieve its interest with the least intrusion on individual privacy. This limit is established by the idea that privacy is still a value for democratic institutions, even though under some circumstances the obligation to protect general autonomy justifies the state's intruding on an individual's privacy. To put the point differently, the maximum amount of government intrusion into privacy must be the minimum intrusion that can achieve the compelling interest that government has at stake. For example, if the police had probable cause to believe that a bomb was going to explode in a building in an area where innocent people could be killed or injured, the police should not be prevented from entering the building for the purpose of deactivating the device. Here the privacy interest of the person owning the building is outweighed by the state's duty to protect the autonomy of all. However, the state would not be justified in carrying out a general search of the building once the bomb had been located. In this latter situation, autonomy in general is in jeopardy when the state can, on its own, decide when to conduct a search.

Before concluding this chapter, we should take up two additional objections regarding the overall justification for a general right to privacy based in autonomy. The first objection is: Since the analysis of the current chapter purports to draw from understandings of a more general quality than those specifically associated with the Constitution, the treatment falls into a kind of popular picture, which is ultimately very undemocratic. Or, to put it differently, the treatment seems to resolve the Madisonian dilemma of having to reconcile self-government with the rights of the minority by favoring the latter group under the guise of protecting autonomy.[40]

But this objection fails by presuming that protecting privacy at the first level or autonomy at the second is necessarily going to conflict with majority rule. In fact, the way privacy is defined at the first level prevents it from conflicting with any basic interest in the relevant group of actors. As for the second level, privacy may conflict with other interests the government might want to foster. However, in that instance, the protection against overbearing majorities and minorities is the determination of which interest better fosters autonomy in general. Since protecting autonomy also protects democracy (by guaranteeing that each citizen can determine his or her interests), relying on autonomy as the criterion does not impinge on majority rule but, in fact, promotes it. As Mill would be quick to point out, protecting privacy at the second level ensures, first, that government does not do what individuals can do better; second, that individuals be allowed to improve their own mental faculties by obtaining relevant information and exercising judgment; and third, that government not be given unnecessary power.[41]

Still another objection is that the approach of this chapter fails to explain why privacy can be so important to persons or cultures where autonomy is not sought or valued. It should be noted that nothing in the above analysis requires that to protect privacy one must value autonomy. Indeed, there may be other bases for justifying a right to privacy that are not related to autonomy.[42] All this chapter claims is that in a democratic society where autonomy is valued as a fundamental end, privacy must be similarly valued.

The considerations of this chapter have been focused at three levels. At the lowest level are the rule-governed activities in terms of which people act autonomously. Here questions of privacy arise when the actions of one person or group are alleged to intrude on the interests of another. At this level, the test for determining whether an action is permitted is whether it is self-regarding. At the middle level, the question is not whether an action has violated someone's privacy but whether the rules that define the autonomous activity themselves limit privacy. For example, does a statute prohibiting adult consensual homosexual acts limit an individual's autonomy? The point is to discover what the rules defining autonomous activities should be. At this level, the primary concern is not with privacy but with autonomy. Consequently, the test is: What rules would better protect autonomy in general? Finally, at the highest level, the concern is to adjudicate between conflicting rights that promote autonomy but to different degrees. At this level, the test is not which right better protects autonomy in general (presumably they both protect it) but which better fosters maximal autonomy. Whichever right that is, the government is justified in promoting it. Thus, these three levels summarize answers to the principle normative questions that have been raised in the law of privacy.

PART
TWO
PRACTICE

LEGAL EPISTEMOLOGY AND PRIVACY

4

So far I have assumed that justification for a legal right to privacy grounded in political morality would satisfy those in the legal profession of the merits of my claim. Now I will show why this should be true. On its face, moral justification of a right is not the same as legal justification. Even so, in a context where what is at stake is a fundamental constitutional right, moral justification may be not only all that is available but exactly what is needed. In setting forth the reasons for this position, I will show how my theory accords with a broad interpretative theory of legal decision making. I also will show what is wrong with a recent theory of privacy that attempts to avoid an appeal to political morality as well as what is wrong with one that treats only a utilitarian view of legislatures without regard for the role of courts in recognizing nonexplicit fundamental constitutional rights.

As a caveat to this discussion, I should say something about what authority means in this context. In traditional legal parlance, an authority (such as a constitutional provision, a statute, or a past case that is on point) is a kind of reason for how a case should be decided that a judge is not free to ignore. The definition becomes blurred when the court (as in the United States Supreme Court) is the highest in the land, for there is no higher court in which to appeal, and the justices have life tenure. Even so, the high courts of countries like the United States, which follow the doctrine of *stare decisis* (the view that present cases should be decided consistent with past-case decisions) are obliged to at least take into account the decisions in relevant prior cases. Consequently, though in the United States the Supreme Court can choose to overrule a prior case, in order to do so it must first show why the prior case no longer fits the conception of the Constitution held by a majority of justices. Here political morality enters as the basis for those conceptions held by the justices.

Dworkin's Interpretative Theory

Little has been better said about the need for incorporating political morality into judicial decisions other than what Ronald Dworkin has said. The strict constructionist (such as Bork) believes that the language the framers used when they wrote the Constitution is the only basis upon which the Supreme Court can properly make constitutional decisions. The rationale follows a contractarian line. Where the framers used vague language, the view is that the Court can rightfully consider, in deciding an issue of constitutional interpretation, only what the framers had in mind given their historical time and circumstances.[1] Thus, the strict constructionist would recognize only a very limited set of constitutional rights because she or he considers only what a limited group of people thought at a particular moment of history.[2]

Dworkin tells us that the theory of meaning on which the strict constructionist view is predicated is too narrow in that it ignores a distinction philosophers have recognized but lawyers are only now beginning to appreciate. "Suppose I tell my children simply that I expect them not to treat others unfairly. I no doubt have in mind examples of the conduct I mean to discourage, but I would not accept that my meaning was limited to these examples, for two reasons."[3] First, one expects children to apply a general rule to situations one may not have thought about or even could not have imagined. Second, if one became convinced that a particular instance of a general rule one thought to be correct was, in fact, in error, one would not claim that the general instructions were wrong, although one might admit to having misunderstood their application. In such a circumstance, one would be inclined to say that the children were meant to be guided by the "concept" of fairness, not by any specific "conception" one may have had in mind.

Dworkin reminds us that the Constitution appeals to various moral concepts; it does not prescribe specific moral conceptions. When the Constitution condemns violations of due process, it appeals to the meaning of due process. It does not afford special standing to any specific view on what should constitute a violation of due process. On the other hand, when the court determines whether a violation of due process exists, the court's view on what would constitute a violation is at the heart of the matter. In other words, when the Constitution appeals to due process, it poses for the court a moral issue. When the court lays down its conception of due process, it attempts to clarify and resolve that issue.

This says to the court attempting to decide a constitutional question that it must look beyond the letter of the constitutional text, even beyond the more concrete beliefs that the framers may have had in mind. Dworkin argues that the court must consider, for example, in the death penalty decision, not whether capital punishment was standard and unquestioned when the constitutional provision against cruel and unusual punishment was adopted. Rather, the court must consider whether, responding to the framers' appeal to the concept of cruelty, they can "now defend a conception that does not make death cruel."[4] For, if the Founding Fathers had meant to provide particular conceptions to govern the court's decision making, they had available to them the language with which to do that. The fact that they did not use this language indicates that this was not their intention.

The objection from political skepticism about the objectivity of moral principles does not work to deny these as a source of law because, as Dworkin notes, we surely do not want to say that a person does not have "a moral right against the state if for some reason the state would be wrong to treat him in a certain way, even though it would be in the general interest to do so."[5] Consider, for example, that before 1954 it was legal to require black children to be educated in all-black schools.[6] Surely we would not say such a situation was just, even though to change it might make a great many people unhappy. Nor does the argument from democracy work. The idea that the court should not usurp the place of the legislature in representing the majority will is like asking those in political power to be the sole judge of their own actions.[7] This opens the door to tyranny by the majority. Nor does it work to shoot down the absurd idea that "law based on principle will lead the nation to a frictionless utopia where everyone is better off than he was before." There is quite a difference between appealing to an invisible hand of history and appealing to a principle because it is a moral principle.[8] So the question becomes, To what should courts look?

Dworkin believes the courts should not give deference to arguments of policy over arguments about principle. The difference is that an argument of policy seeks to "justify a political decision by showing that the decision advances or protects some collective goal of the community as a whole." In contrast, "arguments of principle justify a political decision by showing that the decision respects or secures some individual or group right."[9] An analysis of the two reasons that are often offered in support of the former approach reveal that the latter is more suited to adjudication. First, people of a community should be governed by those officials who were elected by the majority. This is necessary to prevent tyranny by the minority. Second, if judges are allowed to make new law and apply it retroactively, then those who acted prior to the change of the law would be subject to unjust punishment.[10] At first glance, the two reasons support the idea that adjudication should be as unoriginal as possible, but on reflection they present more powerful objections to judicial decisions being based on policy rather than on principle.

With policy, the first reason makes sense because policies are political compromises among individual goals and purposes in search of the common interest. Likewise, with policy, the second reason also makes sense, since we all agree that it would be unjust to punish someone in the name of a new duty. In comparison, the case for basing judicial decision on principles is stronger than either of these two policy rationales.

With principle, the first rationale offers little objection because an argument based on principle does not rest on assumptions about the nature and intensity of the different demands and concerns distributed throughout the community. On the contrary, an argument of principle fixes on some interest presented by the proponent of the right it describes, an interest alleged to be of such a character as to make irrelevant the fine discriminations of any argument of policy that might oppose it.[11]

The second rationale does not apply against an argument on principle, for if the party claiming a right truly has that right, then there is already a corresponding duty on the other party's part and not a new duty imposed by the court.[12] The analysis applies symmetrically in the standard constitutional civil case and asymmetrically in cases involving constitutional criminal procedure.[13] Regarding the latter, a defendant who is innocent has a right to be let go, while the state has no corresponding right to hold the defendant who is guilty. This is because in a criminal case we do permit, also as a matter of principle, certain restrictions on state behavior, such as those regarding the gathering of evidence.

What, then, should courts look to when deciding fundamental rights questions? Dworkin believes that a judge must rely on a constitutional theory that is shaped by a combination of principles and policies that jointly justify the scheme of government. Such a theory can come about only by an integration of political philosophy with "institutional detail."[14] This means that the judge must weigh different possible theories against the broader institutional scheme and then elaborate the contested concepts that the successful theory employs." In short, the judge needs to decide what rights people have against the state, and the only way to do this is by fusing constitutional law with moral theory.

But, on which moral theory should a judge rely? In determining the answer to this question, Dworkin suggests that we consider a literary example.

Suppose a group of Dickens scholars propose to discuss David Copperfield as if David were a real person. They propose to say, for example, that David attended Salem House, that he was industrious and so forth. They might well develop the following ground rules governing these various assertions:

   (1) Any proposition about David may be asserted as "true" if Dickens said it, or said something else such that it would have been inconsistent had Dickens denied it.

(2) Any proposition may be denied as "false" if Dickens denied it, or said something else such that it would have been inconsistent had Dickens said it.[15]

Under the rules of this example we know that the statement that David attended Salem House is true and, correspondingly, that the opposite statement is false. We would also have to admit about many other statements that we could not judge if they are true or not. But, if we were now to relax the rules to allow further propositions about David to be true if, for example, they would very likely be true of a real person who had the properties of David, then we will have many fewer cases of questions where there is no right answer. Accordingly, we could relax the rules even further to allow a proposition about David to be true because it provides a better fit than its negation with propositions already established. Here the measure of fit might be the story's dramatic quality or it might be a particular psychological view of the characters.

Dworkin believes a well-developed legal system, such as British and American models, can be seen to resemble this form of literary exercise.[16] Under this view, a proposition such as that Tom's action violated Jane's right to privacy is true if the best justification for the body of privacy propositions already settled provides a better case for the violation than the contrary proposition, but it is false if the best justification provides a better case for the contrary proposition.[17] Here the measure of fit is the degree to which a particular political view is able to account for what is settled law.

While Dworkin acknowledges that legal reasoning makes use of normative as opposed to narrative consistency, and that the former is more complicated, he nevertheless argues that the analogy can be drawn. Consequently, in the same way that we would draw on the rules of the literary game if we were attempting to decide whether David had a sexual relationship with Steerforth, we could draw on the rules of the legal game if we are attempting to decide whether a particular privacy proposition provides the best justification for the body of privacy propositions taken as settled.

Dworkin argues that there are two dimensions for judging whether a theory provides the best justification of available legal materials: the dimensions of fit and political morality.

The dimension of fit supposes that one political theory is *pro tanto* a better justification than another if, roughly speaking, someone who held that theory would, in its service, enact more of what is settled than would someone who held the other. . . .

The second dimension—the dimension of political morality—supposes that, if two justifications provide an equally good fit with the legal materials, one nevertheless provides a better justification than the other if it is superior as a matter of political or moral theory; if, that is, it comes closer to capturing the rights that people in fact have.[18]

In my work, I first seek to determine what legal privacy means and then I offer a justification for why it should be valued as a right. In doing so, I follow Dworkin's notion of fit to arrive at a conception of privacy that is likely to reproduce more of the settled law of privacy than any definition previously considered. This is evident from the fact that my definitions of a private act and a private state of affairs, which I rely on in developing my conception of privacy, were arrived at from a consideration of the objects that are most often categorized under the term *legal privacy*. Moreover, the value of the definitions at the level of generality that I obtain is that they assist in criticizing other privacy cases that are more controversial.

As for Dworkin's second element, I ground my theory of the right to privacy in a theory of political morality that has autonomy as one of the fundamental ends of democratic government. In this way, I am not only able to explain why a democratic society should seek to protect privacy, but also I am able to account for the relative strength of the right to privacy compared to other constitutional rights. Finally, I note that the political theory I employ can, as I suggest in the text, be expected to reproduce justifications for many other constitutional rights. The grounding might be different from what it could be were some of these rights considered separately. But it will be a grounding that will be able to encompass more, rather than less, of the rights we take as settled.

Mohr's Privacy Justification

In Richard Mohr's recent book *Gays/Justice: A Study of Ethics, Society and Law*,[19] the arguments for an understanding of the legal right to privacy are not very different from my own method of analyzing the concept of legal privacy. (I look to a host of privacy cases from several different areas of the law; Mohr looks to various explicit rights provisions of the Constitution.) In contrast to my work, however, Mohr uses his method of analysis to justify a general right to privacy; whereas, I answer the question of justification with an argument based in political morality.

Mohr distinguishes his view from Dworkin's when he states that although others argue "that political philosophy should largely determine what rights there are . . . , my own suggestion is less venturesome and heady than these interpretive theories which have The Good as the wind in their sails."[20] Mohr's approach to deciding what rights are implicit in the Constitution is to make a reflexive application of the Fourteenth Amendment's equal protection clause to the Constitution per se. In a footnote, Mohr argues that Dworkin's analogy to literary interpretation leaves too much room for political theory and therefore too much room for judges to do what they want to do. The problem with Dworkin, according to Mohr, is in the analogy to literary interpretation. As Mohr explains, in contrast to a "detail-laden and event-packed 500-page novel," the Constitution is "a rather thin tome."[21] The First Amendment has only forty-five words; the Fourteenth Amendment's equal protection clause has only fourteen—and all very general. Consequently, political theory, according to Mohr, must, under the Dworkian model, do the whole job of providing content to constitutional rights, in effect making our rights "whatever five justices think they are."[22]

I think Mohr conflates two very different things. On the one hand is political theory, on the other the personal likes or dislikes of the justices. If Mohr's criticism is that justices will follow those political theories that reproduce only their own personal moral reflections, then I think he undervalues Dworkin's view. First, recall that Dworkin requires that the political theory "fit," by which he means that it reproduce more of what is settled law than any known alternative view. Second, if two or more theories have equal fit (an unlikely situation) then the superior is the one that captures the rights people actually have. This latter claim is an appeal to moral theory.

Mohr's countermove to this response is to claim that Dworkin cannot rely on precedent "to fill in a great deal of "literary detail" [because he] is unable to clarify why precedent should be given any special weight within his scheme, especially when precedents are generated out of theories of constitutional interpretation different than his own."[23] However, I do not believe that this move works either. Dworkin's notion of fit requires that the theory reproduce what is settled law, not what is controversial. Only then, and if there is still a choice left among theories, does Dworkin's method of interpretation affirmatively state that the theory is superior that produces the rights people actually have, presumably under some moral theory.

Mohr argues that fundamental rights, like privacy, are not derived from natural law or cultural consensus or wide majorities or "the Good," but "are *positively suggested* as principles by the specific explicit provisions" of the Constitution.[24] Mohr's claim is epistemological rather than causal or substantive. It is that explicit constitutional provisions direct us to more general precepts, which are the source for other implicit provisions like that protecting marital contraception.

Mohr seems to have arrived at this view from a claim that Justice Douglas makes in the contraception case *Griswold v. Connecticut.*[25] "The foregoing cases suggest that specific guarantees in the Bill of Rights have penumbras, formed by emanations from these guarantees that help give them life and substance."[26]

Mohr points out that the critics of Douglas's penumbral theory have simply misunderstood the metaphor. They have taken his metaphor to mean that certain rights, like the right to marital contraception, have their source and substance in the penumbras of various explicit guarantees. This, Mohr claims, is not the source of these implicit guarantees. Their source, like the source of the more explicit guarantees, resides instead in more general precepts that give rise to all rights.

The "penumbra" metaphor can be spelled out as follows: The specific explicit guarantees of the Constitution are areas of full illumination. Rights to marital contraception and the like are areas of half light and half shadow. And what the state may bar or require is an area of total shadow. Privacy understood as a general right is the source of light producing *both* explicit *and* implicit provisions of the Constitution. The critics of Douglas who cynically claim that he found the right to privacy "lurking in the shadows" of the Constitution have simply misconstrued his careful metaphor.[27]

That this is what Douglas meant, Mohr believes, is made further evident by the fact that following his penumbral claim Douglas "begins to enumerate specific provisions of the Bill of Rights which are a 'facet' of [this more general] right to privacy."[28] Out of these specific provisions of the Bill of Rights one begins to discern the scope and content of the background values, which in turn give rise to the implicit guarantees.[29]

Never, however, does Mohr state precisely the scope and content of these background values, even how many there are, what their degree of generality is relative to the explicit and recognized implicit precepts and to each other, or whether they are all of the same degree of generality. Instead, he goes on, from his discussion of Douglas's strategy, to state that the equal protection clause of the Fourteenth Amendment directs judges to look for and provide a consistent interpretation of these background values. In particular, Mohr says

that the values that inform specific [constitutional] guarantees [like freedom of speech, press, et cetera] also apply to unmentioned guarantees which express similar values. The Clause commits the Constitution to a rule of consistent application of principles at the level of constitutional guarantees, though not to any principle that just happens to be a good one or even the best one.[30]

Having sketched a method for determining the scope and content of the values behind the explicit precepts of the Constitution, and having stated that they should be consistently applied, Mohr next looks at what translates these general values into rights. Here Mohr claims that the Ninth Amendment's proviso that "the enumeration in the Constitution, of certain rights, shall not be construed to deny or disparage others retained by the people" steps in to give the implicit outcrops of these general values their force and substance.[31]

In sum, Mohr claims that the Fourteenth Amendment's equal protection clause directs judges to look for background values that underlie the specific explicit constitutional provisions. These specific explicit provisions, in turn, set the scope and content for the various background values. Once scope and content are clear, the Ninth Amendment comes in to convert these background values into fundamental implicit rights.

How the Fourteenth Amendment directs judges where to look Mohr does not make clear, except to say that "the Clause commits the Constitution to a rule of consistent application at the level of constitutional guarantees."[32] But, this is nothing other than a philosopher's way of saying that the clause provides a formal principle for constitutional decision making. Historically, the more interesting question has been not whether the clause requires that like cases be treated alike but whether the state has classified a group of people in such a way so as to deny them a fundamental right.[33] This, of course, means that there have to be fundamental rights. Where such rights are not clearly stated or implied their existence may be in doubt. At this point, we no longer have a formal question but rather a material one. To resolve it requires the application of a political theory about the kind of government we have.

While I applaud many of the things Mohr says in his book, I believe his method is incapable of justifying a general right to privacy. Putting aside whether I agree with Mohr's interpretation that Douglas was building an epistemic as opposed to a substantive case for some general principles, including privacy, it seems to me that even if this is what Douglas had in mind, the idea that the Constitution has unmentioned guarantees is problematic. To the strict constructionist, for example, this amounts to heresy. Even if we assume that the framers did intend background values, how can we verify the contents of these values? Mohr's analysis does not seem to help here, for the explicit precepts are too specific to give us a determinate criterion. Moreover, is it not just as plausible that the framers limited the guarantees in the Constitution to address only specific issues (like speech, press, and so on) in order to avoid a more general interpretation? The old maxim of statutory construction *inclusio unis est exclusio alterius*[34] seems equally applicable here. I am not saying that I agree with this position (as is evident, I do not), but without an appeal to political morality it seems as plausible as any other. In short, I do not think that Mohr can avoid getting his hands wet with political theory by extracting the Constitution from the very scheme of government it was meant to create.

Like Mohr, I feel that privacy is an implicit constitutional right. Unlike Mohr, however, I consider political morality in that I conceive of privacy in relation to autonomy, democracy, and other fundamental ends of government and not just in relationship to explicit constitutional guarantees. In this regard, I produce a justification for privacy that grounds private acts in a broad principle of autonomy a priori and private information and states of affairs in the very structure of democratic government a posteriori. That this bears resemblance to the United States is incidental, for as I have argued above, privacy should be part of any democratic society that had autonomy as one of its fundamental ends. Thus, while I arrive at a justification for a right to privacy that in fact provides much of what Mohr would want such a right to provide, I arrive by a different method, and one that I believe is sound.

Hixon's Utilitarian Approach to Privacy

Richard Hixon's recent book *Privacy in a Public Society: Human Rights in Conflict* is both philosophical and sociological.[35] It advances the novel proposition "that privacy affords an escape from the obligations and burdens of public life and threatens collective survival."[36] Hixon claims that twentieth-century America has become obsessed with protecting individual privacy at the expense of the society's well-being. Part of the fault rests with the courts who have usurped the place of the legislature in deciding privacy questions, and part of it is due to a change in our culture in which people have become afraid of being manipulated by forces beyond their control.

While I have few quarrels with Hixon's sociological claim, I have a definite difficulty with his philosophical proposal. Still, because I believe that both of his arguments cast light on how courts should decide privacy cases (the second because it shows that privacy is a value at least in American society and the first because it says courts should play little, if any, role in privacy decisions), I shall present both aspects of Hixon's view but in reverse order. Since they are methodologically dissimilar, this should not do disservice to his thought. Moreover, it will provide me the opportunity to make my philosophical objections comfortably at the end of the discussion.

With respect to cultural change, Hixon reminds us that our notions of *community* and *individual* have radically changed over the past four centuries.[37] Hixon states that at one time the term *community* indicated actual social groups. Later it came to refer to a quality of relationship, as in holding something in common or having a sense of community identity or characteristics. From the seventeenth century onward, the term referred to a more immediate social environment, such as a locality rather than a society, and the former was in contrast to the more formal and organized "state."

The term *individual* is often confused with *individualism* and *individuality*. *Individuality* had its origins in the breakdown of medieval social, economic, and religious structures. It came to represent the uniqueness of the individual and his or her membership in a group. In contrast, *individualism* came into use in the nineteenth century and referred primarily to "the primacy of individual states and interests."[38]

According to Hixon, these differences in usage followed along with changes in culture. Hixon notes that in the eighteenth and early nineteenth centuries, privacy in Britain was associated with a movement that had begun in the twelfth century to enclose common fields, meadows, and pastures into consolidated farms and small hedged fields.[39] This meant the old way of life that was tied to community property changed from general dependence to some private independence. It also gave rise, in a developing stratified economic system of landlord-tenant and owner-worker, to private-property legal rights.

In twentieth-century United States, Hixon notes, these differences manifest themselves more psychologically than culturally. People are worried today about being manipulated and about losing their personal privacy. Lost, according to Hixon, is the idea of personality as "self-mastery" or "self-supremacy," which was popular in the nineteenth century. People have withdrawn into "self-aggrandizement" and privacy has become a form of retreat from the pressures of the outside world.[40] This fits the view developed earlier in Chapters 1 and 2 that the desire for privacy has expanded and that privacy is a form of negative freedom.

Because of this psychology, Hixon believes, our sense of community has taken on the dual role of being a haven for a necessary private life (as in the marriage relationship or business communities) and a place for a "creative public commitment." No longer does it represent a return to "small town harmony" or a "compromise for the current tough-minded self-interest movement."[41] In effect, advancing technology and the growth in population has made it necessary to balance the need to be with others and the need to be alone.

With respect to the law, Hixon suggests that the legislature and not the courts should decide privacy questions along the same lines that governed Jeremy Bentham and his followers.

First, Bentham recognized that law and social reform cannot provide happiness, but can only promote the conditions that will enable citizens to procure happiness for themselves. Applied to privacy, this means that not all elements of the private life may need to be protected, at least not without the benefit of reason and utility. Second, Bentham believed that reforms can succeed only if they are appropriate to the circumstances of society, "consonant with the feelings, habits, and desires of men, and commensurate with the material resources available." Applied to privacy, this means that perceptions and yearnings need to be tempered (albeit delicately) by reality. . . .

Bentham insisted as the third cardinal point that no reform measures should be undertaken, or even proposed, without assurance that the legal apparatus had sufficient command of the necessary resources—physical, human and institutional—"to give a high probability that the ends in view could actually be achieved." This suggests that, in the case of privacy, we have relied too heavily upon the courts instead of appropriate legislatures for the enactment and protection of individual rights. Representative government is simply a better forum for the determination of utility law.[42]

Part of the reason for Hixon's view that the legislature and not the courts is the best place to decide privacy questions seems to be the belief that certain "natural" rights, like privacy, do not lend (or at least, as yet, have not lent) themselves to objective clarification of both their ground and content. For this reason, Hixon believes it is simply inconceivable that the law should recognize a natural right to privacy. While the law may prohibit certain intrusions on one's solitude and seclusion, it is not able to guarantee "the need for autonomous behavior in the first place."[43] Hixon claims that the most the law could do is to establish a mechanism for detecting certain kinds of intrusions on privacy. That Hixon believes the courts have gone astray in attempting to ground in the Constitution a fundamental right to privacy is bolstered by the conclusion he draws.

It should be apparent by now that privacy is best conceived of and dealt with as a utility right, based upon natural desire or right, but really only viable if made a legal right with other societal needs and rights in mind. Because privacy is so nebulous in concept, it is well-suited for utilitarian resolution. To the glib charge that utility theory does not take seriously the distinction between individuals, James Griffin insists that it is a mistake to think our moral "intuitions" are always better engaged by such slogans than by the principle of utility. Thus, he says, "there is nothing in the formal conception of utility that rules out one value's being incommensurable with another," but it may be necessary on occasion to sacrifice some rights so that a greater number of others may be upheld.[44]

My problem with Hixon's view is its utilitarian formulation. In his view, whether Hixon believes it important or not, the possibility (if not the probability) exists that no serious controversial claim to privacy will ever be upheld. In part, this is because legislators must cater to the majority sentiment on issues to which the majority (or a well-organized, highly funded minority) have strong emotional commitments. The openly gay or lesbian teacher who wants to continue to teach and the woman who seeks an abortion represent two such examples. Indeed, Hixon admits as much when he states that although the right to privacy is a core matter of sovereignty in one's life, insofar as it can relate only to the personal commitments at the center of one's life, its extension is rather limited, the right, for example, tells us nothing about why telephone tapping, electronic eavesdropping, or access to one's medical or financial records should worry us. Indeed, Hixon believes that one might ask which is the greater danger, "public intrusion in private life or private subversion of public life?"[45]

Clearly, Hixon does not believe that either the teacher or the woman in my examples has any special claim to privacy outside the context of what society would be willing to grant. This is unfortunate, for in effect it makes the society, with all its prejudices, the judge and jury in its own case. But, it is also wrong for a more fundamental reason. Unless we are willing to concede that those who make our laws will rationally deliberate on each and every issue and judge not for the interests that are strongest but for the interests that are right (a proposition whose rationality may itself be in doubt), then we may find ourselves creating a society based on the lowest common denominator of social values. For even on the assumption that freedom of speech would remain intact (and here I am following Mill), there is something appreciably one-sided when issues that affect people's lives and over which the question of harm is obvious can be discussed only in the abstract because one side continues to stifle any active form of expression.

One point Hixon makes with which I am sympathetic concerns the impact of individual freedom on the legitimate interests of others. Hixon notes that today's misadventures are not the fault of Bentham or other nineteenth-century reformers; instead, they are the fault of a society that has obscured its values and has resisted the notion of a public dimension to individual privacy.[46] Hixon claims that it is questionable what society gains when our freedom to choose is without a serious consideration of the effects upon others.

Like Hixon, I do not believe that a society in which anything goes is a society that can long endure. Moreover, because I have not abandoned, as Hixon has, the notion of a fundamental right independent of utility, I may be even more cautious about adopting principles that could intrude upon the equal rights of others. For this very reason my consideration of the right to privacy pays much attention to individual interests that may be affected by the actions of others. At the same time my theory does not usurp the rights of individuals because it precisely delineates the related notions of a self-regarding and other-regarding act.

In sum, the theory of privacy presented above is appropriate for legal decision making in two ways. At the lower court level, it provides a consistent framework for deciding novel cases for which there is no clear precedent. At the higher court level (and, in particular, at the Supreme Court level), the theory provides a reason for not only making new decisions but also reevaluating past decisions to insure consistency. Most importantly, the theory fills an important void in constitutional privacy law by providing a normative scheme of government under which the courts (as the ultimate protectors of rights) should be able to objectively and conclusively decide privacy questions.

APPLICATIONS 5

   In this chapter, I give the same attention to privacy issues involving gays and lesbians as I do to other privacy issues, reflecting the fact that generalizations from lesbian and gay issues can be made to other privacy questions. In all, I will consider ten different applications for the conception of privacy sketched out in the previous chapters: the openly gay or lesbian teacher; gay or lesbian parenting and marriage; surrogate motherhood; privacy and AIDS; adult consensual sodomy statutes; the justification of abortion; data banks and electronic fund transfer services; pornography and drugs in the home; employer drug and polygraph testing; and the right to die. All are current problems that will soon be or are now being addressed by the courts.

   While some of these areas may not specifically inform the analysis of privacy (the computer data bank and electronic fund transfers, for example, raise privacy problems only because of their great efficiency), all of them (with the possible exception of the abortion issue, which also raises the question of agency) are dependent for their resolution on the analysis of the concept of privacy and the justification of the right set forth in Chapters 2 and 3. Although it is not my intention to fully resolve all the privacy problems in these areas, I shall offer a sketch of the basic issues and how my analysis might be used to resolve them. In this way, I hope to lay the groundwork for courts and legislative bodies to more readily address these matters.

Criteria for Dispute Resolutions

In this section, I shall specify the criteria for deciding disputes in which someone has claimed an intrusion on his or her privacy. In doing so, I recognize that the information to be supplied has already been presented in Chapters 2 and 3 in connection with resolving certain theoretical problems regarding the concept of privacy and its normative justification. The value of restating the information here is to give it a central location in resolving cases in which privacy is an issue.

Assume John performs an act (perhaps he opens a letter addressed to Jane) that Jane believes impinges an interest of hers. Assume further that Jane wants to recover for John's having performed the act and brings suit against John for invasion of privacy. (An analogous example might be cast in the future tense when John wants to do something that Jane does not want John to do.)

The first question that arises is whether John's having done the act can be described in a manner that does not affect Jane's interest. (Perhaps the envelope contained a grocery-store receipt.) If it can, then John has a plausible defense against Jane's claim. The defense is plausible if the action as described (let us say in a complaint Jane files against John) does not suggest a conflict with Jane's interest when considered independently of additional facts (such as some personal item on the receipt) or causal theories. In legal terminology, the question is whether or not John has "stated a defense." On the assumption that John has stated a defense, the next question is whether or not the defense holds up. That is, do the actual facts of the situation support the defense John is making? If they do not, because some interest of Jane's is at stake, is the interest important enough to warrant protection as a limitation on autonomy? In other words, does the state have a compelling interest to limit this sort of infringement? In general, if Jane's interest is cognizable by the courts, the language of compelling state interest is not used (since Jane and John are private citizens); the courts just protect the interest. Still, underneath this protection is a compelling interest of the state to ensure that disputes among individuals are resolved peacefully.

Here we are concerned with evaluating the claim in terms of

the normal standards of evidence in which Jane is given the opportunity to show that John's act did affect an interest of hers that the courts will protect. Jane's expectations are relevant in order to determine which of her interests, if any, are at stake. In some cases, like those involving informational privacy, Jane's expectations may be discovered from the conventions surrounding the action, such as whether the information was conveyed behind closed doors. In other words, what appears from the mere description of the action not to affect another's interest may in reality affect an interest of another.

How far the courts will go in tracing the causal sequence connecting John's action with its effect on Jane's interest is a problem of proximate cause. While the details of resolving proximate cause problems are beyond the scope of this work, needless to say a court should be reticent to hold that there is no privacy where the intrusion on the interest of another is due to some unforeseeable event.[1]

A different type of question from the factual one just discussed is how to resolve conflicts of rights involving privacy. I have claimed that all conflicts of rights involving privacy can be resolved on the basis of which right better fosters maximal autonomy. The test is: the right that better fosters maximal autonomy is the one the law is bound to recognize. The justification of this claim is set forth in Chapter 3.

For example, if Brown, a reporter for the *National Enquirer*, reports on what has happened to Jones, who as an adult has escaped the public eye but who as a child prodigy was a celebrated mathematician, Brown and his newspaper should, under our theory, be liable to Jones for the tort invasion of privacy. This is true despite a defense by the newspaper based on freedom of the press. For no significantly useful information is obtained with respect to the conception of autonomy, which is based on the freedom to discover what is in one's own interest, by allowing a newspaper to report on the private life of a citizen under these circumstances. Obviously, the same would not be true were the newspaper reporting on a public official, a public figure, or even a private person in a public setting.

A third type of question arises where the state in its governmental capacity is a party because it is trying to limit some individual or group's privacy. Here the issue is to determine whether the interest the state is asserting is sufficiently compelling to override individual privacy. The test is whether or not the state can show that the interest it seeks to protect is more essential to fostering autonomy in general than is protecting the individual's privacy. Where a compelling interest is shown, privacy provides a regulatory standard against which the maximum intrusion permitted the state is the minimum necessary to satisfy its interest. The justification of this test is also to be found in Chapter 3.

An illustration of this test is the following. Assume Allen, an airline passenger, attempts to evade the security monitoring station at an airport just before he boards his flight. The security people at the station discover this fact and immediately stop and frisk Allen for explosives, guns, or other potential weapons. In this situation, the security people are completely justified in invading Allen's privacy to the extent specified. For, given the nature of airline terrorism and skyjackings, the state has a compelling interest in this situation to guarantee the safety of all persons flying on board commercial airlines. If in the process of conducting the search, the security people come across contraband that indicates possible smuggling, such is the luck of Allen. Even so, the situation would be quite different and unjustified if, under the circumstances posited, the state extended its search to Allen's home or even the trunk of his automobile.

In sum, there is a two-step procedure courts should follow when deciding disputes involving a claim to privacy. First, the court should determine whether the claim to privacy is even plausible. Second, if the claim is plausible, then depending on whether the issue at stake is one of compelling state interest or conflict of rights, the court should decide the claim along the aforesaid lines.

The Openly Gay or Lesbian Teacher

Earlier, I referred to the situation where Jim, a public school teacher, announces that he is gay in a public forum in the community or school district where he is teaching.[2] Roger, a parent, objects to having his child taught by a gay teacher, perhaps because the parent believes this would influence his child's sexual orientation or in some other way harm the child. It was also noted that such a conflict with a derivative interest would not render implausible Jim's claim to privacy for two reasons. First, it was necessary to demonstrate the psychological connection to the child's sexual orientation before the conflict could even be established. Second, because Jim is a public employee, one has to show a compelling reason for the state to protect Roger's interest over Jim's. In other words, there is nothing in Jim's mere statement or the work Jim does that would presuppose the effect Roger is complaining about.

Even so, this does not mean that Roger's alternative claim will necessarily be overlooked and that Jim will be able to keep his job. If Roger is able to prove that allowing Jim to continue to teach would in fact impinge on an interest of Roger's then Jim may be fired. But here the facts become critical. If Roger is to prove that an interest of his is being affected, the interest in question would have to be one the courts could recognize. That is to say, a court would have to be able to assess Roger's claim in terms of the normal standards of evidence that a court would use in evaluating any claim.[3] Otherwise, there would be no such thing as a private act.

Thus, if Roger should assert, as the basis for his claim, that Jim's being allowed to continue to teach would cause Roger to lose favor with God, a court should not take account of it. The truth of such a claim cannot be assessed on the basis of the standards of evidence normally relied on by courts. Indeed, the most that could be shown (and this is not enough) is that the claim is consistent within a given religious tradition. Whereas, if Roger asserts a causal psychological theory (such as that Roger's being allowed to teach would have a coercive effect on the sexual development of the students) as the basis for the claim that Jim should not be allowed to teach, a court could determine the adequacy of the claim using the same rules of evidence it uses to judge the adequacy of any causal scientific theory, namely, relying on the testimony of recognized experts in the field.

In fact, it is very unlikely that Roger would be able to prove such a causal psychological theory for several reasons. First, research shows that one does not learn to be gay. Although there are different theories about the development of sexual orientation, the overwhelming majority of authorities agree that the sexual orientation individuals develop is due to either biological or genetic factors or to the environmental conditioning they receive long before they reach school age.[4] Indeed, most gay and lesbian individuals were raised by unambiguously heterosexual parents.

Whether the state even has a compelling interest in this issue is questionable given that it is not clear that homosexuality is in any legally cognizable sense harmful. What causes homosexuality is probably caught up in what causes heterosexuality, a fortiori, in what causes sexuality at all. To separate out homosexuality for particular attention is to make a value judgment that is not scientific and that usually belies an underlying prejudice. Whereas, treating homosexuality as merely one species of sexuality generally avoids this prejudice and allows for a freer and more scientific understanding of how sexuality, including homosexuality, bisexuality, and heterosexuality, develops.

Arguments against some typical reactionary objections are as follows. First, that the approach opens the door to beastiality and pederasty is without foundation. The fact that society is willing to recognize as legitimate a variety of nonharmful forms of consensual sexual expression among adults in no way binds it to recognize nonconsensual sexual expressions.

Second, gay men and lesbians are no more prone to child molestation, a charge that is sometimes rendered against allowing gays to teach, than straight men and straight women. Statistics show that most child molestation occurs between heterosexual men and young girls.[5]

Third, homosexuality is not a disease, nor is it a mental disorder. In 1973, the American Psychiatric Association removed homosexuality from its list of psychiatric disorders and resolved that "homosexuality per se implies no impairment in judgment, stability, reliability, or general social or vocational capabilities."[6]

The association further stated that "in the reasoned judgment of most American psychiatrists, homosexuality does not constitute any form of mental disease."[7] Similar resolutions were adopted in 1970, 1973, and 1975 respectively by the American Anthropological Association, the American Bar Association,[8] and the American Psychological Association. In 1975, the American Medical Association resolved "to support in principle repeal of laws which classify as criminal any form of non-commercial sexual conduct between consenting adults in private, saving only those portions of the law which protect minors, public decorum, or the mentally ill."[9]

Fourth, the experiences of countries like England, France, Holland, and Finland, where homosexual conduct has been decriminalized for years, indicate that "there is no greater incidence of homosexuality in these countries than in the United States."[10] "Moreover, there have been no adverse side effects in the 21 states that have now decriminalized consensual sodomy between adults in private."[11] This indicates that the population of lesbians and gay men will not be affected because of the number of people who are openly recognized to be gay or lesbian.

Fifth, the argument that gay and lesbian sexuality does not produce children and, therefore, society has a right to prevent any potential encouragement of a gay or lesbian life-style does not stand up to critical scrutiny. As David A. J. Richards has noted, the Augustinian procreation model that has dominated our moral understanding of human sexuality is based on a rather remarkable fallacy.

Augustine starts with two anthropological points about human sexual experience: first, humans universally insist on having sex alone and unobserved by others, and second, humans universally cover their genitals in public. Augustine argues that the only plausible explanation for these two empirical facts about human sexuality is that humans experience sex as intrinsically degrading because it involves the loss of control; this perception of shame, in turn, must rest on the fact that the only proper form of sex is having it with the controlled intention to procreate; sexuality is intrinsically degrading because we tend to experience it without or independent of the one intention that alone can validate it. Assuming, *arguendo*, the truth of Augustine's anthropological assumptions, it does not follow that humans must find sex intrinsically shameful. These facts are equally well explained by the fact that people experience embarrassment in certain forms of publicity of their sexuality, not shame in the experience of sex itself.[12]

As a consequence of this fallacy, society has come to misidentify and misdescribe "the privacy required to express intimate sexual vulnerabilities."[13]

In fact, this [Augustian] conception of sexuality relies on and expresses an overdeveloped willfulness that fears passion itself as a form of loss of control, as though humans cannot with self-esteem indulge emotional spontaneity outside the rule of the iron procreational will. Such a conception both underestimates the distinctly human capacity for self-control and overestimates the force of sexuality as a dark, unreasoning, Bacchic possession whose demands inexorably undermine the rational will. It also fails to fit the empirical facts, indeed, contradicts them. Human, as opposed to animal, sexuality is crucially marked by its control by higher cortical functions and thus its involvement with the human symbolic imagination, so that sexual propensities and experience are largely independent of the reproductive cycle. Consequently, humans uses sexuality for diverse purposes—to express love, for recreation, or for procreation. No one purpose necessarily dominates; rather, human self-control chooses among the purposes depending on context and person.[14]

Moreover, in the case where a lesbian or gay person wanted to have children or where there was a need for a larger population (something neither the world nor our society currently needs), greater acceptance and openness would encourage the possibility of various types of healthy sexual relationships that could bring forth children.

For all these reasons then it would appear that Roger would have an almost impossible task if Roger sought to have a teacher fired merely because the teacher was known to be gay or lesbian or in another context advocated its permissibility.

Sixth and finally, the argument that we should not establish a bad moral example by allowing known "practicing homosexuals" to teach, even if not everyone will follow their example, is equally specious. If one's sexual orientation is not a matter of choice, then where there is no harm to another, it is not morally reasonable to say that two adults should not be able, by consent, to fulfill their sexual and emotional needs. Even from a religious point of view, which in itself is not a precedent for law (since religious opinions tend to vary and are not objective), there is much disagreement as to whether discrimination against gays and lesbians should be allowed.[15] Some recent scholarship suggests that traditional religious condemnation of homosexuality may have involved misinterpretations of historical biblical texts.[16] Consequently, there is little if any factual basis to support discrimination.

Before closing this section, I should say something about advocacy in the classroom. If education in primary and secondary schools is never to raise controversial topics, as is often currently true, then we do children and society a disservice, for we advance the misunderstandings and stereotypes that tend to divide people. This has long-term effects, for children become adult citizens who vote on questions of public policy that affect the lives of others.

This does not mean that a lesbian or gay teacher should overtly advocate any life-style. I should think it equally offensive for a straight teacher to advocate the joys of heterosexual marriage. The classroom is not the place to proselytize. It is a place for learning. But learning does not occur where teachers and students cannot freely and fully discuss issues relevant to their subjects. Nor does it occur when boards of education and parent groups so whitewash textbooks that nothing remains that might stimulate the student's interest or imagination or encourage the student to question. It seems to me that the current sorry state of primary and secondary education in the United States is at least in part due to the fact that we have shifted or ignored the student's interest in his or her own education. We have been so concerned to protect what many have been unwilling to question that we have robbed young people of the opportunity to become fully autonomous individuals. This situation must change.

Here it may be objected that a key function of education, at least at the lower level, is to instill a set of values and that others may have a very personal interest in what those values are. Still, because we live in a pluralistic society, it cannot be said that any private set of values warrants offsetting a public right, particularly since no set of private values could provide a compelling state interest as we have defined it. Consequently, values that should be taught are those that encourage respect for difference and diversity (provided only that the fundamental rights of all persons are being respected) and the institutions of democratic rule.

Gay and Lesbian Parenting and Marriage

Should lesbians or gay men have custody of their own children? Should they be allowed to adopt children? Should lesbians or gay men be allowed to marry or enter into domestic partner relationships? The first of these three questions has already attracted court attention. The second and third promise to become political issues in the near future.

Because the general principles that govern custody and adoption are quite similar, I shall not separate these issues for the purposes of this discussion. However, with regard to the adoption issue, state statutes govern, as long as they are not constitutionally impermissible, and these vary from state to state. Therefore, particular questioning of a specific state's adoption law will have to include an analysis of the requisite statutes.

Whether a gay or lesbian parent should be granted custody or adoption rights to a child or allowed to retain custody is at least in part a privacy question. For the question could be phrased, Would the consequences of the custody or adoption of a child impinge in the first instance on a legitimate interest of the child? Nothing in being gay or lesbian in itself suggests conflict with a basic interest of the child. This means, then, that the question is one of derivative interests that the state may have a compelling reason to protect.

In the United States, courts do not treat the issue of child custody on the basis of privacy or any other fundamental right but rather as falling exclusively under the principle of what is in the best interest of the child. I maintain that while the best-interest-of-the-child principle is correct, it is not independent of fundamental rights concerns. I refer to the kind of justification we would be likely to offer for the principle.

The best-interest-of-the-child principle should not be grounded in intuitions or emotions, for the law should not open itself up to the possibility of unsupported or unprincipled speculation. Similarly, the principle should not be based on irrational or speculative and unsupported notions of what is "good" for the child. This latter point is made in the face of a half century of witness to the effects of mind-ordering propaganda. Such propaganda has in almost every instance, from the great illusion machine of Nazi Germany to the stereotyping of blacks and other minorities in this country, caused debilitating and painful effects, which subsequent generations have had to bear. This suggests that the kind of good we as a society are entitled to seek when deciding what is in the best interest of a child is the same good that we seek for ourselves in the democratic state, namely, what will help the child to develop into a fully autonomous person. (Additionally, I would include for the child, as for ourselves, all other goods that government is intended to secure.) In this regard, I return to the promotion of autonomy in general (in its fullest sense, which recognizes the equal rights of others) as the only proper starting point for an analysis in this area.

My emphasis on autonomy, however, does not mean that I favor wealthy persons over poor persons in custody disputes. While it may be true that wealthy persons are more able to ensure that some portion of a child's development toward autonomy is advanced, such as through providing the child with higher education opportunities, this picture is too simplistic. It takes no account, for example, of the relevance of love, attention, respect, and a willingness to show that these can be manifested in a parent-child relationship. Since all these qualities are important in the child's total development, no one quality should count for substantially more than another. They all work together.

What does not work, and is an area where some courts have gone astray, is assuming that children are better off in heterosexual families than in gay or lesbian families. In *In re Jane B.*,[17] the court took custody away from a mother who had been previously granted custody after her divorce solely because the mother and her school-age child were living in the same apartment with the mother's partner. The court found on *controverted* evidence that the change of circumstances (from the time custody was originally granted) caused by the mother's having a live-in lover was emotionally disturbing to the child and warranted the finding that it was not in the best interest and welfare of the child to be living in that environment. The court also ruled that the mother could visit the child but could not have the child overnight or have any other "homosexuals" present.

The basis on which I claim that such decisions are wrong was stated in the last section; namely, one does not learn to be gay or lesbian, and homosexuality is not a disease nor is it harmful in any legally cognizable sense. Consequently, to restrict custody or adoption on the basis of such a standard is to lower the criteria recognized by the law in other situations to the level of stereotyping and prejudging.

The argument that the child's life would be easier with a heterosexual parent than a lesbian or gay parent, because we are a society that stereotypes, is also not justified. Even putting aside the number of children being raised in single-parent households, to allow this type of prejudice is to promote it. Granted, a child should not suffer the negative social attitudes of society, but who is at fault for these negative social attitudes? At one time, not too long ago, it was thought that racially mixed marriages should not be allowed because (among other reasons) the children that might be produced would not be accepted by either race. Was it correct for the court to strike down such laws in *Loving v. Virginia?*[18] Unless it can be shown that there would be actual psychological damage to the child, a gay or lesbian couple should not be denied the opportunity to raise the child. Otherwise, we will only continue the stereotyping that exists when people have no alternative images against which to compare.

This approach does not treat persons (in this instance, children) as means rather than ends. My point is not that gay and lesbian parents should be allowed custody of or to adopt children in order to bring about social change. That would be a wrong approach to human beings since it fails to recognize them as having rights and to be deserving of respect. My claim is only that if there is no legitimate reason for a lesbian or gay parent or couple to be thought unfit to have custody, to decide they are unfit because of irrational beliefs that others might hold is to use both them and the child (in violation of their rights) to perpetuate an immoral end.

The objection that gay and lesbian relationships are not permanent and, therefore, they should not be allowed to have children also fails. Many such relationships are indeed permanent,[19] which might be surprising in light of the fact that except for

Denmark (which now recognizes same-sex marriages) and Madison, Wisconsin; Seattle, Washington; Takoma Park, Maryland; and Berkeley, Los Angeles, Santa Cruz, and West Hollywood, California (which passed domestic partner ordinances offering limited legal recognition to gay relationships), the law usually does not recognize gay relationships, much less encourage their permanence. More often, the law discourages such relationships through federal and state tax laws that do not grant gay and lesbian couples the same joint tax rate privilege as traditionally married couples enjoy and state sodomy laws that label gay people criminals for engaging in sexual intimacy.[20]

In a society that truly affirms autonomy as a fundamental end, lesbian and gay relationships should be granted recognition when consenting adults freely choose such relationships. Furthermore, there is no reason to believe that such relationships are unhealthy to the individuals involved or an impingement on the legitimate interests of any person. In this day of AIDS, a committed gay relationship may be healthier (depending on the type of commitment) and safer than remaining single. Gay and lesbian relationships display many of the same commitments that traditional marriage displays, with less of the stereotypical role playing that has only recently become less common in traditional marriages. This may be a result of lesbians and gays having witnessed firsthand the debilitating effects of institutionalized stereotyping on the human psyche. Indeed, those who argue most against such marriages and gay rights in general often do so as part of a broader political agenda that focuses not on homosexuality but on the preservation of the traditional nuclear family.[21] In this context, gays and lesbians are made the scapegoats for what others view as society's ills. Whether lesbian and gay relationships are a threat to the traditional family depends on how one construes the term *traditional family.*

Clearly, if a traditional family involves the kinds of sex-role stereotyping that has historically been a part of Western family life, then, yes, gay and lesbian relationships may challenge the traditional family. Lesbians and gays will have had a similar cultural indoctrination as straight people (for example, men brought up to be providers and women to be nurturers), but the equality between the partners will enhance the worth of these individuals' roles in the relationship and will allow both partners to share in both roles. Thus, gay and lesbian relationships may serve as a model to straight relationships by enacting the belief that traditional sex-role stereotyping does not have to be a part of family life.

Surrogate Motherhood

Another area of recent controversy that is likely to become more prominent in the development of the law of privacy in the near future is surrogate motherhood.[22] A surrogate mother is a woman who agrees to be artificially inseminated with the sperm of a man from a childless couple.[23] As part of the contract, the surrogate mother agrees to bear the child to term and upon birth to relinquish all rights to the child.[24] This latter requirement is legally necessary (given two-person adoptions) to allow the biological father's wife to adopt the child. The surrogate mother also agrees not to develop a parent-child relationship with the child.[25] In return, the biological father promises to pay all the medical and hospital bills resulting from the pregnancy and birth as well as a sum, usually between five thousand and ten thousand dollars, to the mother for bearing the child. The issue becomes problematic only when the courts must become involved either to enforce the terms of the contract or to determine whether state adoption statutes (which prohibit the selling of babies) apply to surrogate motherhood contracts.

Where courts are asked to become involved, the question is one of public policy. Should the courts uphold surrogate motherhood contracts, or are such contracts a form of baby selling? Do surrogate motherhood contracts undermine the family, or to they support family structures? What is in the best interest of the child? Does the biological father have a right to privacy with regard to these contracts? All of these questions are related, given that courts usually rely on the best-interest-of-the-child principle. Moreover, except where the best interest of the child clearly dictates otherwise, the issues should be resolved on right to privacy considerations. (As will be explained below, where the best interest of the child dictates otherwise, the privacy right is overridden.)

Initially, the question might be put in terms of the contract itself. Who has a prima facie claim to privacy? Clearly, under the above definition of privacy, the biological father has a prima facie privacy claim at least against all persons other than the surrogate mother. Generally, nothing in the description of a surrogate motherhood arrangement suggests consequences that are in direct conflict with the interest of any other person.

Between the biological father and the surrogate mother, privacy may or may not be a factor. The description of the surrogate motherhood arrangement includes the fact that the mother freely agrees to relinquish all rights to the offspring. Thus, there is a prima facie claim by the father not to have their privacy (regarding their choice) impinged upon by a court because of a subsequent change of heart on the part of the natural mother.

As with all prima facie claims, this too can be overcome, by showing that the natural mother was unable to freely consent, was a minor, or was under duress (not of her own making, and not within what she could have foreseen) at the time she entered into the contract. These would be questions for a court to decide based on whether the consequences of the arrangement did impinge upon a legitimate interest of the natural mother. Moreover, these same questions would also bear on whether such a contract is void from the outset (as where there is no informed consent) or voidable after the fact (as where the mother is a minor) under contract law, independent of the privacy considerations.

In addition, because a potential surrogate mother's action may not always be taken on freely (perhaps because she is poor and has an urgent need for income), the state may have a compelling interest to regulate (though not eliminate) such contracts. For example, the state may want to ensure that women with low income know of and have access to financial assistance from appropriate state agencies before they enter into a contract. Also, the income from such contracts should be taxed just as any business income to avoid undue enticement. In addition, the state may limit entry into such contracts to women who have had children before and who have received appropriate counseling (in order to insure informed consent). Finally, the state should educate citizens to the subtle and often insidious ways in which sexism becomes institutionalized in otherwise neutral institutions like family and how the effects of a male ideology can stilt the development of a public psyche. In this regard, the state should encourage the idea that there are virtually as many opportunities for women as there are jobs. The reason to educate about the effects of ideology is not to create the idea that government should regulate family or other private matters but to reveal how some good and important limitations on government (like privacy) can be malignly used to oppress women and other groups in our society.[26] The emphasis on job opportunities is not to diminish motherhood, but to offset the view that only certain roles are open to women (a problem often compounded by socioeconomic circumstances).[27] Because of complex and interrelated social, economic, and psychological factors, these questions require legislative action at the outset, which can then be assessed by the courts in terms of how well autonomy in general is served.

This raises a question.[28] Do surrogate motherhood contracts inherently exploit poor women? The question seems perplexing (once the concern about institutionalized sexism is removed) because any contract to provide a service that may be fraught with danger could be viewed as exploitive of those who need money enough to take the risk. This is a concern about capitalism itself. Hence, if there is a question at this level of abstraction, it should be evaluated in terms of a theory regarding exploitive contracts in general. Because this would move us away from surrogate motherhood contracts in particular and would raise questions much broader than the confines of this book, I will not attempt to resolve this issue.

Still, if the point of the objection is that no contract providing for performance of a dangerous service (i.e., one that has definite foreseeable risks) should be coerced, the rationale is that either the party who agreed to the contract did not know the risk involved or was in so desperate a situation as to be unable to freely consent. This is, then, a general reason for voiding any contract on the basis of its being an adhesion contract. It is also a reason for legislation in this area. Otherwise, surrogate motherhood contracts would seem to be no different than other contracts. Consequently, except where there is serious reason to doubt free consent, a surrogate mother contract should be enforced. This means that if the surrogate mother chooses to carry the fetus to term, she should be required to give custody to the natural father. If the surrogate mother chooses not to carry the fetus to term, then she should repay the money she received.[29] The surrogate mother could never be specifically required to carry the fetus to term if she chose not to. Under the Thirteenth Amendment's prohibition against indentured servitude[30] and probably under *Roe v. Wade*,[31] the mother would be liable only for monetary damages, which in this situation would be the advances from the natural father. The former limitation, coming as it did at the end of the Civil War, represents a compelling interest of the state that can historically be shown to promote maximal autonomy in general. The latter represents a fundamental right of a woman to control the use of her own body.

Next is the question of the privacy relationship between the biological parents and the unconceived child. Surely, there is no impingement of any interest when the contract is made, since the offspring has not even been conceived. Indeed, even after conception the offspring has only potential interests until it becomes a person (a point that will be more fully discussed under "The Justification of Abortion," below). Consequently, a surrogate motherhood contract that does not attempt to specify the qualities of the child after birth when custody is transferred is not a limitation on autonomy. Moreover, although the contract affects the offspring at the point of birth and immediately thereafter (especially if the mother has to wean the child before it is given up), there is no basis upon which to claim that the newborn has any interest in where it is to be placed other than that the placement be in its best interest. Therefore, the consequence of the arrangement in respect to where the newborn is to be placed does not on its face impinge upon any legitimate interest of the child. To the contrary, questions of whether the placement is in the best interest of the child would have to be decided on the basis of outside evidence in order to negate the contracting parties' presumptive prima facie claim to privacy.

Were the evidence to suggest that the best interest of the child might not be well served by upholding the contract, then and only then would the court be justified in annulling the contract. But again, this would be a factual matter that would have to be considered from the standpoint of overcoming the biological father's presumptive claim to privacy.

Certain factors, such as the amount of money the biological parents make (as long as it is enough to provide basic support for the child), should not be considered in isolation from other factors such as the kind of home life the child would have and whether the child would be given love and respect and encouraged to become all that it can be. These items comprise the best interest of the child. Consequently, from the standpoint of fostering autonomy, no special standing should be given to wealthy persons over poor persons. Even in the situation where the only difference between the natural mother and the biological father is the amount of money they make, it would be inappropriate to use this as a criterion (again, so long as basic support is provided for) since the elevation of such criteria can lead to disrespect for poorer people and a consequent loss of autonomy in general. Under this circumstance a random arbitrary choice would be appropriate.

Likewise, there is no validity to the argument that surrogate motherhood contracts need be a form of baby selling. One cannot sell to the biological father what he already has a right to. On the other side of the coin, a contract specifying that payment is contingent on a live birth or on the infant's possessing certain qualities (regarding health, hair color, and so on) would be void under this interpretation of privacy, for this suggests the mother is selling a future interest in another human being. Since the description of a sale would necessarily impinge upon the child as an autonomous being, a court should find such a provision in a contract to be null and void. This means, then, that the most these contracts can require is payment for the service of bearing a child. As for the egg, which is not a person, a small payment might be appropriate, especially since most states allow men to be paid for contributions to sperm banks.[32] Allowing women the same right would seem to be nothing more than fair.

Nor are such contracts likely to undermine the family, assuming, *arguendo*, that the nuclear family should be preserved. The fact that such contracts allow childless couples to have and raise children is an enhancement of the family structure. Even when entered into for reasons other than infertility or hereditary disease, such contracts do not necessarily undermine the family. Obviously, if a person's reasons were frivolous, that would bear on his or her competency to be a parent, and the best interest of the child would become the deciding factor.

Finally, surrogate motherhood contracts should not be considered void because they undermine adoptions. First, no person has a duty to adopt someone else's child, although society has a compelling interest, based in maximizing autonomy, to provide for all unwanted children. Second, there is no guarantee that sufficient adoptions will be available to all those who may want children. Lastly, there is no reason a biological father should not be allowed to have his own child, regardless of whether he may choose to adopt a child. This latter restriction would be an impingement on the biological father's autonomy. Moreover, it would be using childless couples to treat society's needs.

For the aforementioned reasons, the conception of privacy I have articulated supports surrogate motherhood contracts. It also supports court interference with such contracts, but only when the best interest of the child overrides the presumptive privacy claim of the biological father. In this regard, the best-interest-of-the-child principle is again seen in the context of the fundamental right to privacy.

Privacy and AIDS

In March 1984, when researchers confirmed that a woman who had received a transfusion of blood that had come from a gay man had contracted AIDS,[33] a major effort was launched to develop a test that could guarantee the safety of the nation's blood supply.[34] Since that time, several antibody tests have been developed for the purpose of screening for the AIDS virus.[35] In addition, a number of states have passed statutes affecting who can have access to the test results.[36]

All of this has led to concerns about privacy that have been expressed by Tom Stoddard, when he was legislative director of the New York Civil Liberties Union.

Our greatest fear is that employers, insurers, and others will latch onto test results to screen out those people they don't want to serve. That will lead to unnecessary suffering.

This test can lead to a list of people who are assumed to be gay. The test is widely overinclusive and will implicate a majority of people who impose no threat at all. It could become a list of undesirables, a list of people who are viewed as disease spreaders who will be unable to hold their jobs, their insurance.[37]

In a similar vein, with respect to military testing, Ron Naiman, speaking for the National Gay Task Force, stated: "While it's reasonable to administer the test to people who would be subject to battlefield transfusion . . . we don't see a reason to test people with desk jobs in Arlington."[38]

The privacy-related problem, with the screening and diagnosing of AIDS, centers on trying to balance the legitimate interest of the state to halt the spread of this epidemic versus the rights of individuals to selectively disclose information that could have devastating consequences for them. Also, in this balance is the interest of the state (in capitalistic societies) to allow insurance companies the maximal amount of economic freedom consistent with the national interest of making available at least a minimal degree of health care to all persons. The national interest here may manifest itself through different means but is essentially an interest to provide a basic amount of health-care protection at the least direct cost to the state. How, then, is the balance to be struck?

The answer depends on recognizing that the state's interest in protecting the health and physical well-being of its citizens is more compelling than its interest in protecting privacy, because health and physical well-being are essential to the very possibility of autonomy. Consequently, the former interest generally overrides the interest to protect privacy in individual cases.

But here an important caveat must be noted regarding the legal institution, which recognizes both of these rights: Intrusion on the privacy of any individual must be no greater than the minimum necessary to achieve the state's interest to secure the health and well-being of its citizens in general. This accommodation should be thought of as mandatory over any alternative that would deny either the legitimate interest of the state or the privacy of individuals. The underlying rationale is the commitment of the legal institution to autonomy as an end, which allows privacy to play the regulatory role of limiting how far the state can go in achieving its interest.

Thus, in screening for the AIDS virus, a compelling interest of the state (over any privacy interest of the individual) is to require blood banks to test donations of blood before such donations are dispersed to the public. It is not a compelling interest of the state, however, that a blood bank create a computerized list of persons whose blood tests are positive, since testing the individual blood donations would adequately protect autonomy without any invasion of privacy. Furthermore, absence from such a list might be relied upon in emergencies to avoid testing of blood where a donor had previously donated. Since a donor could have become infected since the last donation, this result could prove more detrimental to society's interest than any delay caused by a testing of the new donation. Therefore, the presence of such a list would not be justified on the basis that it protects an interest more fundamental than privacy.

The best reason a blood bank may have for maintaining such a list is that it diminishes the probability of a false negative on a subsequent donation. However, a less intrusive means on privacy for achieving the same result is to run a second test. Obviously, this would incur greater costs, but considering the interests involved (both privacy and health), such increased costs might be justified. In any event, if a blood bank maintains such a list, it must assume responsibility to insure the privacy of donors. This can be bolstered through the enactment of laws that require blood banks with such lists to meet stringent requirements for protecting confidentiality. The blood bank's responsibility can also be enhanced by allowing civil suits against those who through negligence or intention release such information. In either case, justification for the enactment of such laws is that they would further promote the democratic end of autonomy.

A more difficult question arises in the context of medical treatment. Should health-care workers be allowed to order an HIV test on anyone who submits to general treatment?[39] Should they be allowed to order the test if a nurse is accidentally pricked with a needle and does not want to wait through the incubation period to discover the results? Should surgeons be allowed to require the test before surgery if they are to incise the patient? The interests of the medical community are enormously important, but so are the interests of the patient, who may find him- or herself uninsurable. Fortunately, there have been relatively few instances of health-care worker infections even though the number of needle pricks is comparatively high. More important, there are now available universal health-care precautions (such as wearing gloves of a certain gauge plastic when administering medications through needles) that the Center for Disease Control recommends to prevent spread of the disease. Clearly, the cost of taking appropriate precautions will be high and ultimately will have to be borne by everybody. However, these precautions also prevent the spread of other diseases and very well should be part of regular health-care protocol. Consequently, financial investment may be what is necessary to walk the fine line between health-care workers' safety and patient privacy.

Regarding state monitoring of individuals, say through "contact tracing" of persons believed to be in high-risk groups (which in one proposed version involves tattooing individuals who test positive),[40] the risks to autonomy are even greater. Such monitoring has the effect of limiting the privacy of both those originally identified as seropositive for the AIDS antibody (which is believed to be an indication of the presence of the virus in the system) and of those with whom they have had contact. Such monitoring might be justified if it reasonably could be expected to provide information that could halt the spread of this deadly epidemic by providing a warning to persons who might come in contact with infected individuals. The problem with this point of view, however, is that public identification or monitoring of individuals who test positive may cause them to turn away from seeking medical treatment. Moreover, any attempt to publicly identify those who are seropositive for the virus could give a false sense of security to those who come in contact with someone who became infected after the time of the examination or within the period when the infection would not show up.[41] Furthermore, through the use of grants (like the one endowing the National Institute of Health's study project on AIDS)[42] other methods can be designed that are less intrusive on individual privacy and scientifically more reliable for studying the spread of this disease. Consequently, it is not evident that the state has a compelling interest to identify and monitor individuals merely on the basis of a positive test for the AIDS antibody.

It would of course be reckless and irresponsible for a person who has tested positive to be sexually active without first advising the party with whom he or she wishes to become intimate of the HIV status or taking medically reasonable steps to avoid transmission of the disease by limiting the opportunities for exchange of body fluids (through mutual masterbation or the use of condoms in conjunction with spermicides containing Nonoxynol-9).[43] Still, even these instances of transmission can be limited if all parties have access to relevant information on protection.

Similarly, it would be gross recklessness for prison authorities not to take steps to insure against forceable sexual assault.[44] Obviously, the facts must be evaluated in each situation. Still, in these instances, it is the individual or the prison that is potentially disregarding the autonomy of others. Only in cases where there is actual disregard of the autonomy of others, as, for example, in cases of sexual assault or criminal deception but not simple prostitution (where autonomy is not violated) is the state justified in requiring the assailant to submit to an HIV test. Only under circumstances where there has been a threat to the autonomy of others does the state have a compelling interest to invade privacy.

For more general health-care policy, the focus should not be only on abstinence from sex, although this may be the safest choice. I doubt, however, that it is good public policy. First, most people will not comply with abstinence, just as they will not give up driving to avoid risks on the road, although they may be willing to use seat belts. Second, both parties to any sexual act can take reasonable (medically cautious) steps to protect themselves by lowering the probability of infection. Clearly, in an environment where people are informed about "safe" sex practices, the risk of AIDS may be substantially reduced.

But this puts a burden on government to insure that people are informed, for no other institution is as capable of dealing with the question of public health. More important, in dealing with this question government must do so in an open and scientifically reasonable manner. Information should not be withheld because some may be offended in their personal, moral, or religious beliefs. If such information is not made available, the autonomy of those who are uninformed may be compromised. This point is particularly applicable to school sex education programs, which may be the only means by which young people can learn about this disease. Consequently, government has an obligation to require adequate sex education courses for students, as this will help to foster autonomy in general.

With respect to the military, no compelling reason seems to exist for testing those who are not likely to be called upon to provide immediate blood transfusions. Moreover, such testing could serve as a check on the private lives of individual members of the armed forces. While it is true that persons in the military are subject to more restrictions on their private lives than those outside the military (as, for example, the fact that they cannot belong to partisan political organizations), in most cases, the rationale behind these restrictions is in service of the basic end of autonomy. For instance, the restriction against involvement in partisan political activities can be seen as a way of preventing these institutions from becoming mere extensions of the military's influence. However, no such protection of autonomy seems to be served by requiring the whole of the armed forces to be tested for the AIDS virus antibody.[45]

Still, it could be argued that such testing is justified in order to limit increased health-care costs in the defense budget for those who may have contracted AIDS while in the service. Essentially, this is the same sort of argument an insurance company might make on behalf of testing before granting coverage. Since I specifically address the insurance argument next, it suffices to note here that the defense budget could be treated analogously to that of an insurance company. In other words, to the extent that an insurance company should be allowed reimbursement from a general government fund designed to protect against losses due to AIDS, so might the defense budget be similarly protected.

With respect to insurance, the question is one of economic incentives. Should the government restrict insurance companies from setting whatever qualification requirements they deem appropriate to protect their investments? Here it is important to understand that insurance companies do not exist in a vacuum. They are heavily regulated, even though they are privately run, because insurance companies provide an important public function. In the United States, there is no national health insurance, in part because private health insurance companies have lobbied against it. Consequently, if insurance companies are going to monopolize this function of government (namely, to provide for health care for all citizens as part of promoting maximal autonomy in general), then they must take on the same burdens and responsibilities as government in this area.

Autonomy enters in at the level of the shareholders, whose interest is to protect their economic position. But in this case, autonomy can be limited to the extent that government has a more compelling interest to protect the health and physical well-being of (including making adequate health care available to) its citizens. Since a lack of health care would restrict autonomy in general, even though it might enhance the freedom of shareholders in the setting of company policy, the government is certainly warranted to take steps against the exclusion of any identifiable class of persons or group from receiving such health care. Moreover, if insurance companies are allowed to choose whom they are going to insure based on the results of an antibody test, the likelihood that this information may filter down to employers and others (who will wonder why some of their younger employees do not qualify for health insurance) is greatly increased. Consequently, the negative impact on privacy is increased.

Accounting for the legitimate economic interests of shareholders, an accommodation that would allow for both the provision of health care and the protection of shareholder investments would be for the government to establish a fund to cover the costs associated with persons who contract AIDS. Such a fund would be available for withdrawals either by an insurance company or by persons who contract AIDS, depending on whether the insurance company had chosen to afford coverage for illnesses associated with AIDS. In the event the insurance company had chosen to refuse coverage, no antibody test would be required. If the insurance company had granted coverage, the antibody test would be required only if the applicant were seeking to purchase insurance well in excess of the amount customary for a person in his or her economic circumstance. In either instance, the justification for the government's picking up this tab would be that AIDS represents a national health crisis of epidemic proportions.

Still, one might object that the government has no duty to pick up the health-care costs for those who became infected after information on the transmission of the disease had been made generally available to the public. Such an argument might claim that requiring taxpayers to pay for health services in this context is paternalistic at best and unjustified at worst. The problems with this view are threefold. First, it assumes that everyone has access to the same information, which means that the government has been doing all that it reasonably could to make that information available. Given that former president Ronald Reagan never used the word *AIDS* until 1985 (more than four years into the epidemic) and that Surgeon General C. Everett Koop admits to having been prohibited from discussing it before then, this is a highly doubtful assumption. Second, the argument assumes that because government has a duty to provide general health care, a recipient must owe a duty to the society (a duty to oneself would logically not suffice) to protect his or her own health. While the former duty follows from the obligation of a democratic government to protect autonomy, the latter duty has no clear foundation. Consequently, those who would rely on a breach of the latter "duty" to excuse the former must first show that it exists. In short, the burden of proof to show the existence of a duty owed to the society to protect one's own health is on the opponents of health care in the instance described. This is necessary if we are not to sacrifice a clear right for what is only the breach of an alleged duty.

A third assumption the above argument makes is that those

who endanger their health know of the dangers and what could be done to prevent them. One obvious problem with this assumption is that we cannot distinguish between those who become infected before and those who become infected after information about the spread of the disease became known, for even today we do not know the incubation period. Consequently, for many cases, this assumption is without merit.

Even so, the assumption does direct us to recognize another important point about AIDS, namely, that there are degrees of safety involved. Should, for example, someone be denied government-supported health care because they may have used a condom that broke or used a condom without a prescribed lubricant? Should they be held to forfeit health care because they engaged in sexual activity at all? What justifies drawing the line at one place and not at another? Without clear and convincing answers to these questions, there can be no support for this assumption.

One might claim to be justified in denying health care in this context on the ground that autonomy is served by using a few people as examples of responsible behavior. But this view is flawed not only in that we may not be able to know who had what knowledge, but also because it seeks to use some autonomous individuals for the benefit of other (presumably a greater number of) autonomous individuals. This is not equivalent to fostering autonomy in general, which also promotes autonomy for the individuals involved with the disease. On the contrary, this utilitarian approach suggests, without moral justification, that one can benefit one group of people by setting up another group as a warning. Consequently, there is no reason from the standpoint of promoting, let alone protecting, autonomy to use some autonomous individuals merely for the sake of other autonomous individuals.

Another view that favors denial is that while government may have a duty to provide everyone health care, when a person decides to harm his or her health (for example, by smoking or by engaging in potentially harmful sexual activities), that person in effect waives the right to such health care. In other words, health care in this context is available only to those who become ill through no fault of their own. The problem with this argument is that, first, it illogically assumes that a decision to take on a health risk is tantamount to a decision to waive health care. If this were true, then health care would be available only to people who live extremely isolated lives. Second, the argument assumes that protecting autonomy is the only justification for government action. In fact, as was discussed earlier, protecting autonomy in general is a particular responsibility of democratic government, which holds autonomy as a fundamental end. Still, a democratic government is a species of government in general. If it is true that a moral responsibility of government is to provide humane health care based on need alone because this is not something that individuals can do for themselves, then the problem of providing health care to someone who is partially to blame for an illness is eliminated. Certainly, to promote maximal autonomy, this would be required. In any event, since privacy is not at stake here, this matter is better dealt with under a broader theory of the moral responsibilities of government.

Finally, there is the issue of children with AIDS attending school.[46] Recently, in more and more cases courts have held that school districts may not refuse to admit a child who has AIDS.[47] The rationale that is usually relied upon is that a person cannot contact AIDS by casual contact.[48] Nevertheless, the issue becomes emotional when the medical practitioners who assert this claim qualify it with phrases like "there are no reported cases" or "the probability is."[49]

Even so, medical practitioners are not wrong in their careful use of language; nor are courts wrong in ordering schools to admit children with AIDS. The fact is that in this physical world, information is often incomplete, and thus there is very little about which any of us can be absolutely certain. When we cross the street or walk next to a building, we cannot be sure that a car will not hit us or that an earthquake will not cause the building to come toppling down on us. Still, we do not hesitate to make probability judgments, since crossing a street and walking next to a building are events familiar to us. A difficulty arises when we are asked to believe what is not familiar and the consequences of a mistake are grave.

Nevertheless, we may have to accept the opinions of experts unless we are willing to become experts on every issue. Still, we do not have to be naïve in accepting the opinions of experts.[50] Especially on matters of importance to us, we should ask critical questions, consider alternative points of view, and demand that those who ask us to accept their view explain why we can discount whatever risk may be involved. More important, we should do all this with as much cool headedness as is possible. Only in this way can we be assured that our decision will be both the best in light of what we know and the decision most likely to respect the legitimate interest of all parties concerned.

In the case of AIDS, the casual contact a child is likely to engage in at school will not likely spread the disease according to most medical authorities.[51] Consequently, recognizing the legitimate interests of the child with AIDS to live as normal a life as possible, the children without AIDS to be free from disease, and all parties to be provided a good education (which includes knowing how to survive and accept people with different infirmities), the courts are correct when they order school districts to admit children with AIDS.

Adult Consensual Sodomy Statutes

The rationale that has been typically relied upon to justify state adult consensual sodomy statutes[52] is fivefold. First, it is argued that the protection of the right to privacy extends to only two aspects of sexual behavior: marital intimacy and procreative choice. Second, it is claimed that the prohibition against adult consensual sodomy will prevent harm that might otherwise befall the participants. Third, a prohibition against consensual sodomy will prevent the spread of sexually transmitted diseases. (Today, this argument is extended to emphasize the desire to limit the spread of AIDS.) Fourth, prohibiting consensual sodomy will uphold the public morality. Fifth, prohibiting consensual sodomy will protect the institution of marriage. Do these reasons provide an appropriate justification for the limits they impose on privacy?

Regarding the first rationale, the real question is whether coverage of the privacy right extends beyond marital intimacy and procreative choice. Does it, for example, extend to the free choice of two unmarried adults (regardless of gender) to engage in sexual activities in the home? Certainly, it would seem to under the definition of privacy specified earlier. In Chapter 2, we stated that an act is private with respect to a group of other actors if and only if the consequences of the action impinge in the first instance on the basic interests of the actor and not on the interests of the specified group of actors. "Impinge in the first instance" meant that no conflict would be apparent from a specification of the basic interests of the group of actors and a description of the action itself. The purpose of limiting the coverage of the privacy right to only the basic interests of the specified group was to avoid the possibility that a derivative interest (which is made up of assumptions about facts or social conventions) might be substituted for a basic interest. The idea is that these various assumptions are often called into question (both as to their genuineness and their importance) in cases in which privacy is an issue.

Applying this definition of the privacy right to the first rationale for state adult consensual sodomy statutes, it is clear that coverage of the right in the constitutional area is broader than both marital intimacy and procreative choice. For example, it would protect two unmarried adults (regardless of gender) who choose to engage in sexual activities outside the view of others. In this situation, it is plausible that no basic interest of any other person would in the first instance be impinged upon. As with the gay or lesbian teacher, one could not validly assert as a basic interest the mere knowledge that such activities were permitted when there was a preference that they not be. That would beg the question. What is really at stake is a derivative interest containing an underlying assumption (such as that the activities were immoral) or a social convention (such as that everyone should get married before having sex) that has given rise to the interest. Consequently, the first rationale for the enactment of state adult consensual sodomy statutes is clearly too narrow to justify an intrusion on privacy.

With respect to the second rationale, the problem seems to be one of clarification as well as justification. Exactly what kind of harm is sought to be prevented by the enactment of adult consensual sodomy statutes is not obvious. This important question requires a response if such a statute is to be supported on this basis. Even on the assumption that a real harm exists, why should the state (given the presumed consensual nature of the activity) be thought to have a compelling interest to prevent the harm? In other words, the state, under this rationale, appears to be acting in a paternalistic capacity with respect to its citizens. But the state would be justified in imposing such restrictions only if one of the parties is a minor or mentally incapable of assessing his or her actions in terms of personal interests. Indeed, given my view of autonomy (as the freedom of all persons to discover what is in their own interest), these levels of agency would be the only situations where other interests could be considered more important than privacy.

Proponents of the state's view typically assume that such statutes are necessary in order to protect the physical or psychological well-being of its citizens. Their basis for this view is either another fundamental end of government (such as the safety of the individual) that claims to ignore the issue of autonomy altogether or, alternatively, the view that the state has a compelling interest to safeguard existing autonomy (in the sense of the individual's overall well-being) rather than to promote maximal autonomy at the risk of diminishing existing autonomy. The former view fails because it is not necessarily true that autonomy drops out of the picture. To the contrary, protecting autonomy may be part of what is necessary for the state to safeguard the well-being of its citizens. The latter view leads to a fundamental paradox.

The paradox hinges on whether one can assert one's privacy, which is based on the value of autonomy, in order to be able to give up a portion of one's autonomy. The paradox is resolved in the democratic claim that the individual is best suited to decide what is in his or her own interest, as long as valuable information for making such a choice is not being withheld or the individual is not mentally deficient or younger than the age of consent. Indeed, were the individual not given deference here, the possibility of government intrusion on an individual's autonomy would be greatly enhanced. Consequently, we discover another situation in which the state would not be justified in restricting the range of private actions, and thus why any statute that attempts to restrict autonomy within the private sphere for the sake of maintaining autonomy is not justified.

Such a statute would not be justified even if the risks the persons were taking (and note that it is unlikely that everyone in a whole group takes on the same risks) increased their likelihood of becoming a burden on society. As argued above, it is not clear that there is a duty owed to society (as opposed to oneself) to protect oneself. Of course, this does not mean that society has an obligation to pay by taxation for injuries to individuals who act recklessly. However, the determination of whether an individual is truly reckless must take into account a broader set of factors including what information is reasonably available to them. No doubt one might also want to take into account such superrogatory concerns as compassion, but this reaches a different dimension of moral reasoning.[53]

The third rationale, prohibiting the spread of sexually transmissible diseases, would be a sufficient condition for enacting adult consensual sodomy statutes were it not true that criminal statutes cover instances of sexual assault, rape, or incest. Otherwise, the spread of such diseases can occur only if the recipient is a party to the consensual activity.[54] We can assume that in most cases individuals have an interest not to be the recipients of such diseases. In addition, existing state laws allow civil actions by persons who become infected with such diseases against those who by negligence or recklessness cause the infection. What remains to be done is to provide adequate education on how to prevent the spread of such diseases.

Such considerations as these address the state's legitimate health concern in a matter that is less obtrusive to an individual's right to privacy than is enactment of adult consensual sodomy statutes. Moreover, since the above alternatives presume a degree of sexual expression, they are more likely to influence the behavior of persons who remain sexually active regardless of the law. Therefore, they would probably work as well as, if not better than, sodomy statutes at limiting the spread of sexually transmissible diseases.

Next, the question of whether or not there exists a legitimate ground for state interference with the individual's privacy depends on whether state support of a particular view of morality is more fundamental to fostering autonomy in general than protection of individual privacy. That such a view of morality could meet this requirement seems unlikely. The nature of such a limitation likely would be to restrict the possibility of individuals discovering what is in their own interests, for such restrictions tend to permit a much narrower range of behavior than would be permitted if privacy is protected. Indeed, even if it were thought that a particular view of morality was in the interests of the citizens in general, unless this could be shown beyond a reasonable doubt, given the government's compelling interest to promote autonomy, the view would not provide a justifiable basis for restricting individual privacy.[55] On this account, then, enacting adult consensual sodomy statutes is not justified.

Finally, with respect to the fifth rationale, while it may be conceded that the state has an interest in protecting the rearing of children, it is less clear in what specific institutional arrangement such an interest must manifest itself. The traditional Western marital and nuclear-family structure is clearly not the only viable alternative. Other alternatives include single parenting, extended family structures (such as the kibbutz), domestic partnerships, or (as argued earlier) gay and lesbian marriages.

Even if the traditional nuclear family were accepted as the ideal, it does not necessarily follow, however, that legal prohibition of sodomy is truly conducive to promoting this ideal. Such statutes operate by *coercing* individuals to refrain from private actions that they otherwise would perform. Consequently, they provoke resentment of, rather than enhance respect for, the institution they seek to protect. Moreover, they are usually very difficult to enforce. As for the argument that such statutes set a certain "moral tone," the fact that they so severely limit freedom of choice is contrary to treating autonomy as a fundamental end.

If privacy is to be protected as a fundamental right, the burden of proof to show why adult consensual sodomy statutes are necessary must be placed on those who want to restrict privacy in this area. Otherwise, we open the door to erosion of privacy and with it individual autonomy as a landmark end of democratic government.

We can conclude that current court decisions allowing states to restrict adult consensual homosexual activity unjustifiably impinge on individual privacy. The Supreme Court, in its 1986 decision in *Bowers v. Hardwick*,[56] was mistaken in holding that such statutes do not violate an individual's fundamental right to privacy. In light of the arguments presented here, the Court should at its earliest opportunity reconsider that decision.

The Justification of Abortion

One of the most controversial questions for contemporary society concerns the justification of abortion. Can a woman validly choose as a matter of privacy the right to terminate her pregnancy, thus causing the death of the fetus? The question of choice under these circumstances raises several issues, not all of which involve privacy. (See also the section "The Right to Die," below.)

The first issue concerns the fetus's status. Standard political rhetoric relies on such phrases as "when life begins" or "when human life begins." Such phrasing tends to beg the question and to produce equivocal interpretations of the word *life*. Does *life* refer merely to biological life and, if so, should that be enough to stop all abortions? What does the word *human* add to the word *life?* Should day-after pills, which prevent a fertilized egg from attaching to the wall of the uterus, be restricted?[57] Should all abortions be stopped because the fertilized cell possesses 46 chromosomes? Or does *life* mean having experiences that one is aware of (essentially being sentient or conscious), or being an agent? If so, then the question needs to be answered: What is it about having experiences or being an agent that affords one rights?

These approaches assume general agreement on the core question of the attributes we associate with human beings and for which we think of human beings as possessing rights. In fact, no such general agreement exists. The more salient point, however, in the context of a democratic society, is the one factor that all parties to the discussion would admit is determinative of personhood, namely, agency, that feature of autonomy (being able to act on one's own interest) that is both voluntary and purposive. The idea of agency being expressed here encompasses mental as well as physical actions. Consequently, if democracy holds autonomy as a fundamental end, it must recognize agency as an essential element in the realization of that end. As Gewirth has noted, "voluntariness and purposiveness . . . are the most general features distinctively characteristic of the whole genus of action, where 'action' consists in all the possible objects of moral and other practical precepts."[58]

By focusing on the issue of agency, which has discrete, discernable attributes, it is possible to frame the normative question underlying the abortion debate more usefully. Stating the issue this way implicitly suggests that the fetus may not possess the requisite attributes, for it may not be anything close to being an agent, at least until well into the pregnancy, if at all. All of its thoughts and desires (assuming it even has any) may be exclusively outside of its control. Consequently, we have begun to lay the groundwork for placing the burden of proving that the fetus has rights on those who would deny a woman's right to have an abortion.

The restatement is also important for another reason. Were the fetus shown to be a person (in the sense of possessing those attributes that would make it an agent), then clearly no claim to privacy between the mother and the fetus would be plausible. The plausibility of the claim, under our privacy definition, depends on one being able to describe the action of the mother without describing it as an impingement on a basic interest of the fetus. Abortion, connoting the death of the fetus, prevents the possibility of such a description. Consequently, were the fetus shown to be a person, there would be no problem from the standpoint of privacy (although there may be one from the standpoint of liberty, which I will discuss below) with the state restricting abortions.[59]

Still, it may be argued that given the gravity of the possible interest involved, it is wrong to place the burden of proving that the fetus is a person on those who would seek to restrict abortions. It should be placed instead on those who would seek to allow choice. Indeed, this argument would seem persuasive if it were as plausible to think of the fetus as a person as it is to think of it as not being a person. However, given the many views of what constitutes a person, our intuitions on the issue are not clear.[60]

Certainly, if agency is the deciding criterion, there is very little reason to think of the unborn (especially at an early stage in the mother's pregnancy) as possessing the requisite voluntariness and purposiveness to be an agent. The unborn does not exhibit voluntary actions since it is living off the mother and is necessarily confined within her. Nor is there any reason to think that at an early stage in the pregnancy the fetus would possess, even remotely, any purposes that could truly be called its own. The same could not be said of even the newborn infant, which possesses, even if only to a rudimentary degree, most of the features we associate with adult human beings.

Perhaps it may be plausible to think of the fetus as a person if the time period in question is postviability (i.e., past the period when the fetus could survive outside the womb).[61] Then, at least, it is arguable that the fetus is in much the same position as a newborn baby without its independence from the mother. Moreover, improvements in medical technology may push back the period of viability, although so far they have not significantly done so.

In contrast, at an early stage in the pregnancy, thinking of the fetus as a person in the relevant sense seems largely implausible. Where exactly one should draw the line is unclear, since there is a range between plausibly believing that the fetus has rights and believing that it does not. Nevertheless, the fact that the line may be difficult to draw does not mean that the boundary does not exist. Indeed, it is with respect to just such boundary questions that those who would seek to limit a woman's right to choose an abortion should bear the burden of proving the fetus is a person.

There is an injury to the mother's autonomy (in some cases a social or economic injury, in others a threat to life or health) by not allowing her the choice of an abortion. Although it is reasonable to disregard a lesser injury to the mother if it is necessary to avoid a plausibly greater harm to another, it is not reasonable to disregard even a lesser harm to the mother if it is to offset only an implausibly greater harm to another. Consequently, as long as it remains that the fetus is not even plausibly a person, within whatever non-question-begging definition of personhood we adopt, then the burden to prove otherwise should remain on the opponents of abortion.

It is also not satisfactory to take a halfway measure of supporting the right to choose abortion but only in cases of rape, incest, or
serious threat to the mother's life. If the view is that the fetus is a
person, then an innocent third party is being killed in each of
these three situations. On the other hand, if the view is that the
fetus is not a person, what justification is there for restricting a
woman's right to choice? In short, the standing of the fetus issue
has to be dealt with up front and along the lines articulated above.

This raises the question: Should there be any restriction of the
mother's autonomy in order to allow the fetus to develop into an
agent? In other words, given that autonomy is a fundamental end
of democratic government, should not the state seek to protect
the development of the fetus where there is no comparable cost to
the mother? The key here is the comparable cost. Clearly, at an
early stage of pregnancy there is little reason, in terms of the
fetus's state of development, for a woman not to exercise her right
to an abortion. Conversely, at a late stage there is much greater
reason; perhaps only a serious threat to maternal health would be
sufficient justification. Again, the question is where to draw the
line. Viability seems to provide a good place, because at that point
the fetus could survive independent of the mother.

This, then, brings us to the even more difficult question in the
choice controversy. What does one do either after viability or in
the face of proof that the fetus is a person, if its continued development poses a serious health threat to the mother? While
strictly speaking this is no longer a privacy question (since in this
case an interest of the fetus would be impinged); nevertheless, I
have chosen to include it here since the issue cannot be separated from the abortion debate. Needless to say, what I suggest
here will be dependent on the facts of the situation.

In "A Defense of Abortion,"[62] Judith Jarvis Thompson argues
from the standpoint of self-defense that even if we assume the
fetus to be a person, abortion is not always impermissible. First, it
is permissible for the woman to defend against a life threat posed
by the unborn, even if to do so involves the fetus's death. Second, a
woman has a prior claim to her own body that others are not free
to ignore. Third, even in situations where the threat is less than
life threatening, nobody (including the fetus) has a right to use

one's body unless one consents. Fourth, only if one voluntarily indulges in intercourse knowing that it might lead to a pregnancy and without taking proper precautions is it even plausible to say that the abortion is unjust. But even this limitation would not apply where the mother's life was in jeopardy, since nothing in the mother's choices can be reasonably construed as acquiescence to a life-threatening situation. Finally, that some women may choose to bring the fetus to term does not afford a right in the fetus to be brought to term.

A response is that self-defense is the wrong measure in the case where the unborn is viewed as a person, since the unborn is itself not guilty of any crime.[63] But while the unborn may not be guilty of a crime, it is immediately threatening harm to the mother. Consequently, at least in the case where the harm is life threatening, it is not unreasonable for the mother to defend herself.[64]

Needless to say, with any potentially painful medical procedure, care must be taken to minimize trauma to both the mother and the developing fetus. This humanitarian requirement follows from the fact that all sentient beings (agents or not) commonly share the avoidance of pain.

Finally, most moral arguments that are relied upon to establish the immorality of abortion do not stand up to critical scrutiny. Take a Kantian point of view, for instance. From this perspective one might argue that because everyone wills their own birth and life, and because it is wrong to act from a maxim that cannot be universalized, no one can have an abortion without contradicting herself. The approach is flawed, however, since not all maxims that we would take to be moral should be universalized. For example, we might think it perfectly moral for a person to be a farmer, without all people becoming farmers, or for a person to tell a lie in order to save many lives, without all people telling lies (as, for example, if a Gestapo agent asks where the Jewish family is hiding).

Similarly, an argument based on natural law theory such as Aquinas's would not suffice to show that the abortion of a person is immoral per se, because natural law theory is itself too much in doubt. First, modern science has made a powerful case for believing that human beings are not part of a divinely preordained plan but have come about by a random set of events called evolution.[65] Second, what constitutes the "natural" in natural law is not precise under Aquinas's formulation. For example, why is it natural to have intercourse during an infertile period but unnatural to have intercourse using contraception? Why is heterosexuality more natural than homosexuality? If *natural* is a substitute for *statistically average*, the question is, Why would one want to be statistically average? Does *natural* mean not found in nature other than man? But many of the actions that "natural" law supposedly prohibits (such as homosexuality) are found in nature.[66] If *natural* is supposed to mean morally right, the use begs the question. Finally, in Aquinas's formulation of natural law, there are internal inconsistencies. On the one hand, Aquinas says that one must not kill, as a derivation of the natural law precept that one should do no harm to anyone.[67] On the other hand, a specification (also permitted by the theory) of a natural law precept that the wrongdoer may be punished allows for capital punishment.[68] Since Aquinas has no way to make consistent these two outcomes on the basis of his theory (such as by finding an exception for a grievous crime), the theory is internally contradictory.[69]

The second issue concerns the state's compelling interest to protect the health and well-being of all its citizens, including pregnant women. (Here well-being is understood to include both the psychological and medical health of women at various points in a pregnancy.) For the sake of clarifying this second issue, I am assuming that fetuses are not persons. The obligation to protect the health and well-being of citizens follows at least in part from the state's commitment to foster autonomy in general. Consequently, under this theory the government is permitted to act through general legislation to limit the use of public funds or facilities for abortions without a physician's consent where there is a substantial threat to the life and well-being of a mother. But the nature of such a limitation and the extent to which it limits a mother's choice must be supported by objective medical evidence. The evidence must show that the limitation in question is required in order to avoid a serious health risk to pregnant women. The restriction on how far government can restrict a woman's right to an abortion on the basis of health concerns is justified by the fact that in a compelling state interest situation, privacy does not drop out of the consideration but remains to regulate governmental intrusion. Thus, the maximum intrusion that the government is permitted in restricting a woman's right to an abortion is the minimum amount necessary to achieve its compelling interest of protecting the health and well-being of all pregnant women. Too often states have attempted to use this device as a way to discourage women from having abortions.

A third issue concerns restricting abortions in order to foster a particular moral view. Here the question must be whether fostering such a view is more fundamental than protection of individual privacy to fostering autonomy. It is unlikely that a limitation on a woman's right to an abortion based on moral grounds could ever meet this requirement. Even if it were thought that a particular moral view was in the interest of citizens, unless this could be shown beyond a reasonable doubt, it would not provide a justifiable basis for restricting individual privacy. Such a view tends to be much narrower in the behaviors it permits than would be treating autonomy as a fundamental end of democratic institutions. Consequently, such an argument is insufficient to justify a restriction on abortions.

In *Webster v. Reproductive Health Services*,[70] the Supreme Court upheld the provisions of a Missouri abortion statute that prohibited abortions from being performed in public hospitals, prohibited public employees from performing abortions, and prohibited the use of public funds in abortions. In short, while the decision does not prohibit all abortions, it does significantly impact the right to choice by causing increased health and medical costs (which has a disproportionate effect on poor women) and by decreasing accessibility to places where abortions can be performed. In addition, Chief Justice Rehnquist and Justices White and Kennedy, in their plurality decision, stated that the trimester system, established in *Roe v. Wade* (which prohibited the state from placing any limits on abortions in the first trimester, gave the state limited control to restrict abortions in the second trimester but only for the purpose of protecting maternal health, and gave the state complete control to restrict abortions in the third trimester for the purpose of protecting the unborn but only so long as the mother's life was not in jeopardy), should no longer be required. Because this argument occurs only in the plurality opinion, it does not affect the current state of the law. Nevertheless, given Justice Scalia's concurring opinion that *Roe v. Wade* should be overruled and Justice O'Connor's concurring opinion, which specifically does not affirm *Roe*, it is reasonable to assume that in an appropriate case, which may come up as early as next term,[71] the Supreme Court will overrule *Roe v. Wade*. The fact that *Webster* has narrowed *Roe v. Wade* and its progeny indicates that it is highly likely that eventually *Roe* will be overturned. Even if the Court does not directly overrule *Roe*, if in a future case it follows the plurality opinion and seriously damages the trimester system, it will in fact achieve the same result. In this regard, *Webster* represents a potential for a substantial cutback in the privacy rights of women. More important, *Roe* (as the first case to clearly raise the question of whether there is a right to privacy in the performance of certain acts) when combined with the Supreme Court's holding in *Bowers v. Hardwick* (which held that there was no constitutional right for two adults to engage in consensual homosexual conduct in the privacy of their home)[72] presents good reason to question whether the Supreme Court is still committed to the view that privacy can reach activity.

Two additional points should be noted about the *Webster* case. First, the Court did hold as constitutional a provision in the Missouri statute that required a doctor who believes that the woman is twenty or more weeks pregnant (twenty-four weeks begins the third trimester) to perform tests to determine the fetus's gestational age, weight, and lung maturity, as long as this is subsidary to a finding of viability. The effects of this aspect of the decision are to place additional costs on women seeking abortions and to burden the medical profession with regulations about how viability is to be determined. Second, *Webster* let stand the Missouri legislature's statement in the statute's preamble that except for what is currently allowed by law (namely, abortion), life begins at conception. These aspects of the case further portend the ultimate overruling of *Roe v. Wade*. As Justice Blackmun stated in his dissent, "for today, at least, the law of abortion stands undisturbed. For today, the women of this Nation still retain the liberty to control their destinies. But the signs are evident and very ominous, and a chill wind blows."[73]

A separate but important issue concerns the role of the father in an abortion decision. Should the father have any say in the decision of whether a woman is allowed to have an abortion? The father has an interest that would be impinged in the first instance if the abortion were allowed; thus, privacy is not an issue. The problem in this situation is that the father's interest cannot be protected without impinging on the woman's interest. Moreover, the woman's interest is immediate, physical (as well as emotional), and ongoing in a way that the father's interest is not. The father is physically detached from the developing fetus and therefore separate from the direct psychological effects of pregnancy. In such a situation, it is usually better for the parties to decide among themselves how best to handle the situation. Where agreement is not possible, however, the state has a compelling interest to protect the woman's right to choose, and this includes not coercing her into continuing the pregnancy. Since the effects of the pregnancy are most immediate with the woman (not to mention any risks, either physical or psychological), this obligation on the part of the state is necessary to guarantee autonomy in general.

The father would not have a monetary damage claim against the mother, for, unlike the surrogate mother situation (where damages are accessible as advances on the contract), here there is no way in which to assign damages. In states where fault is a basis for divorce, a ground might be a woman's failure to continue a healthy pregnancy, but only where there is no empirically ascertainable physical or psychological harm to the mother and there is convincing evidence that prior to the conception the mother agreed to the pregnancy. In response to the argument that granting the husband the right to divorce on this basis plays into a male ideology, since often women in our society are socially conditioned to meet certain expectations of men,[74] one must remember that the real issue here is not whether or not the couple would remain together under such circumstances but whether or not either spouse in such a situation would legally be entitled to alimony. A decision on alimony should weigh multiple factors.

These factors include the ground for the dissolution of the marriage along with all other elements that made up the marriage, including whether both parties had careers, what other children were brought into the marriage, how long the marriage lasted, the kinds of expectations that existed between the parties, and so forth. These questions involve facts and must be decided case by case.

Situations such as these raise deeply emotional issues. A society bent on limiting abortions should approach the situation not from the standpoint of trying to limit autonomy, but from the point of view of providing adequate and honest sex education in the schools, health (especially prenatal) care, financial support for raising children, and an awareness of the effects of the institutional and cultural sexism that permeates our society. Needs in these areas often make abortions seem necessary.

Computer Data Banks and Electronic Funds

Transfer Services

Alexander Solzhenitsyn observed that "as every man goes through life, he fills a number of forms for the record, each containing a number of questions . . . There are hundreds of little threads radiating from every man."[75] Computer data banks are able to store much of these threads, which can be analyzed and processed by computers at speeds thousands of times faster than through earlier conventional methods. The effect of this technology on privacy is that now information gathered from census and tax files, medical and credit reports, arrest and criminal records, or even magazine subscriptions has a greater potential than previously for being used as an instrument of control. The situation is exacerbated by the current popularity of owning a personal computer that can link up to commercial time-sharing services (should the security be broken), which may hold much of this information in storage.

More specifically, one privacy issue that arises in this context is that much personal information may be available without the individual's knowledge or consent, since very few laws exist pertaining to the ownership of such information.[76] A related issue is that computer compilations of information in the public domain (such as information about a person's organizational affiliations, religious beliefs, charitable contributions, income, and history of support of various causes), along with whatever statistical inferences may be drawn from them, have become so comprehensive and inexpensively available as to be usable by a wide group of interested parties (like political candidates, charities, etc.) to affect others.[77] Still another privacy issue concerns the problem of devising adequate security procedures to guard against leaks of information, given that many users may have legitimate access to valuable information.[78] There is also the problem that large information-gathering systems, which might be used to create profiles of the ideal juror or might show tendencies toward juvenile delinquency or antisocial behavior, could be used to do away with the possibility of an impartial jury[79] or to provide a basis for governmental monitoring of the lives of certain persons who do not fit the profile.[80] Moreover, because many bureaucratly produced decisions (as in such areas as health benefits, student loans, or tax returns) rely only on such profiles, the probability increases that information released through computer data banks may not always be reliable.[81]

A related problem concerns the widespread availability of systems for electronic funds transfers. Such systems are often used between large corporations or institutions such as automatic clearing houses, which receive, sort, and redistribute financial information to participating banks to debit or credit accounts. Perhaps the most familiar of such services are the automatic teller machines, which are widely available to consumers to make deposits or withdrawals twenty-four hours a day. The obvious privacy issues raised by these electronic funds transfer systems concern the availability of personal information to third persons, the possibility of governmental or private surveillance through system data files, and the claims of consumers to be able to see, challenge, and correct personal data contained in these systems that might be used, for example, to deny them credit.[82]

Because resolving these issues may raise technically complex questions, legislation is necessary in order to determine the best practical approach. Courts are simply ill equipped to perform this task, for their efforts must be focused on narrow problems of specific cases. And indeed some legislation has been tried[83] and other legislation recommended to handle these problems in a sensitive way.[84] From the perspective of this book, the question is not which method is best, but whether or not a call for such legislation is justified. Clearly, that some governmental action should be taken to protect against threats to privacy seems justified. First, it should be noted that the only obvious argument for failing to protect privacy in this area seems to be that protecting privacy would limit the efficiency of the systems and give rise to increased user costs. Second, in neither the computer data bank nor the electronic funds transfer situation is there any support for the view that the nonprivacy interest at stake is more fundamental than privacy to fostering autonomy. The very existence of such systems presupposes at least the minimal degree of autonomy of being able to choose how to live or spend money. Third, even in this highly technological age, when the availability of such systems seems important for economic growth and international competition, it is doubtful that such reasons justify intrusions on privacy. Little would be sacrificed in the way of growth or competition if the state allowed these systems but placed limits on their use for the protection of privacy. In fact, the additional costs associated with protecting privacy might be offset by increased usage once privacy was insured.

There is no counterargument from the point of view that protecting some means for obtaining economic efficiency is essential to protecting autonomy. What is at stake is not giving up all protection of economic efficiency but guaranteeing that the particular means of protection chosen also protect privacy. Consequently, a level of governmental involvement with respect to computer data banks and electronic funds transfers seems justified in order to protect individual autonomy.

In *Whalen v. Roe*,[85] a group of physicians and their patients brought a suit challenging the constitutionality of New York legislation requiring that a copy of every prescription for certain drugs be supplied to the state and that provided protection for the information in the state's possession. A three-judge district court held the statutes unconstitutional. On appeal, the United States Supreme Court reversed on the ground that the legislative scheme did provide protection for the information obtained. In this regard, the Court did recognize for the first time in *dicta* a *constitutional* (non–Fourth Amendment) *right to informational* privacy. The Court, per Justice Stevens stated:

> We are not unaware of the threat to privacy implicit in the accumulation of vast amounts of personal information in computerized data banks or other massive government files. The collection of taxes, the distribution of welfare and social security benefits, the supervision of public health, the direction of the Armed Forces, and the enforcement of the criminal laws all require the orderly preservation of great quantities of information, much of which is personal in character and potentially embarrassing or harmful if disclosed. The right to collect and use such data for public purposes is typically accompanied by a concomitant or regulatory duty to avoid unwarranted disclosure. Recognizing that in some circumstances that duty arguably has its roots in the Constitution, nevertheless, New York's statutory scheme, and its implementing administrative procedures, evidence a proper concern with, and protection of, the individual's interest in privacy.[86]

Since *Whalen*, the Supreme Court has decided *Nixon v. Administrator of General Services*,[87] in which the former president challenged the constitutionality of a federal law that would have allowed the public access to his papers and tape recordings after preliminary screening to separate out personal communications. On holding the law constitutional, the Court, per Justice Brennan, stated:

> In sum, appellant has a legitimate expectation of privacy in his personal communications. But the constitutionality of the Act must be viewed in the context of the limited intrusion of the screening process, of appellant's status as a public figure, of his lack of any expectation of privacy on the overwhelming majority of the materials, and of the virtual impossibility of segregating the small quantity of private materials without comprehensive screening.[88]

The decisions in *Whalen* and *Administrator of General Services* can be seen to comport with the theory stated here. In *Whalen*, the state arguably had a compelling interest in the prescription records. Even so, the Court recognized a fundamental right to informational privacy, which could be intruded upon only to the minimum extent necessary for the state to achieve its compelling interest. This is the meaning of the Court's acknowledgment that the statutory scheme and administrative regulations had taken into account the privacy interest of individuals. Similarly, in *Administrator of General Services*, the Court noted the "limited intrusion of the screening process" as one of the factors to be taken into account when balancing the privacy interest of a major public figure. The Court applied a "flexible balancing" standard as opposed to the compelling state interest standard[89] but did not explain the difference in terminology. Clearly the state has a compelling interest in seeing to it that the public papers of a former President of the United States are opened to public scrutiny, as long as they do not compromise the national interest. An explanation for not using the compelling state interest standard might be its association with cases where the government almost always loses and here the state was going to be given access to Nixon's papers, but such an explanation buries the analytical structure of the standard and suggests without explanation that not all claims of privacy are of the same weight. It is clearer to say that all valid privacy claims are important but that in some circumstances other important factors necessitate their being overriden. Moreover, since the screening process seemed to be the only way to separate Nixon's few private records from the overwhelming number of public records, the conclusion adopted by the Court comported with the requirement that the maximum amount of intrusion on Nixon's privacy be the minimum necessary to achieve the state's compelling interest. Perhaps this is the underlying meaning of flexible balance.

Finally, in *United States Department of Justice v. Reporters Committee for the Freedom of Press*,[90] we have a case that arose "out of requests made by a CBS news correspondent and the Reporters Committee for the Freedom of the Press for information concerning the criminal records of four members of the notorious Medico family." The FBI had provided the requested data on only three of the Medicos after their deaths. In their complaint in the district court, the respondents sought the "rap" sheet on the fourth member of the family. The district court granted the state's motion for summary judgment, thus denying the appellant's right to the information. The court of appeals then reversed the district court. At issue was whether the individual's "interest in the non-disclosure of any 'rap' sheet the FBI might have on him was the sort of 'personal privacy' interest the Congress intended the law enforcement exemption of the Freedom of Information Act to protect."[91] In holding that the disclosure of the sheet to third parties would constitute the kind of unwarranted invasion of privacy the statutory exemption was meant to protect against, the Court, per Justice Stevens, cited its earlier constitutional *dicta* in *Whalen* for the proposition that a centralized computer file posed a threat to privacy.[92] The Court then went on to interpret the law enforcement exemption under the Freedom of Information Act.

The privacy interest in maintaining the practical obscurity of "rap" sheet information will always be high. When the subject of such a "rap" sheet is a private citizen and when the information is in the Government's control as a compilation, rather than as a record of "what the Government is up to," the privacy interest protected by Exemption 7(C) is in fact at its apex while the FOIA-based public interest in disclosure is at its nadir. Such a disparity on the scales of justice holds for a class of cases without regard to individual circumstances; the standard virtues of bright-line rules are thus present, and the difficulty attendant to ad hoc adjudication may be avoided. Accordingly, we hold as a categorical matter that a third party's request for law-enforcement records or information about a private citizen can reasonably be expected to invade that citizen's privacy, and that when that request seeks no "official information about a Government Agency, but merely the records the Government Agency happens to be storing, the invasion of privacy is unwarranted."[93]

In contrast to *Administrator of General Services*, the Court's holding in *Reporters Committee for Freedom of the Press* recognized a congressional intention in the FOIA, that whatever may be the public's right to know in the context of a public official or a public figure, that right is substantially diminished in the case of a private person not currently involved in a public event. Although this was not a constitutional decision but one based on statutory interpretation, were the FOIA not to have provided for this exemption, then under my theory the Court would have been proper to rule the *application* of the FOIA to this case as unconstitutional.

What these three cases suggest is that after a long period of development in the law of privacy, the Supreme Court has finally recognized a constitutional right to privacy of information independent of Fourth Amendment concerns. What will become of this right in the subsequent development of privacy law (such as what will become of the constitutional right to perform private acts) remains to be seen. However, based on the theory set forth herein, there is hope for the view that the future development of both of these facets of constitutional privacy will be developed along lines that would promote maximal autonomy.

Pornography and Drugs in the Home

Two issues that are stirring much debate and will continue to do so concern the possession and use of pornography and illegal drugs in the home. Until recently, the possession of pornography in the home has been firmly protected, and, by extension, it might have been argued that the same should hold for drugs.

In the 1969 case of *Stanley v. Georgia*,[94] the Supreme Court held that the First Amendment protects persons in their homes from statutes regulating what books they may read or films they may watch.[95] As the Court stated it, "the mere private possession of obscene matter cannot constitutionally be made a crime."[96] However, *Stanley* has since been narrowed by the Supreme Court's recent decision in *Osborne v. Ohio*.[97]

In *Osborne*, the majority refused to apply *Stanley* to an Ohio statute that made it a crime to possess pornographic photographs of children in the home. The majority reasoned that *Stanley* involved a paternalistic attempt by the state, which could not override First Amendment protections.[98] By contrast, in *Osborne*, Ohio was trying to protect the victims of pornography by limiting the demand.[99]

When the two cases are read together, *Stanley* is still the controlling law with regard to the possession of adult pornography, but now the state can intrude into the home for the sake of restricting the availability of child pornography. The decisions thus read as a limitation on the rationale police can use to intrude on one's seclusion or solitude. They prohibit paternalistic intrusions for the sake of the pornographic user as well as moralistic intrusions the state may be inclined to support.

One would expect that a similar rationale should govern the private use of drugs in the home. Thus, the state in its police power should be prohibited from regulating private drug use in the home if the primary reason it would have for doing so is the protection of the user or the promotion of a particular moral standard. The "Just Say No" campaign against drug use would not warrant intrusion into one's solitude. Still, if the state can show that its primary motive is neither legal paternalism nor legal moralism but protection against the effects of drug use outside the home (such as increased accidents on the job, addiction, crime, etc.), then the *Osborne* rationale would open the home to invasions by the state in the pursuit of the prohibition of illegal drugs.

For our purposes, the question could be put narrowly in terms of whether the *Osborne* case was correctly decided or more broadly in terms of whether the state has any compelling interest to limit the possession or use of pornography or drugs in the home. Let us begin by asking whether there is even a prima facie claim to privacy in such cases.

A statement that one possesses pornography or uses drugs in the home does not entail a conflict with any other person's interest in the relevant group of citizens that the state has a duty to protect, because there is nothing in the mere description of these acts that without a causal theory would suggest harm to another. Consequently, the home possessor or user has a prima facie claim to privacy from unwarranted intrusions by any other persons including the state.

The more interesting question arises at the second level of analysis. Does the state have a compelling interest to overcome the privacy claim of the possessor or user? Currently, eighteen states have statutes that outlaw the possession of child pornography.[100] Almost all states prohibit the possession of certain dangerous drugs. One way to look at the problem is to ask whether the reasons behind these statutes support a compelling interest of the state.

In preventing child pornography, the state has a compelling

interest to prevent the exploitation of children in order to insure autonomy. The interest arises from the fact that children are generally not able at an early age to distinguish between exploitation by adults who have special influence over them and those who are acting for their own interest. Consequently, in its role of *parens patriae* the state may operate on behalf of children by imposing various kinds of criminal prohibitions on the sale and distribution of child pornography. Exactly how far the state can go in imposing such restrictions is itself not unrestricted, however.

As in any case where the state has a compelling interest that allows it to interfere with privacy, the maximum amount of intrusion is the minimum necessary to meet its compelling interest. This means that the state cannot take any actions but those that will achieve its interest and have the least intrusive effect on privacy. In *Osborne v. Ohio*, Justice Brennan, in his dissent, stated that Ohio had other options available to help eradicate child pornography, including laws against creation and distribution.[101] Presumably, such laws would carry high penalties and thus discourage distributors. Moreover, as such laws become regularly enforced, the price of the material increases, making it less desirable for purchase. This latter effect tends to limit demand. Where the Court erred in *Osborne* was in not realizing that its duty of analysis did not end once it had determined that the state had a compelling interest to protect the exploitation of children by child pornographers. Thus, the Court's restriction on this area of privacy was unnecessarily intrusive on a fundamental right.

A related analysis applies in the context of the use of illegal drugs in the home. Here the issue is whether the state has a compelling interest in criminalizing the possession and use of drugs in private.[102] One approach is to ascertain the empirical effects of the different kinds of drug use. Presumably, if some drugs have no effects beyond those that accompany their occurrent use, then the state would have no reason to prohibit their use in the home. On the other hand, drugs whose effects carry over from the private to the public sphere may very well command a compelling interest of the state to prohibit them if that is necessary to protect autonomy in general. This last issue of whether continued criminalization or some other approach will better protect autonomy must be examined.

Enough Americans (perhaps as many as thirty-five million) have at one time or another used drugs,[103] creating a widespread, lucrative black market worth billions of dollars. This has meant that there is very little incentive for those who deal in drugs to give up the trade. Even the threat of the death penalty will probably have little effect given the actual dollars involved, the fact that some of these people are outside of American territorial limits, and the difficulty of identifying them. More important is the fact that the street price of most drugs, controlled by the black market, is so high that (especially for addicts) the need to raise money is very strong. This has led to a rise in the crime rate as more and more drug users find it difficult to support their habit.[104] It has also led to the availability of drugs to children, many of whom begin stealing at an early age and will, no doubt, undertake other criminal endeavors to support their habit.[105] Another side effect is that the intravenous use of needles has become a prime source for the spread of AIDS,[106] and still another side effect is the average 37.7 percent overload of the criminal justice system.[107] (One source estimates that it costs $14,750 to detain a typical suspect from indictment to sentencing.[108])

As a result of these factors, a surprising alliance has arisen between those on the left (including the American Civil Liberties Union) and some on the right, like William F. Buckley and former secretary of state Charles Schultz, who argue for the decriminalization of drugs.[109] What this spells for future policy is still unclear.

If criminal penalties cannot stop the use of illegal drugs and are counterproductive by creating more crime, then the above analysis provides a persuasive argument (from the standpoint of protecting autonomy) for legislation to decriminalize drugs. This, however, would not translate as removing restrictions on their use. Certainly we could maintain criminal sanctions for the use of drugs while operating a car or other vehicle, or for dispensing them to minors, just as we do with alcohol. These actions are sufficiently limited in scope so as not to create the kind of economic market that gave rise to the current situation. Moreover, of the ten billion dollars that the Bush administration's 1990 budget allocates to the "war" on drugs, 70 percent has been earmarked for enforcement, including police officers, prosecutors and judges.[110] This money might better be spent through the surgeon general's office helping educate people about drugs and creating more rehabilitation programs. Distributing clean needles to addicts, with information about rehabilitation programs and the dangers of drug use, would help curb the spread of AIDS, much as it has in the Netherlands.[111] In short, we are more likely to maximize autonomy in general by educating society to the dangers of substance abuse than by criminal prohibitions, which seem to make the problem more acute.

Employer Drug and Polygraph Testing

Can employers validly require mandatory drug or alcohol testing of prospective or current employees? The question is becoming increasingly controversial as more and more employers—both public and private—require as a condition for employment or as a condition for remaining employed that their employees pass a "substance abuse" test.

What makes such tests controversial is the clear differentiation of interest between employers and employees. On the employer's side, a 1985 survey by the national cocaine helpline found that 75 percent of its respondents used drugs on the job, 44 percent dealt drugs to fellow employees, and 25 percent used drugs daily at work.[112] While such results as this may be skewed to the population surveyed, there is evidence to suggest that between 10 and 23 percent of American workers use drugs at work, that 91 percent of those who use cocaine do so during working hours, and that half of this group buys and sells drugs on the job. It is estimated that loss of productivity from employee drug and alcohol abuse cost American industry approximately one hundred billion dollars in 1986. Alcohol was implicated in thirty-seven deaths in the railroad industry over a nine-year period.[113] The pilot in an airplane crash that killed two crewmen may have been smoking marijuana while flying. Not unexpected are the instances of employee theft in support of a habit, which in one case amounted to $250,000 worth of computer equipment.[114] Under such circumstances, employers have an interest to protect themselves from liability for impaired workers' negligence, lost productivity, and outright theft.

On the employee's side, supplying urine samples on demand is "fundamentally offensive." This is particularly true where the employee is obligated to urinate under observation to insure the reliability of the sample. Some employees are concerned that their employer will learn about a medical condition (such as epilepsy) from medications detected in the urine. (Epilepsy is often controlled by the use of prescription drugs, which are detectable in urinary analysis.) Another reason employees dislike testing is the possibility of a false positive result. The employee may be concerned that a mistake in the testing could result in labeling her or him a drug user, with potential loss of job and long-term stigma.[115] Such concerns clearly suggest that the employee's privacy is invaded, especially where the employee has not been involved in an incident in which the question of drugs might have arisen. Since such concerns in the case of private employees are not currently cognizable by the courts, unless the test is shown to discriminate against drug addicts or other minorities,[116] some commentators have argued for legislation to help sort out the various important interests involved.[117]

In contrast, where the employee works for a public employer, he has the benefit of traditional Fourth Amendment privacy protection.[118] Under this guise, some courts have held that an employee can be tested only where there is a "reasonable suspicion" of drug use,[119] while other courts have found a "diminished expectation of privacy" based on the general nature of the employee's job,[120] or have allowed administrative search warrants.[121] This area of the law is in need of a more consistent analysis. To this end, then, the remainder of this section should provide courts with clear guidelines at least for the public employer.

To begin with, it should be noted that what is at stake is not the information that is obtained about the employee, but the inference that the employer who has that information is inclined to make about the employee. In this respect, the first privacy question is whether the employee has a prima facie claim to use illegal drugs with respect to the public employer. Once this question is decided, we can take up the question about the privacy issues involved in cases of misinformation (false positives) or irrelevant information (epilepsy).

Under our definition of a private act, it is certainly true that the mere description of an employee or potential employee using an illegal drug does not suggest a conflict with any basic interest of the employer. The reason is that the employee may be using the drug in off hours and the drug may be of a kind that has no lingering effect on the employee's performance at work. Since instances of drug use that meet these conditions exist, it cannot be concluded that a description of the mere use of an illegal drug necessarily impinges upon an interest of the employer. Consequently, it must be the case that an employee has a prima facie privacy claim to the use of an illegal drug with respect to her or his employer.

Having said this much, it should immediately be noted that an employee's prima facie privacy claim will not hold up against a subsequent discipline or discharge by a public employer if indeed the drug used is discovered to have hindered the employee's performance on the job. The claim here is that, initially, it is not the public employer's business what substances the employee may use in off hours.

Still, that claim may not secure the employee from on-the-job drug testing or the prospective employee from testing as a condition for employment where it is reasonable to expect that the job in question requires a high degree of skill, accuracy, and quickness of judgment if human life or property is not to be endangered. Under such circumstances, the state in its capacity as public employer is likely to have a compelling interest to require drug testing. This would likely be true for fire fighters, police officers, surgeons, ambulance attendants, airline pilots, air controllers, bus drivers, truck drivers, train operators, shut-down attendants at nuclear power plants, and others. It is less likely true for janitors, telephone operators, most clerical personnel, and many others. In positions where impairment of mental or physical function can have disastrous effects on life or property, the state would have a compelling interest to test for drugs in advance of any incident that might occur because of their use.

This brings us, then, to the question of misinformation or the discovery of irrelevant information. Here the point is that such information is in itself potentially harmful to the employee, depending on how it is handled. In order to avoid a false positive, a second test should be required to confirm the result. In order to avoid the discovery of embarrassing or irrelevant information, as in the case of some medical conditions, the employer should be required to guarantee that only the results of relevant information become part of the employee's record. Moreover, a statement to this effect should be included in the company's written personnel policy. Otherwise, our limitation on intruding into an area of privacy because of a compelling state interest, namely, that the maximum amount of intrusion be no more than the minimum necessary to achieve the state's compelling interest, will not be satisfied.

Before closing this section, we need to take up the issue of employers' using polygraphs ("lie detectors") to screen prospective and current employees for various purposes. One important difference between this situation and drug testing is that the accuracy of the polygraph is uncertain.[122] An important side effect of an individual's not passing a polygraph test is that he or she may become unemployable. Moreover, unless polygraph testing is carefully regulated, employers may use it to screen out those considered "undesirable" for reasons unrelated to their ability to perform the job. From the standpoint of privacy, then, the use of polygraphs raises substantial questions.

Given their unreliability, are polygraph examinations ever justified? If the polygraph were accurate in the same sense that drug tests are accurate (namely, that subject to a small margin of error in the results there are no basic questions of interpretation), then the analysis governing its application would follow that governing drug testing. Indeed, one might think that even given the inaccuracy of interpretation, polygraphs should be allowed for at least sensitive jobs. Take, for example, the case of the government worker being considered for access to classified information. Agencies that investigate the backgrounds of such persons usually take into account the testimony of neighbors, coworkers, and friends, which may not be fully accurate. Even so, questions are usually resolved within the context of one or several interviews. If a neighbor says, "I am not sure about this person," the appropriate follow-up would be, What is it that gives rise to your suspicions? If the suspicion can be stated objectively, the investigator can independently determine its validity.

In contrast, where a polygraph examination is involved, interpreting the results has theoretical as well as practical difficulties. For example, if the prospective employee answers no to the question Have you ever stolen anything? and the machine records a deceptive answer, how is that answer to be interpreted? We know nothing about the context of a possible theft and very little about the psychological state of the examinee. While the former may be susceptible to further questioning by the examiner, the latter may not. Even if the examinee admits to a wrongdoing, is the correct interpretation that being fundamentally a moral person the examinee feels guilt about it or that the examinee has made a practical judgment that he or she could not get away with a lie? What if the examinee once stole a candy bar? If the examinee holds this information back, is it because he or she believes it irrelevant in light of his or her subsequent moral development (it may have happened ten years ago), or is the examinee seriously attempting to deceive the examiner? Is it even the examiner's business if it was an incident from the examinee's youth? Do we not run into the problem that in order to determine whether it is the examiner's business or not we have to expose a lot of private information? Perhaps the examinee, having overcome guilt feelings, may be able to lie with impunity. If so, might the examination leave us with a pack of good liars? Such possibilities are less likely where there is independent fact finding. They are also less likely with interviews, since the interviewee will usually exercise judgment in creating an impression of the subject and the examiner can ask follow-up questions. These concerns, when combined with the fact that such tests are open to abuse, override any compelling interest the state might have for requiring such tests.

This discussion has focused primarily on public employment and has omitted police criminal investigations. Obviously, the same objections would hold in that context as well. Moreover, there is the Fifth Amendment right against self-incrimination, which makes a more compelling case against polygraph testing.

In this section, I have focused on the public, rather than the private, employer, because private employers are not subject to constitutional or Fourth Amendment restrictions but only to torts restrictions, and there are no torts limitations in this area. However, this is purely a historical accident and does not follow out of the theory. To the contrary, the justification for the theory, while clearly regulating the relationship of the citizen to the state, would also prescribe that the state act to insure the privacy of its citizens with respect to each other. For this reason, either legislation should be enacted to rectify this limitation of the current law of privacy or a judicial review in an appropriate case should be undertaken in order to determine whether common law tort privacy might be properly construed to extend more protections to employees in the private sector.

The Right to Die

On June 25, 1990, the United States Supreme Court rendered its seminal decision in *Cruzan v. Director, Missouri, Department of Health*.[123] The case involved the question of whether parents and coguardians could order the withdrawal of life-sustaining treatment from their twenty-five-year-old daughter after she sustained severe injuries in an automobile accident resulting in a loss of cognitive faculties, with no possibility of recovery.

In the early morning of January 11, 1983, Nancy Cruzan was found lying face down in a ditch approximately thirty-five feet from where her automobile had overturned. No respiratory or cardiac functions could be detected. By the time paramedics arrived and were able to restore cardiac and spontaneous respiratory functions, Nancy had been in a state of anoxia (or deprivation of oxygen to the brain) between twelve and fourteen minutes. Normally, deprivation of oxygen to the brain approaching six minutes would result in permanent brain damage. Exploratory surgery showed a laceration of her liver, and a CAT scan indicated no significant brain abnormalities. For three weeks following the accident Nancy remained in a coma. Subsequently, because Nancy's condition seemed to improve somewhat, her (then) husband gave permission for a gastrostomy feeding tube to be surgically implanted. A substantial period of time passed during which valiant efforts were made to rehabilitate Nancy without success. Thereafter, Nancy's parents, as her guardians, brought this action to have her taken off further nutrition and hydration.

The trial court found that Nancy had normal respiration and circulation but was oblivious to her environment except for certain reflex responses to sound and possibly painful stimuli. The trial court also found that she had suffered anoxia of the brain, resulting in irreversible cerebral cortical atrophy and massive enlargement of the ventricles, which were filled with cerebrospinal fluid where the brain had degenerated. Her highest cognitive functions seemed to be her response to sound and pain stimuli. Her four extremities had irreversible muscular and tendon damage and she had no cognitive or reflex ability to swallow food or water. Still, according to the medical experts, as long as Nancy continued to receive nutrition and hydration, she could live another thirty years. She was not dead or terminally ill. The trial court also found that while Nancy never executed a living will, there was evidence that on one occasion she stated to her roommate in a somewhat serious conversation "that if sick or injured she would not wish to continue her life unless she could live at least halfway normally."[124] Based on these findings, the trial court granted the parents petition to discontinue nutrition and hydration.

The Missouri Supreme Court reversed this decision. Reviewing the case *en banc,* the court stated that the United States Supreme Court had never extended the right to privacy to decisions about the termination of life-sustaining treatment and had in *Bowers v. Hardwick*[125] specifically resisted the expansion of the right to privacy to encompass adult consensual homosexual behavior, implying that no further extension was envisioned. The Missouri Supreme Court went on to characterize the state's compelling interest in this area as involving the preservation of life, not the quality of life. It then rejected the argument that Cruzan's parents were entitled to order withdrawal of nutrition and hydration on the ground that Missouri's Living Will statute requires that the intention of the patient to terminate life-supporting procedures must be established by "clear and convincing" evidence. The informal discussion Nancy had with her roommate did not satisfy this standard.

In affirming the Missouri Supreme Court, the United States Supreme Court treated the matter as one involving a Fourteenth Amendment liberty interest protected under the due process clause rather than a general right to privacy. This gave the court the opportunity to apply a lesser standard of protection (as is typical in due process cases, since the question of fairness usually requires the balancing of different interests) than the compelling state interest standard, which attaches to fundamental privacy rights. Consequently, greater power was afforded to the state to regulate the new right. As Chief Justice Rehnquist's majority opinion stated:

It cannot be disputed that the Due Process Clause protects an interest in life as well an interest in refusing life-sustaining medical treatment. . . .
    In our view, Missouri has permissibly sought to advance these interests through the adoption of a "clear and convincing" standard of proof to govern such proceedings.[126]

Not every justice who joined the majority opinion was satisfied with its rationale. Justice Scalia, though concurring in the result, thought that the federal courts had no business in this field. Justice O'Connor's concurrence noted:

I also write separately to emphasize that the Court does not today decide the issue of whether a state must also give effect to the decisions of a surrogate decision-maker. In my view, such a duty may well be constitutionally required to protect the patient's liberty interest in refusing medical treatment.[127]

In dissent, Justice Brennan stated: "Although the right to be free of unwanted medical intervention, like other constitutionally protected interests, may not be absolute, no state interest could outweigh the rights of an individual in Nancy Cruzan's position."[128]

Similarly, Justice Stevens stated: "Only because Missouri has arrogated to itself the power to defend life, and only because the Court permits this usurpation, are Nancy Cruzan's life and liberty put into disquieting conflict."[129]

At stake in this case is the scope of the right to privacy. Does the right to privacy include the right to die, or can the state assert a compelling interest in the fact of life regardless of its quality?[130] At least sixteen states have had to deal with the question of removal of life-sustaining treatments, some in reference to patients who were terminally ill, others, like *Cruzan*, in reference to patients who were not terminally ill.[131] Of the former group, *In re Quinlan* is certainly the most famous.[132]

Karen Quinlan also had suffered severe brain damage as a result of anoxia. The medical experts who examined her diagnosed her condition as terminal. They further claimed that she could not survive without the respirator to which she was attached. As a result, her father sought a court order allowing him to disconnect the respirator so Karen could die quickly, but nevertheless, Karen Quinlan continued to live nine years after the respirator was disconnected. The Supreme Court of New Jersey, noting the heavy medical intrusion on Karen's body, found a right to privacy to terminate her "noncognitive vegetative existence." It thereby granted her father's request, stating: "We think that the State's interest *contra* weakens and that the individual's right to privacy grows as the degree of bodily invasion increases and the prognosis dims. Ultimately, there comes a point at which the individual's rights overcomes the state's interest."[133]

In *Cruzan*, the Missouri Supreme Court cited one commentator to support the legislative notion in the Living Will statute that "where the patient's right to refuse medical treatment is constant, the patient's condition and prognosis would no longer seem relevant."[134] The court went on to decry the *Quinlan* decision as opening the door to the *judicial* approval of suicide, a situation that could not arise where the state's compelling interest is in the fact of life and not its quality.

The question for our analysis is: what should be the state's compelling interest in cases such as *Cruzan* and *Quinlan?* Is it an ultimate regard for life per se? Is it a regard for the quality of life? Or is it something else? Our earlier discussion of abortion is apropos.

There a fundamental right of the mother was being challenged on the basis of a presumed right of the unborn. It was argued that such a challenge could succeed on the basis of a compelling state interest only if the plausibility of treating the fetus as a person (in the sense of its being an agent) could be established. In other words, the fetus would have to possess at least minimum voluntary control over its life for its own purposes, even if only in the sense of not being subject to exclusively uncontrollable thoughts and desires.[135] Anything less could not be justified, as it would mark a clear intrusion on a prima facie right of the mother.

A similar analysis should govern here. What we have is the flip side of the abortion question. Where there is very little reason to suppose that the vegetating body is a person in the relevant sense, the state can have no compelling interest, based solely on the fact of life, to intrude into a guardian's decision about what further efforts should be undertaken to keep the body alive.

The concern not to open the door to guardians' being able to kill unwanted relatives or charges merely because the latter possess a handicap or retardation or disability is also met by this analysis, which is not based on degree of quality of life (as, for example, would be the situation if one said that beyond a certain degree of retardation life is no longer worth living). Instead, the analysis is based on whether the body in question can either currently or prospectively be properly described as an agent. What is at stake is not quality of life, or life per se, but agency.

If the body can properly be described as an agent, either currently or prospectively, then the state has a compelling interest in protecting it. The reason for emphasizing agency over life per se or quality of life is that agency is a necessary condition for being able to engage in autonomous actions. Life per se and quality of life may play a role only when they are part of agency. Otherwise, they have no independent significance.

In *Cruzan*, it seems clear from the findings of the trial court that Nancy was not an agent. Consequently, the reliability of her statement to her roommate is relevant only if there is a reasonable medical possibility that eventually she may return to being an agent. In other words, what is at stake, under these circumstances, is her prospective psychological state—whether she will eventually be able to engage in purposive activities. If medical data supports a conclusion by physicians knowledgeable about Nancy's condition that in time she could return to being an agent, then the state would have a compelling interest to protect Nancy's agency. Otherwise it would not.

Does this position contradict our earlier abortion position? Since most unborn fetuses will eventually become agents, why should they not also be treated as prospective agents? In the case of abortion, it was argued that the right to terminate a pregnancy cannot be restricted as long as the fetus is not an agent and there is no threat to the mother's health. In seeming contrast, it is argued here that patients who are comatose cannot be allowed to die merely because their agency is suspended. How are the two positions to be reconciled? The answer lies in the fact that the comatose patient has not lost the essential cognitive abilities for agency. Whereas with abortion, the essential abilities for agency have not yet developed. In other words, for there to be prospective agency, it must be true that the body in question has not suffered such brain damage as to make even the future capability for minimal voluntary and purposive action impossible.

Being an agent, then, should be construed not to mean actual agency, but rather actual or prospective agency. Otherwise a person who was asleep could justifiably be killed. In the abortion situation, the body is only potentially an agent. Whereas, with the temporary vegetative state situation the body is a prospective, though not an actual, agent.[136] The point might be put this way. When General Motors receives a delivery of raw materials for assembling automobiles, the proper description of what General Motors has is not automobiles but what will eventually become automobiles, all things going as planned. On the other hand, when I say that my automobile is on the fritz, I mean not that I do not have an automobile but that my automobile is not currently in working condition. Instead, were I to say that my automobile was "totaled," I would mean that I no longer own an automobile, only a pile of junk. In putting the point in this way, the linguistic distinctions betray logical differences. Where abortions are performed prior to viability (as in the General Motors situation), the body is not yet a person. Whereas in the situation of the patient in a vegetative state (as in the situation with my automobile), the personhood of the body depends on whether recovery to agency is possible.

The objection that time, in the development of the unborn, plays the same role that treatment plays with respect to the comatose patient does not work. In the former situation, before a certain period of development, it would not be proper to say an agent exists, even though the building blocks, from which an agent might eventually arise, are present. In the latter situation, by contrast, the features of agency essentially exist even though the patient's condition prevents him or her from performing voluntary acts for his or her own purposes. As soon as the patient ceases to be inhibited, he or she will be able to exercise agency. Where it becomes clear that the inhibition is permanent, as with a persistent vegetative state, agency is no longer possible. Hence, the state should no longer have an interest in preserving the patient's life.

Thus, the method for approaching privacy issues regarding vegetative bodies is no different than the method regarding abortion. The conclusions derived from this analysis are consistent in the application of the principles.

It should be noted historically that following the Supreme Court's decision in November 1990, a second hearing was held before Probate Judge Teel in which the Cruzans introduced the testimony of two coworkers who testified that they remembered Nancy's saying she would not want to live like a vegetable.[137] This time the state of Missouri withdrew from the case saying that it had no further role because the legal issue had been decided. The judge ruled in favor of removing the feeding tube on December 14, 1990, and two weeks later, on December 26, Nancy Cruzan died.

Another interesting question arises: Does the state have a compelling interest to preserve the life of a terminally ill patient? As with the comatose patient, there is the question of whether a doctor, at the request of her or his patient or the patient's guardian, should be allowed to remove the patient from life-supporting treatment, whether such treatment is a respirator, a medication, or other type of medical support. There is also the question of whether, under these same circumstances, a doctor should be allowed to administer a drug that, in effect, puts the patient to sleep. (The problematic distinction between active and passive euthanasia need not be dealt with here since the argument applies regardless of which way the act is characterized.) If at the time the doctor is to act the patient is in a persistent vegetative state (i.e., no longer an agent), then the same analysis as above would apply here. An important question arises, however, where the terminally ill patient has not ceased to be an agent. Certainly, if the patient is either in constant excruciating pain or drugged into oblivion, very little is gained from saying that the state has a compelling interest to preserve the patient's life. Under these circumstances, however, the analysis is not based on whether the patient is an agent. The analysis is the straightforward one of whether autonomy is better served by preserving the patient's life or by leaving that choice up to the patient (or the patient's guardian) and her or his physician. Under these circumstances, the latter alternative seems preferable if privacy is to be respected as a fundamental right. As for ensuring that physicians act only for the best interests of the patient, the state would have a compelling interest to mandate the establishment of hospital ethics boards to review any situation that poses such a question before action is taken.

What about a person who is neither terminally ill nor in a vegetative state but who does not want to continue to live? Under these circumstances, would the state have a compelling interest to interfere with the person's freedom of action in order to protect his or her life? The answer is affirmative, but only to the extent that the state is protecting individual autonomy against a psychological or physical condition that clearly is interfering with rational thought. Once that interference is removed or it becomes clear that the individual has truly weighed all the alternatives (what I mean by rational in this context), further interference with the individual is not justified. Generally, the state should ensure that there is available adequate medical and psychological care to deal with such a situation. Such situations are tragic at best, and therefore they should be dealt with sensitively if human dignity is to be preserved.

Epilogue
AUTONOMY: THE
ULTIMATE QUESTION

The concern of this book has been to develop a theory of legal privacy that explains precisely what privacy is and shows how it is justified. With respect to the latter, I have argued that because democratic government in the Western sense values autonomy as a fundamental end, it must also value privacy as a fundamental right. This then raises the question, Why should a democratic society value autonomy as a fundamental end? The answer cannot be found by analyzing the concept of democracy without circularity. One can certainly imagine democratic governments that grant their people the basic freedoms of speech, press, and the right to vote but do so for reasons unrelated to the promotion of autonomy. What this suggests, then, is that the justification for autonomy, as a fundamental end of democratic government, must lie elsewhere.

Autonomy (when properly understood) must be a basic requirement of morality or, if not, then at least it must be accepted as such in the tradition and culture of the society in which it is to operate. The first approach is normative, the second empirical. In support of the first approach, the works of Alan Gewirth and John Rawls provide a promising beginning.[1] Although Gewirth's work has been criticized for not giving adequate attention to the problem of autonomy,[2] the value of that criticism is in doubt.[3] Moreover, the work by David A. J. Richards has drawn a promising connection between the ethical foundations of constitutional and criminal law and the broader philosophical structures of both Gewirth and Rawls.[4]

> The substantive criminal law and cognate principles of constitutional law rest on the same ethical foundations . . . Whether one uses Rawl's maximizing contractarian hypothesis or Gewirth's universalization of rationally autonomous people, the consequence is the same for purposes of the criminal law. Certain basic principles are agreed to or universalized as basic principles of critical morality, because they secure, at little comparable costs to the agents acting on them, forms of action or forbearance from action that rational persons would want guaranteed as a minimal condition of advancing the responsible pursuit of their ends.[5]

In support of the empirical approach, Hixon's sociological study, although skeptical about the motivations underlying the quest for ever greater autonomy in contemporary society, nonetheless attests to its existence:

> Early in the present century, another vision of self emerged, a different emphasis on self-development and mastery, a new way of presenting the individual in society. Susman saw this as part of significant change in the social order, which he diagnosed as "American nervousness" over the rash of utopian writings, the appearance of systematic sociological and economic analysis in the academic community, the perceived need for "objective" and "scientific" data to solve social ills, and the development of psychological and psychiatric studies. These in turn suggested the need for a new kind of man to meet the new conditions.
>
> From this study of advice manuals that appeared after the turn of the century, Susman learned that the vision of self-sacrifice began to yield to one of self-realization. . . . That shift gave impetus—which continues today if best-seller lists are any indication—to the concern for personal autonomy and privacy.[6]

Obviously, the normative approach is the more appealing in that it would apply universally. But even within the empirical approach, I have shown that any society that values autonomy as a fundamental end must by definition value privacy as well. Whether either or both of these two approaches ultimately prove correct, one thing is certain: Western democratic societies fundamentally value autonomy. The strength of this commitment is borne out by the Senate confirmation hearings that led to the rejection of Supreme Court nominee Robert Bork.

It is fair to say that one reason Robert Bork lost Senate confirmation is that he had expressed doubts about whether a general right to privacy could be grounded in the Constitution.[7] The events leading up to the killing of the nomination included an outpouring of criticism by various groups from around the country. Whatever the merits of particular criticisms, what cannot be doubted is that they exhibited a broad-based consensus for the view that government should stay clear of the private lives of individual citizens.[8]

A possible counterargument against my view is that critics of Bork were not necessarily responding to autonomy in all its implications but rather were merely advancing their own agendas (abortion rights, gay and lesbian rights, freedom of expression, and so forth). What this argument fails to recognize is that in a democratic society autonomy is the ability to discover, amidst numerous competing interests and compatible with a like freedom for all, what one's own interests are. Since providing for the discovery of one's own interests is the only aspect of autonomy that one must value in order to formulate a general right to privacy, the fact that people disagree on applications of the right is of no paramount significance. Therefore, my theory does not succumb to the objection that we are justified only in looking to the concrete intentions of those making up the consensus.

Beyond this issue, the criticisms of the Bork nomination brought to life a deeper concern regarding how we select judges. Should they be chosen because they conform to a particular ideology (liberal or conservative), or should that selection be based on qualifications in the sense that they know the law and are willing to apply it in an impartial manner? The Bork nomination showed that the two questions cannot be separated. Putting aside any tradition in this country that a president appoints justices who share his or her ideology (or even whether such an approach to selection makes democratic sense), it is clear that political theory is part of constitutional decision making. The argument that judges should act independent of political philosophy is simply not valid. In a judge's decision—indeed, even in his or her approach to a decision—broad political points of view are exhibited. This is true even where the appointee expresses a high degree of deference to past precedent. The only difference is that the political philosophy at stake coincides with the political interest of senators to appease, or at least not alienate, a majority of their constituents, who may not all share the same points of view. What made the Bork nomination so poignant and distressing was that the candidate had a well-developed political theory that many people came to believe would alter their legal rights, especially to privacy, under the Constitution.

Conclusion

If I have succeeded in this book in presenting a conception of legal privacy with clear content and a firm grounding in political morality, then certain things can be expected. First, cases that are traditionally recognized as privacy cases and over which there is little controversy will fit my paradigm. Second, cases with which the courts have had difficulty or, if decided, are controversial nonetheless,[9] can now be reevaluated. The significance of this latter point may be to put rights to privacy for gays, lesbians, women, and other oppressed or marginalized groups on a stronger footing. This in itself would be enough to warrant the effort in writing this book.

Still, one might hope for additional benefits from this research. If with respect to this latter group of cases, the criteria for reevaluation affords us a reason for pulling away from the adage that "the law is whatever the courts say it is," if it opens up a new place for moral theorizing in the law, if it helps to resolve the longstanding debate over the relationship of morality to law,[10] then the philosophy of law will be given a level of credibility and concreteness heretofore unknown, and democratic societies will be better off as a result.

Notes

Preface

1. Roe v. Wade, 410 U.S. 113 (1973).

2. Alexander Bickel, *The Least Dangerous Branch: The Supreme Court at the Bar of Politics* (Indianapolis: Bobbs-Merrill, 1962), pp. 263–64.

3. Ibid., p. 249.

4. Ibid., p. 261.

5. David A. J. Richards, *Sex, Drugs, Death, and the Law: An Essay on Human Rights and Overcriminalization* (Totowa, N.J.: Rowman and Littlefield, 1982); David A. J. Richards, *Toleration and the Constitution* (New York: Oxford University Press, 1986), pp. 229–81.

Introduction

1. Bowers v. Hardwick, 478 U.S. 186 (1986).

2. President Bush's nomination on July 23, 1990, of Judge David H. Souter to replace William Brennan on the Supreme Court raises an unknown about how the Court is likely to decide many controversial privacy issues. While on the New Hampshire Supreme Court, Souter in 1987 participated in a decision that barred gay people from becoming adoptive or foster parents. But the decision did not prohibit them from running day-care centers. In another decision that same year, Souter joined the majority in allowing a retarded child to file a "wrongful birth suit" in a case that further held that doctors have a responsibility to test for birth defects and to inform pregnant women of the possibility of defects in order to give them the abortion option (Janet Cawley and Timothy J. McNulty, "Bush Selects New Hampshire Jurist to Fill Post," *Chicago Tribune*, July 24, 1990, sec. 1). In a separate concurring opinion, however, Souter noted that the question was never raised whether a physician with scruples about abortion must discharge his or her professional responsibility (Linda Greenhouse, "Scholars with a Low Profile," *New York Times*, July 24, 1990, sec. 1).

3. Robert Bork, "Neutral Principles and Some First Amendment Problems," *Indiana Law Journal* 47 (1971): 1–35.

4. Robert Bork, *The Tempting of America: The Political Seduction of the Law* (New York: Free Press, 1990), pp. 324–25.

5. Dronenburg v. Zech, 741 F. 2d 1388 (D.C. Cir. 1984).

6. Alexander Bickel, *The Least Dangerous Branch: The Supreme Court at the Bar of Politics* (Indianapolis: Bobbs-Merrill, 1962).

7. For a discussion of abstract and concrete intentions as they relate to constitutional interpretation, see Ronald Dworkin, *A Matter of Principle* (Cambridge, Mass.: Harvard University Press, 1985), pp. 48–57. *Contra* Michael J. Perry, *The Constitution, the Courts, and Human Rights: An Inquiry into the Legitimacy of Constitutional Policymaking by the Judiciary* (New Haven, Conn.: Yale University Press, 1982), p. 70.

8. U.S. Constitution, Article 1, Section 3.

9. Brown v. Board of Education, 347 U.S. 483 (1954).

10. Bork claims that his theory of original intent necessitates this result. *See* Bork, *The Tempting of America*, p. 82.

11. Bickel, *The Least Dangerous Branch*, pp. 254–72.

12. Bork, *The Tempting of America*, pp. 133–38.

13. See Ronald Dworkin, *Law's Empire* (Cambridge, Mass.: Harvard University Press, 1986), ch. 2.

Chapter 1

1. Griswold v. Connecticut, 381 U.S. 479 (1965).

2. Stanley v. Georgia, 394 U.S. 557 (1969).

3. Roe v. Wade, 410 U.S. 113 (1973).

4. A closely related discussion of the ideas represented in the paradigm can be found in an article written by Alan Gewirth, "The Basis and Content of Human Rights," in *Nomos XXIII: Human Rights*, ed. J. Roland Pennock and John W. Chapman (New York: New York University Press, 1981), pp. 119–47; also *Human Rights*, ed. Alan Gewirth (Chicago: University of Chicago Press, 1982), pp. 41–51.

5. Joel Feinberg, "The Nature and Value of Rights," in *Philosophy of Law*, 2d ed., ed. Joel Feinberg and Hyman Gross (Belmont, Calif.: Wadsworth Publishing Co., 1980), pp. 277–78.

6. It should be noted that Gewirth discusses the nature of rights and the institutional settings in which they are recognized in the article cited in n. 4, as well as in his book *Reason and Morality* (Chicago: University of Chicago Press, 1978), although he does not incorporate into the paradigm specific designators where this information is to be presented.

7. The example presented is taken from H. L. A. Hart, "Are There Any Natural Rights?" *Philosophical Review* 64 (1955): 179.

8. Wesley N. Hohfeld, *Fundamental Legal Conceptions* (Westport, Conn.: Greenwood Press, 1946), p. 36.

9. Ibid.

10. H. L. A. Hart, "Positivism and the Separation of Law and Morals," *Harvard Law Review* 71 (1958): 606–15.

11. *See Oxford English Dictionary* (1971), s.v. *privacy* for the definition "the quality or state of being private" and then s.v. *private* for the etymological relation to *privatus.*

12. Charlton T. Lewis and Charles Short, eds., *A Latin Dictionary,* s.v. *privo* (Oxford, Eng.: Oxford Clarendon Press, 1879).

13. Griswold v. Connecticut, 381 U.S. at 484.

14. U.S. Constitution, Amendment 4.

15. Semayne's Case, 5 Co. Rep. 91a, 77 Eng. Rep. 194 (1604).

16. "Nullus liber homo capiatur vel imprisonetur, aut disseisiatur, aut utlagetur, aut exeletur, aut aliquo modo destrautur, nec super eum ibimus, nec super eum mittemus, nisi per legale judicium parium suorum vel per legem terre." See Samuel E. Thorne et al., *The Great Charter: Four Essays on Magna Carta and the History of Our Liberty* (New York: Pantheon Books, 1965), p. 132.

17. Semayne's Case, 5 Co. Rep. at 91b, 77 Eng. Rep. at 195.

18. William Blackstone, *Commentaries on the Laws of England,* 4 vols. (Chicago: University of Chicago Press, 1979), bk. 1, ch. 1.

19. Ibid., 4:223.

20. Snydacker v. Brosse, 51 Ill. 357, 359–60 (1869).

21. "The Right to Privacy in Nineteenth Century America," *Harvard Law Review* 94 (1981): 1894–95, note.

22. Samuel D. Warren and Louis D. Brandeis, "The Right to Privacy," *Harvard Law Review* 4 (1890): 193.

23. Ibid., p. 195.

24. Ibid., p. 205.

25. Ibid., p. 201.

26. Ibid., p. 205.

27. Roberson v. Rochester Folding Box Co., 171 N.Y. 538, 64 N.E. 442 (1902). The case will be discussed as part of the broader discussion of the present state of the law. For now it suffices to point out that at least one commentator has thought that the tort of appropriation of identity was the favorite in privacy's early successes in litigation, even though it was not specifically advocated by Warren and Brandeis (Tom Gerety, "Redefining Privacy," *Harvard Civil Rights–Civil Liberties Law Review* 12 [Spring 1977]: 247–48).

28. *See* Semayne's Case, 5 Co. Rep. at 91b, 77 Eng. Rep. at 195; *see also* "The Right to Privacy in Nineteenth Century America," p. 1898.

29. *See* "The Right to Privacy in Nineteenth Century America," pp. 1899–902.

30. Ibid., pp. 1904–6.

31. Roe v. Wade, 410 U.S. at 113.

32. Griswold v. Connecticut, 381 U.S. at 479.

33. Omstead v. United States, 277 U.S. 438 (1928).

34. Ibid., p. 464.

35. Ibid., p. 478.

36. In Weeks v. United States, 232 U.S. 383 (1914), the Supreme Court barred the use in a federal prosecution of evidence seized illegally by

federal officers. In Mapp v. Ohio, 367 U.S. 643 (1961), the Court incorporated the regulation of searches and seizures into the term *liberty* and applied it to the states via the due process clause of the Fourteenth Amendment.

37. Ibid.

38. Griswold v. Connecticut, 381 U.S., at 479.

39. Ibid., p. 484.

40. While substantive due process had its genesis before the turn of the nineteenth century, it was shortly after 1800 that the Supreme Court attempted to limit the power of the states and eventually the federal government to regulate the number of hours and the conditions under which a person could work, unless such regulation was affected by a public interest. "Public interest" here meant that the business either resulted from a public grant or franchise, was subject traditionally to regulation, or "which though not public at [its] inception may be said to have risen to be such and have become subject in consequence to some governmental regulation" (Wolf Packing Co. v. Court of Indus. Relations, 262 U.S. 532 [1923]). In fact, the Court afforded few guidelines to determine whether a state could properly regulate a business in the third situation. Moreover, the Court's seeming probusiness attitude after 1923 became a serious threat to the Court's own survival once New Deal politics came into fashion. This is shown by the serious attention Congress gave to legislation that would have effectively packed the Court and by the adage "a switch in time saved nine" (John E. Nowak, Ronald D. Rotunda, and J. Nelson Young, *Handbook on Constitutional Law* [St. Paul, Minn.: West Publishing Co., 1978], pp. 397–404).

41. Griswold v. Connecticut, 381 U.S. at 486–99 (Goldberg concurring).

42. Ibid., pp. 499–507 (Harlan, concurring).

43. Ibid., p. 499.

44. Ibid., p. 486.

45. Ibid., p. 500. Here it should be noted that Justice Harlan cites Palko v. Connecticut, 302 U.S. 319, 325 (1937). (The case affirmed a lower court's holding that a Connecticut statute permitting appeals to be taken by the state did not violate the Fourteenth Amendment of the United States Constitution.)

46. Omstead v. United States, 277 U.S. 438 (1928).

47. Berger v. New York, 388 U.S. 41 (1967).

48. Ibid., p. 64.

49. Gary L. Bostwick, "A Taxonomy of Privacy: Repose, Sanctuary, and Intimate Decision," *California Law Review* 64 (1976): 1459–60.

50. Katz v. United States, 389 U.S. 347 (1967).

51. Ibid., p. 348.

52. Ibid., pp. 351–52.

53. United States v. White, 401 U.S. 745 (1971).

54. Lanz v. New York, 370 U.S. 139 (1962).

55. William Prosser, "Privacy," *California Law Review* 48 (1960): 389.

56. Ibid., and William Prosser, *Handbook of the Law of Torts*, 4th ed. (St. Paul, Minn.: West Publishing Co., 1971), p. 814.

57. Martin v. Struthers, 319 U.S. 141 (1943).

58. Breard v. Alexandria, 341 U.S. 622 (1951).

59. Ibid., p. 626.

60. Public Utilities Commission v. Pollack, 343 U.S. 451 (1952).

61. Ibid., pp. 462–63. It is interesting to note that Justice Frankfurter disqualified himself from the case, stating: "My feelings are so strongly engaged as a victim of the practice in controversy that I had better not participate in judicial judgment upon it" (p. 467).

62. Melvin v. Reid, 112 Cal. App. 285, 297 P. 91 (1931).

63. Sidis v. F-R. Publishing Co., 113 F. 2d 806 (2d Cir. 1940).

64. Prosser, "Privacy," p. 397.

65. Gerety, "Redefining Privacy," p. 255.

66. Lord Byron v. Johnston, 2 Mer. 29, 35 Eng. Rep. 851 (1816); *see also* Gerety, "Redefining Privacy," p. 257.

67. Time, Inc. v. Hill, 385 U.S. 374 (1967).

68. N.Y. Civil Rights Law, secs. 50–51 (McKinney 1948).

69. Time, Inc. v. Hill, 385 U.S. at 394. (The attorney arguing on behalf of the Hill family was former President Richard Nixon before he held that office.)

70. Ibid., p. 401.

71. Roberson v. Rochester Folding Box Co., 171 N.Y. 538, 64 N.E. 442 (1902).

72. Griswold v. Connecticut, 381 U.S. 479 (1965).

73. Eisenstadt v. Baird, 405 U.S. 438 (1972).

74. Ibid., p. 447 (citing Royster Guano Co. v. Virginia, 253 U.S. 412, 415 [1920]).

75. Ibid., p. 453.

76. Ibid.

77. Roe v. Wade, 410 U.S. 113 (1973).

78. Ibid., p. 153.

79. Ibid., p. 152.

80. Carey v. Population Services Int'l, 431 U.S. 678 (1977).

81. Akron v. Akron Ctr. for Reproductive Health, 462 U.S. 416 (1983); Planned Parenthood Assn. v. Ashcroft, 462 U.S. 476 (1983); Simopoulos v. Virginia, 462 U.S. 506 (1983).

82. Thornburgh v. American College of Obstetricians and Gynecologists, 476 U.S. 747 (1986).

83. "Court Reaffirms Right to Abortion by Barring Variety of Local Curbs," *New York Times*, June 16, 1983, sec. 1.

84. Akron v. Akron Ctr. for Reproductive Health, 462 U.S. at 426.

85. Thornburgh v. American College of Obstetricians and Gynecologists, 476 U.S. at 759.

86. Bowers v. Hardwick, 478 U.S. 186 (1986).

87. Doe v. Commonwealth's Attorney, 403 F. Supp. 1199 (E.D. Va. 1975), *aff'd mem.*, 425 U.S. 901 (1976).

88. People v. Onofre, 51 N.Y. 2d 476, 415 N.E. 2d 936, 434 N.Y.S. 2d 447 (1980), *cert. denied,* 451 U.S. 987 (1981). It should be noted that the Supreme Court had the opportunity in 1984 to reconsider the New York Court of Appeals decision in *Onofre* when it heard arguments in New York v. Uplinger, 467 U.S. 246. *Uplinger* involved the question of whether the state of New York could prohibit loitering for the purpose of engaging in "deviate" sexual intercourse when the conduct ultimately complained of was not illegal under *Onofre.* Instead of deciding this issue, however, the Supreme Court chose, after hearing oral arguments, not to render a decision on the ground that it had improvidently granted certiorari in the case.

89. Bowers v. Hardwick, 478 U.S. at 190.

90. Ibid., p. 191.

91. Post v. State, 715 P. 2d 1105 (Okla. Crim. App.), *cert. denied,* 479 U.S. 890 (1986). Note that seven states prohibit sodomy *only* of persons of the same gender: Ark. Stat. Ann. § 5–14–122 (1987); Kan. Stat. Ann. § 21–3505 (Supp. 1987); Ky. Rev. Stat. Ann. § 510.100 (Michie/Bobbs-Merrill 1985); Mo. Rev. Stat. § 566.090(3) (1986); Mont. Code Ann. § 45–2–101 (1987); Nev. Rev. Stat. § 201.190(2) (1987); Tex. Penal Code Ann. § 21.06 (Vernon 1989). *See* Cass Sunstein, "Sexual Orientation and the Constitution," *University of Chicago Law Review* 55 (1988): 1161, 1164–70 (discussing whether gay men and lesbians comprise a suspect class for equal protection purposes).

92. "Treating Adultery as Crime: Wisconsin Dusts Off Old Law," *New York Times,* April 30, 1990, sec. 1.

93. Two recent circuit court decisions, one in Michigan (Michigan Organization for Human Rights [MOHR] v. Kelley, No. 88–815820CZ [Cir. Ct., Wayne County, Mich., July 9, 1990]) and the other in Kentucky (Kentucky v. Wasson, No. 86-X-48 [Cir. Ct., Fayette County, Ky., June 8, 1990]), have struck down as unconstitutional those states' sodomy statutes under their respective state constitutions' right to privacy. The Michigan statute prohibited both heterosexual and gay sodomy while the Kentucky statute prohibited only gay sodomy. The Kentucky decision will most certainly be appealed. A similar attack is under way against the Texas sodomy statute. *See* D. Olson, "Michigan Overturns Sodomy Laws: Similar Kentucky Decision Also Faces High Court Appeal," *Windy City Times,* July 19, 1990, sec. 1.

94. Webster v. Reproductive Health Services,—U.S.—, 109 S. Ct. 3040 (1989).

95. Ibid., pp. 3056–57.

96. Ibid., p. 3067 (Blackmun, dissenting).

97. Ibid., p. 3067 (Scalia, concurring).

98. Ibid., p. 3057.

99. Hodgson v. Minnesota, 58 U.S.L.W. 4957 (U.S. June 25, 1990).

100. Ohio v. Akron Center for Reproductive Health, 58 U.S.L.W. 4979 (U.S. June 25, 1990).

101. Cruzan v. Director, Missouri, Department of Health, 58 U.S.L.W. 4916 (U.S. June 25, 1990).

102. Ibid., p. 4920, n.7.

103. Ibid., p. 4920.

104. Ibid.

105. Ibid., p. 4927 (Brennan, dissenting).

106. Ibid., p. 4936 (Stevens, dissenting).

107. Stanley v. Georgia, 394 U.S. 557 (1969).

108. Ibid., p. 564.

109. Ibid., p. 565.

110. Osborne v. Ohio, 58 U.S.L.W. 4467 (1990); *see also* "Justices, 6 to 3, Restrict Rights to Pornography," *New York Times*, April 19, 1990, sec. 1.

111. Osborne v. Ohio, 58 U.S.L.W. at 4469.

112. Ibid.

113. Ibid.

114. Ibid., p. 4477 (Brennan, dissenting, citing Stanley v. Georgia, 394 U.S. at 568).

115. Minnesota v. Olson, 58 U.S.L.W. 4464 (1990); *see also* "Justices, 6 to 3."

116. United States v. Orita, 413 U.S. 139 (1973).

117. United States v. Reidel, 402 U.S. 351 (1971).

118. United States v. 12 200-Ft. Reels of Film, 413 U.S. 123 (1973).

119. Paris Adult Theatre I v. Slaton, 413 U.S. 49 (1973).

120. Ibid., pp. 65–66.

121. See Polyvios G. Polyviou, *Search and Seizure: Constitutional and Common Law* (London: Gerald Duckworth & Co., 1982), p. 346 (arguing for the view that the exclusionary rule is a "judicially contrived doctrine").

122. See ibid., pp. 346–48.

123. Edward H. Levi, *An Introduction to Legal Reasoning* (Chicago: University of Chicago Press, 1949).

124. Ibid., pp. 2–3.

125. Ibid., pp. 5–6.

126. Winterbottom v. Wright, 10 Meeson & Welsby 109, 152 Eng. Rep. 402 (1842).

127. Winterbottom v. Wright, 10 Meeson & Welsby at 114, 152 Eng. Rep. at 405.

128. Thomas v. Winchester, 6 N.Y. 397 (1852).

129. Ibid., p. 409.

130. MacPherson v. Buick, 217 N.Y. 382, 111 N.E. 1050 (1916).

131. Macpherson v. Buick, 217 N.Y. 391, 111 N.E. at 1053.

132. John H. Ely, "The Wages of Crying Wolf: A Comment on *Roe v. Wade*," *Yale Law Journal* 82 (1973): 929.

133. Tyler Baker, "*Roe* and *Paris:* Does Privacy Have a Principle?" *Stanford Law Review* 26 (1974): 1165.

134. Roe v. Wade, 410 U.S. at 152.

135. Ibid., p. 155.

136. Robert G. McCloskey, *The American Supreme Court* (Chicago: University of Chicago Press, 1960), p. 224. The idea of a shifting moral consensus has been criticized on normative grounds for failing to incorporate a critical moral assessment to explain the shifts (David A. J.

Richards, *Toleration and the Constitution* [New York: Oxford University Press, 1986], p. 236).

137. Levi, *An Introduction to Legal Reasoning,* p. 73.

138. Catharine MacKinnon, "*Roe v. Wade:* A Study in Male Ideology," in *Abortion: Moral and Legal Perspectives,* ed. Jay L. Garfield and Patricia Hennessey (Amherst: University of Massachusetts Press, 1984), pp. 45–54.

139. Ibid., p. 53.

140. Michael J. Perry, *The Constitution, the Courts, and Human Rights: An Inquiry into the Legitimacy of Constitutional Policymaking by the Judiciary* (New Haven, Conn.: Yale University Press, 1982).

Chapter 2

1. *See* Phillip B. Kurland, "The Private I," *Chicago Magazine* 25 (Autumn 1976): 8.

2. W. A. Parent, "Recent Work on the Concept of Privacy," *American Philosophical Quarterly* 20 (October 1983): 341.

3. Samuel D. Warren and Louis D. Brandeis, "The Right to Privacy," *Harvard Law Review* 4 (1890): 193.

4. Parent, "Recent Work on the Concept of Privacy," p. 341; *see* Francis Beytagh, "Privacy and Free Press: A Contemporary Conflict in Values," *New York Law Forum* 20 (1975): 455; *see also* Edward J. Bloustein, "Privacy as an Aspect of Human Dignity: An Answer to Dean Prosser," in *Philosophical Dimensions of Privacy: An Anthology,* ed. Ferdinand D. Schoeman (New York: Cambridge University Press, 1984), p. 188; Paul Freund, "Privacy: One Concept or Many?" in *Nomos XIII: Privacy,* ed. J. Pennock and J. Chapman (New York: Atherton Press, 1971), pp. 197–98; Milton Konvitz, "Privacy and the Law: A Philosophical Prelude," *Law and Contemporary Problems* 31 (1966): 279; Henry Paul Monagham, "Of 'Liberty' and 'Property,' " *Cornell Law Review* 62 (1977): 414; Richard A. Posner, *The Economics of Justice* (Cambridge, Mass.: Harvard University Press, 1983), p. 272.

5. Parent, "Recent Work," p. 347.

6. A somewhat different objection attesting to the too-broad nature of the Brandeis definition is raised by Ruth Gavison, "Privacy and the Limits of the Law," in *Philosophical Dimensions,* ed. Schoeman, p. 357.

7. Parent, "Recent Work," p. 342; *see* William Beaney, "The Constitutional Right to Privacy in the Supreme Court," *The Supreme Court Review,* 1962, p. 250; *see also* Louis Henkin, "Privacy and Autonomy," *Columbia Law Review* 74 (1974): 1410; Jack Hirschleifer, "Privacy: Its Origin, Function, and Future," *The Journal of Legal Studies* 9 (1980): 657.

8. Parent, "Recent Work," pp. 342–43.

9. Ibid., p. 343; *see* Tom Gerety, "Redefining Privacy," *Harvard Civil Rights–Civil Liberties Law Review* 12 (Spring 1977): 266.

10. Ibid., pp. 343–44; *see* Elizabeth Beardsley, "Privacy, Autonomy, and Selective Disclosure," in *Nomos XIII,* ed. Pennock and Chapman, p. 65; *see also* Charles Fried, *An Anatomy of Values* (Cambridge, Mass.:

Harvard University Press, 1970), p. 141; Charles Fried, "Privacy," *Yale Law Journal* 77 (1968): 483; Hyman Gross, "Privacy and Autonomy," in *Nomos XIII*, ed. Pennock and Chapman, p. 170; Richard Wasserstrom, "Privacy: Some Arguments and Assumptions," in *Philosophical Dimensions*, ed. Schoeman, p. 325; Richard Wasserstrom, "The Legal and Philosophical Foundations of the Right to Privacy," in *Bio-Medical Ethics*, ed. Thomas Mappes and Jane Zembaty, 2d ed. (New York: McGraw-Hill, 1986), p. 113; Alan Westin, *Privacy and Freedom* (New York: Atheneum, 1967), pp. 7, 42.

11. Parent, "Recent Works," p. 344.

12. The abortion example, where the concern is more with the freedom to act than with who knows about our actions, is a case in point.

13. Parent, "Recent Works," pp. 344–45; *see* Irwin Altman, "Privacy: A Conceptual Analysis," *Environment and Behavior* 8 (1976): 8; *see also* Irwin Altman, "Privacy Regulation: Culturally Universal or Culturally Specific?" *The Journal of Social Issues* 33 (1977): 67; Vern Countryman, "The Diminishing Right to Privacy: The Personal Dossier and the Computer," *Texas Law Review* 49 (1977): 868; Roger Ingham, "Privacy and Psychology," in *Privacy*, ed. John Young (New York: John Wiley and Sons, 1978), p. 52; Peter Klipter and Daniel Rubenstein, "The Concept 'Privacy' and Its Biological Basis," *Journal of Social Issues* 33 (1977): 53; Robert Laufer and Maxine Wolfe, "Privacy as a Concept and a Social Issue: A Multidimensional and Developmental Theory," *Journal of Social Issues* 33 (1977): 30–35; Stephen Margulus, "Conceptions of Privacy: Current Status and Next Steps," *Journal of Social Issues* 33 (1977): 19; Richard Parker, "A Definition of Privacy," *Rutgers Law Review* 27 (1974): 280; James Rachels, "Why Privacy Is Important," in *Philosophical Dimensions*, ed. Schoeman, p. 292; Jeffrey H. Reiman, "Privacy, Intimacy, and Personhood," in *Philosophical Dimensions*, ed. Schoeman, p. 314; Ernest Van Den Haag, "On Privacy," in *Nomos XIII*, ed. Pennock and Chapman, pp. 149–68.

14. Parent, "Recent Works," p. 345.

15. Ibid., pp. 345–46; *see* Roland Garrett, "The Nature of Privacy," *Philosophy Today* 18 (1974): 264–84; *see also* Gavison, "Privacy and the Limits of the Law," p. 354; Hyman Gross, "The Concept of Privacy," *New York University Law Review* 42 (1967): 34–35; David O'Brien, *Privacy, Law, and Public Policy* (New York: Praeger, 1979), p. 16.

16. Parent, "Recent Works," p. 345.

17. Ibid., p. 346.

18. Ibid.

19. Ibid. This attempted definition brings to a head a problem lurking throughout Parent's discussion: Parent seems to be treating *privacy* and *private* as completely coextensive—that is, all cases of the private are cases of privacy. But, in such uses as "private property" or "having a sphere of conduct which is of private as opposed to public concern," *private* does not seem to be connected with *privacy*, where Parent treats the latter as referring to a kind of information.

20. Ibid., pp. 346–47.

21. Ibid., p. 348.

22. Ibid. Parent does not explain his use of the word *private* here. The phrase is borrowed from Prosser, who also does not explain it but appears to leave it to judicial interpretation.

23. Ibid., p. 347.

24. Lawrence Tribe, *American Constitutional Law* (Mineola, N.Y.: Foundation Press, 1978), ch. 15.

25. Ibid., p. 887.

26. Ibid.

27. Ibid., pp. 887–88.

28. Ibid., p. 888.

29. Most, if not all, states have adopted a Canon of Judicial Ethics that warns members of the judiciary not to engage in conduct that might even appear as improper.

30. For a discussion of Wittgenstein's idea of family resemblance, see Ludwig Wittgenstein, *Philosophical Investigations*, 3d ed., trans. G. E. M. Anscombe (New York: Macmillan Publishing Co., 1958), pars. 65–66.

31. Gavison, "Privacy and the Limits of the Law," pp. 346–402.

32. Ibid., p. 373.

33. Ibid.

34. Ibid.

35. This formulation of the privacy right is extracted from the line of constitutional cases beginning with Griswold v. Connecticut, 381 U.S. 479 (1965).

36. John Stuart Mill, *On Liberty* (New York: Penguin Books, 1988), pp. 69–70.

37. Ibid., p. 71.

38. *See* J. C. Rees, "A Re-Reading of Mill's *On Liberty*," *Political Studies* 8 (1960): 113–29; Ted Honderich, *Punishment: The Supposed Justifications* (London: Hutchinson and Co., 1969), ch. 6; D. G. Brown, "Mill on Liberty and Morality," *Philosophical Review* 81 (1972): 142–58. Others who have attempted to resolve the problem include David A. J. Richards, *Sex, Drugs, Death, and the Law: An Essay on Human Rights and Overcriminalization* (Totowa, N.J.: Rowman and Littlefield, 1982), pp. 17–20; David A. J. Richards, *Toleration and the Constitution* (New York: Oxford University Press, 1986), pp. 237–42; *see also* Vincent J. Samar, "The Legal Right of Privacy: A Philosophical Inquiry" (Ph.D. diss., University of Chicago, 1986).

39. The idea that freedom and well-being are basic interests is derived from the treatment of freedom and well-being as necessary goods in Alan Gewirth, *Reason and Morality* (Chicago: University of Chicago Press, 1978), pp. 52–65.

40. Even the person who commits suicide because of perceiving his or her circumstances to be unbearable is relying on a derivative interest. In that situation, the basic interest of well-being is probably being combined with the conception that well-being will never be achieved. Such a conception may arise in the context of a serious illness or even a lonely heart.

41. This finding is particularly significant in light of the D.C. Court of Appeals holding, in Dronenburg v. Zech, 741 F. 2d 1388 (D.C. Cir. 1984), rehearing en banc 746 F. 2d 1579 (1984), that there is no constitutional right to engage in "homosexual conduct," and therefore the navy's policy of mandatory discharge for homosexual conduct does not violate either the constitutional right to privacy or the equal protection of the laws.

42. Mill, *On Liberty,* p. 71. Indeed, the definition of privacy presented here represents a nonutilitarian clarification of the concept Mill somewhat more vaguely employed.

43. Alan Westin, "The Origin of Modern Claims to Privacy," in *Philosophical Dimensions,* ed. Schoeman, p. 63.

44. Robert F. Murphy, "Social Distance and the Veil," in *Philosophical Dimensions,* ed. Schoeman, pp. 41–49.

45. Robert Murphy explains how privacy among the Tuareg protects autonomy (pp. 50, 52) and provides social distance (p. 48). Similarly, Alan Westin points out how privacy in less-developed societies protects activity (pp. 66, 69) as well as rights of passage (p. 65). *See also* Stanley I. Benn, "Privacy, Freedom, and Respect for Persons," in *Philosophical Dimensions,* ed. Schoeman, p. 223.

46. Richards, *Sex, Drugs, Death, and the Law,* p. 37.

47. Westin, "Modern Claims," p. 63.

48. Initially, the subject has the burden to make out a prima facie claim to privacy. Once that is established, the burden shifts to the opposing party to show either that a claim to privacy is not justified or that a countervailing rights claim of greater weight is at stake.

49. Frederick Schauer, *Free Speech: A Philosophical Enquiry* (Cambridge: Cambridge University Press, 1982), p. 89.

50. The qualification is not meant to exclude the possibility of a state or the federal government being sued in tort for actions of a proprietary as opposed to governmental character. But this subtlety need not concern us here.

51. In Matter of Farber, 78 N.J. 259, 394 A. 2d 330, *cert. denied,* 439 U.S. 997 (1978), the New Jersey Supreme Court tried to avoid this conflict by holding that the First Amendment did not provide the appellants the protection they sought.

52. Roe v. Wade, 410 U.S. 113 (1973).

53. Ibid., p. 155.

54. Korematsu v. United States, 323 U.S. 214 (1944), which involved the internment of American citizens of Japanese descent during World War II.

55. Beck v. Ohio, 379 U.S. 89 (1964) (expressed strong preference for arrest warrants); United States v. Ventresca, 380 U.S. 102 (1965) (expressed a similar preference for search warrants).

56. Chimel v. California, 395 U.S. 752 (1969).

57. Terry v. Ohio, 392 U.S. 1 (1968) (allows stopping and frisking without probable cause); Schneckloth v. Bustamonte, 412 U.S. 218 (1973) (provides for voluntary consent); On Lee v. United States, 343 U.S. 747

(1952) (allowed informant wired for sound to enter defendant's laundry and engage him in incriminating conversation); People v. Roebuck, 183 N.E. 2d 166 (Ill. 1962) (permitting police to search and seize property that has been abandoned); Warden v. Hayden, 387 U.S. 294 (1967) (permitting entry of premises in hot pursuit of an offender); Vale v. Louisiana, 399 U.S. 30 (1970) (recognized a warrantless search of a dwelling in "exceptional situation" such as the possible destruction of narcotics evidence).

58. In United States v. Leon, 468 U.S. 897 (1984), the Supreme Court recognized a "good faith" exception for law enforcement authorities gathering evidence of a crime where the underlying warrant was ultimately found to be unsupported by probable cause. *See generally* Polyvios G. Polyviou, *Search and Seizure: Constitutional and Common Law* (London: Gerald Duckworth, 1982), for a discussion on the development of the exclusionary rule and how it compares to the law of England and the Commonwealth.

59. Time, Inc. v. Hill, 385 U.S. 374 (1967), citing New York Times v. Sullivan, 376 U.S. 254 (1964).

60. New York Times v. Sullivan, 376 U.S. at 278.

61. Gertz v. Robert Welch, Inc., 418 U.S. 323, 345 (1974).

62. Bowers v. Hardwick, 478 U.S. 186 (1986).

Chapter 3

1. For a discussion of abstract and concrete intentions as they relate to constitutional interpretation, see Ronald Dworkin, *A Matter of Principle* (Cambridge, Mass.: Harvard University Press, 1985), pp. 48–57. *Contra* Michael J. Perry, *The Constitution, the Courts, and Human Rights: An Inquiry into the Legitimacy of Constitutional Policymaking by the Judiciary* (New Haven, Conn.: Yale University Press, 1982), p. 70.

2. Here I take note of the distinction between a concept and a conception in John Rawls, *A Theory of Justice* (Cambridge, Mass.: Harvard University Press, 1971), p. 5, and H. L. A. Hart, *The Concept of Law* (Oxford: Clarendon Press, 1961), pp. 155–59.

3. A closely related discussion of the ideas represented in the paradigm can be found in Alan Gewirth, "The Basis and Content of Human Rights," *Nomos XXIII: Human Rights*, ed. J. Roland Pennock and John W. Chapman (New York: New York University Press, 1981), pp. 119–47.

4. Ronald Dworkin, *Taking Rights Seriously* (Cambridge, Mass.: Harvard University Press, 1978), pp. 22–23.

5. Joel Feinberg, "The Nature and Value of Rights," in *Philosophy of Law*, 2d ed., ed. Joel Feinberg and Hyman Gross (Belmont, Calif.: Wadsworth Publishing Co., 1980), pp. 274–76.

6. Lawrence Haworth, *Autonomy, An Essay in Philosophical Psychology and Ethics* (New Haven, Conn.: Yale University Press, 1986), p. 49.

7. Sir Isaiah Berlin, "Two Concepts of Liberty," in *Political Philoso-*

phy, ed. Anthony Quinton (New York: Oxford University Press, 1967), p. 148.

8. Fundamentally nothing is at stake by my not treating this problem from a utilitarian approach, for the version of privacy advocated here is not substantially different from a version that could be asserted under a rule utilitarian model.

9. Perhaps privacy can be justified on more general moral grounds (see, e.g., Alan Gewirth, *Reason and Morality* [Chicago: University of Chicago Press, 1978], p. 256), but for purposes of this argument on the role of the privacy norm in Western democracies, the more narrow focus suffices.

10. In *Capitalism, Socialism, and Democracy,* 3d ed. (New York: Harper and Row, 1950), Joseph Schumpeter makes this same point when, in presenting his alternative theory of democracy, he says: "The democratic method is that institutional arrangement for arriving at political decisions in which individuals acquire the power to decide by means of the competitive struggle for the people's vote" (p. 269).

11. Alan Gewirth, *Political Philosophy* (New York: Macmillan, 1965), pp. 9–12.

12. The reason for not adopting a classical conception of democracy is to avoid a long-standing philosophical problem. Under the classical model, "the democratic method is that institutional arrangement for arriving at political decisions which realizes the common good by making the people itself decide issues through the election of individuals who are to assemble in order to carry out its will" (Schumpeter, "Two Concepts of Democracy," in *Capitalism, Socialism, and Democracy,* p. 250). One problem with the classical model is making sense of the idea of the common good. In my conception, the problem is avoided by appealing to voter interests, which captures what is at stake in Western democratic institutions.

13. Berlin, "Two Concepts of Liberty," p. 148.

14. Ibid.

15. U.S. Constitution, Amendment Nine.

16. John Hart Ely, *Democracy and Distrust: A Theory of Judicial Review* (Cambridge, Mass.: Harvard University Press, 1980), pp. 34–41.

17. Ibid., p. 34.

18. Ibid., pp. 36–37.

19. Ibid., p. 38.

20. Griswold v. Connecticut, 381 U.S. 479 (1965).

21. Ibid., p. 493 (quoting Snyder v. Massachusetts, 291 U.S. 97 [1934]) (Goldberg, concurring).

22. Ibid., p. 519 (Black, dissenting).

23. Here I also disavow the Kantian use of autonomy as self-legislative in the sense of giving to oneself the moral law. See Immanuel Kant, *Foundations of the Metaphysics of Morals,* trans. Lewis W. Beck (Indianapolis: Bobbs-Merrill, 1959), pp. 49–59.

24. Arguments for affirmative action programs are not excluded here since the validity of such arguments is usually made to rest on rectifying present inequalities due to past discrimination. In other words, since it is thought that the benefits or detriments bestowed on the current generation are the result of a previous period of discrimination, some have argued that it is not necessarily unfair to give greater advantages to the group inheriting the detriment even if it is at the expense of the group inheriting the benefit. See Louis Katzner, "Is the Favoring of Women and Blacks in Employment and Educational Opportunities Justified?" in *Philosophy of Law*, ed. Feinberg and Gross, pp. 356–61.

25. Jeffrey H. Reiman, "Privacy, Intimacy, and Personhood," in *Philosophical Dimensions of Privacy: An Anthology*, ed. Ferdinand D. Schoeman (New York: Cambridge University Press, 1984), p. 314.

26. Stanley I. Benn, "Privacy, Freedom, and Respect for Persons," in *Philosophical Dimensions*, ed. Schoeman, p. 243.

27. Gewirth, Locke, and Rousseau are just a few who have written on this question. *See* Gewirth, *Reason and Morality*, pp. 304–7; John Locke, *Two Treatises on Government* (New York: Cambridge University Press, 1960), nos. 66, 132; Jean-Jacques Rousseau, *The Social Contract and Discourses on the Origin of Inequality*, ed. Lester G. Crocker (New York: Washington Square Press, 1967), bk. IV, ch. 2.

28. Locke, *Two Treatises*, nos. 25–51.

29. Karl Marx and Fredrick Engels, "Manifesto of the Communist Party," in *Basic Writings on Politics and Philosophy*, ed. Lewis S. Feuer (Garden City, N.Y.: Anchor Books, 1959), pp. 7–20.

30. In sum, what we have here is a matrix in which each row and column are designated "active" and "passive," respectively. In the active/active square, privacy can be seen to potentially conflict with such other rights as freedom of speech, press, or religion. In the active/passive (or passive/active) square, privacy is not involved, although other active rights such as freedom of press may conflict with passive rights such as the right to a fair trial. Finally, in the passive/passive square no active rights are involved, and it may be that there are not even any passive rights conflicts.

31. William Prosser, *Handbook on the Law of Torts*, 4th ed. (St. Paul, Minn.: West Publishing Co., 1971), p. 814.

32. Ibid., p. 818.

33. David F. Linowes, *Privacy in America: Is Your Private Life in the Public Eye?* (Urbana: University of Illinois Press, 1989), pp. 107, 126–39.

34. Ibid.

35. Ibid., p. 817.

36. In Sidis v. F-R Publishing Co., 113 F. 2d 806 (2d Cir. 1940), the court probably erred by not holding the New York magazine liable for publishing without permission a follow-up story on the former infant prodigy some years after he had dropped out of sight. Note the discussion in Chapter 1 on this case.

37. *See* Dirk Johnson, "Opening Closets for Others in the Pursuit of Gay Rights," *New York Times,* March 27, 1990, sec. 1.

38. " 'Outing': An Unexpected Assault on Sexual Privacy: Gay Activists Are Forcing Others Out of the Closet," *Newsweek,* April 30, 1990, p. 66.

39. Ibid.

40. James Madison, *Federalist* No. 51 in Alexander Hamilton, James Madison, and John Jay, *The Federalist Papers,* ed. Clinton Rossiter (New York: New American Library, 1961). In Thomas Jefferson's first inaugural address of March 4, 1801, we find: "All, too, will bear in mind this sacred principle, that though the will of the majority is in all cases to prevail, that will to be rightful must be reasonable; that the minority possess their equal rights, which equal laws must protect, and to violate which would be oppression" (Adrienne Koch and William Peden, *The Life and Selected Writings of Thomas Jefferson* [New York: Random House, 1944], p. 322).

41. John Stuart Mill, *On Liberty* (New York: Penguin Books, 1988), pp. 180–83.

42. Schoeman, ed., *Philosophical Dimensions.*

Chapter 4

1. Ronald Dworkin, "Constitutional Cases" in *Taking Rights Seriously* (Cambridge, Mass.: Harvard University Press, 1977), p. 134.

2. Robert H. Bork, *The Tempting of America: The Political Seduction of the Law* (New York: Free Press, 1990), pp. 143–60.

3. Dworkin, "Constitutional Cases," p. 134.

4. Ibid., p. 136.

5. Ibid., p. 139.

6. Brown v. Board of Education, 347 U.S. 483 (1954).

7. Dworkin, "Constitutional Cases," p. 143.

8. Ibid., p. 147.

9. Dworkin, "Hard Cases," in *Taking Rights Seriously,* p. 82.

10. Ibid., p. 84.

11. Ibid., p. 85.

12. Ibid. Further, Dworkin means a claim right as opposed to, for example, a Hohfeldian liberty right.

13. Ibid., p. 100.

14. Ibid., p. 107.

15. Ronald Dworkin, "Is There Really No Right Answer in Hard Cases?" in *A Matter of Principle* (Cambridge: Harvard University Press, 1985), p. 134; *see also* Marshall Cohen, ed., *Ronald Dworkin and Contemporary Jurisprudence* (Totowa, N.J.: Rowman and Allanheld, 1984) (essay by Kent Greenawalt and reply by Ronald Dworkin).

16. *See* Ronald Dworkin, *Law's Empire* (Cambridge, Mass.: Harvard University Press, 1986), in which Dworkin develops a unified interpretive model for morality, legal justification, and political legitimacy. *Contra,* Richard A. Posner, *The Problems of Jurisprudence* (Cambridge, Mass.: Harvard University Press, 1990), in which Posner argues that

Dworkin's concept of interpretation will not limit judicial discretion in hard cases.

17. *See* Dworkin, "Is There Really No Right Answer?" p. 142.

18. Ibid., p. 143.

19. Richard D. Mohr, *Gays/Justice: A Study of Ethics, Society, and Law* (New York: Columbia University Press, 1988).

20. Ibid., pp. 81–82.

21. Ibid., n. 75.

22. Ibid.

23. Ibid.

24. Ibid., p. 83.

25. Griswold v. Connecticut, 381 U.S. 479 (1965).

26. Griswold v. Connecticut, 381 U.S. at 484, cited in Mohr, *Gays/Justice*, p. 72.

27. Mohr, *Gays/Justice*, p. 72.

28. Griswold v. Connecticut, 381 U.S. at 484, cited in Mohr, *Gays/Justice*, p. 73.

29. Mohr, *Gays/Justice*, pp. 73–76.

30. Ibid., p. 83.

31. Ibid., p. 76.

32. Ibid., p. 81.

33. It is with respect to this question that the courts apply to classifications regarding economics or social welfare the easier rational relationship test (in which the government only has to show that the classification relates to some legitimate governmental policy) and to classifications regarding the exercise of fundamental rights, or that are based on race, national origin, alienage, illegitimacy, or gender, the more difficult strict scruity test (in which instead of deferring to the government, a court will inquire as to the degree of relationship the classification has to a constitutionally compelling state interest). See John E. Nowak, Ronald D. Rotunda, and J. Nelson Young, *Handbook on Constitutional Law* (St. Paul, Minn.: West Publishing Co., 1978), pp. 524, 527.

34. "The inclusion of one is the exclusion of the other."

35. Richard F. Hixon, *Privacy in a Public Society: Human Rights in Conflict* (New York: Oxford University Press, 1987).

36. Ibid., p. 93.

37. Ibid., p. 115.

38. Ibid., p. 117.

39. Ibid., p. 125.

40. Ibid., pp. 131–32.

41. Ibid., p. 132.

42. Ibid., pp. 94–95.

43. Ibid., p. 98.

44. Ibid., p. 101.

45. Ibid.

46. Ibid., p. 104.

Chapter 5

1. For an interesting discussion of causation problems in the law, see H. L. A. Hart and A. M. Honoré, *Causation in the Law* (Oxford: Oxford University Press, 1959).

2. Such cases are not uncommon, as, for example, National Gay and Lesbian Task Force v. Board of Educ. of the City of Oklahoma City, 729 F. 2d 1270 (10th Cir. 1984), *aff'd,* 470 U.S. 903 (1985); Acanfora III v. Board of Educ. of Montgomery County, 359 F. Supp. 843 (D.C. Md. 1973), *aff'd,* 491 F. 2d 498 (4th Cir. 1974), *cert. denied,* 419 U.S. 836 (1974); National Gay and Lesbian Task Force v. Board of Educ. of City of Oklahoma City, 33 Fair Empl. Prac. Cas. (BNA) 1009 (W.D. Okla. 1982). Nor is it uncommon that, regardless of any public announcement, a teacher is known or suspected to be gay. Gaylord v. Tacoma School Dist., No. 10, 85 Wash. 2d 348, 535 P. 2d 804 (1975); Conway v. Hampshire County Bd. of Educ., 352 S.E. 2d 739 (W. Va. 1986); *cf.* Ashlie v. Chester-Upland School Dist., No. 78–4037, slip op. (E.D. Pa. May 9, 1979) (involving an analogous situation with a transexual teacher). *See generally Sexual Orientation and the Law* (Cambridge, Mass.: Harvard University Press, 1990) (compiling and critically evaluating much of the law in this area), pp. 85–93.

3. National Gay and Lesbian Task Force v. Board of Educ. of the City of Oklahoma City, 729 F. 2d at 1274; Gaylord v. Tacoma School Dist., No. 10, 85 Wash. 2d at 350–51, 535 P. 2d at 806; Morrison v. State Bd. of Educ., 1 Cal. 3d 214, 229–30, 461 P. 2d 375, 386–87, 82 Cal. Rptr. 175, 186–87 (1969).

4. Baker v. Wade, 553 F. Supp. 1121, 1129 (N.D. Tex. 1982).

5. Janet Shibley Hyde, *Understanding Human Sexuality,* 3d ed. (New York: McGraw-Hill, 1986).

6. For a discussion of the events relating to this action, see Don Clark, *Loving Someone Gay* (New York: New American Library, 1977).

7. Ibid.

8. The Model Penal Code developed by the American Law Institute recommends that criminal statutes covering sexual conduct "be recast in such a way as to remove legal penalties against acts in private among consenting adults."

9. Baker v. Wade, 553 F. Supp. at 1130.

10. Ibid.

11. Ibid. *See also* Rhonda R. Rivera, "Our Straight-Laced Judges: The Legal Position of Homosexual Persons in the United States," *Hastings Law Journal* 30 (1979): 799, 950–51 (which indicates that twenty-two states have decriminalized adult consensual sodomy).

12. David A. J. Richards, *Sex, Drugs, Death and the Law: An Essay on Human Rights and Overcriminalization* (Totowa, N.J.: Rowman and Littlefield, 1982), p. 37.

13. Ibid., p. 38.

14. Ibid.

15. At two hearings on the Chicago Human Rights Ordinance that were held in 1988, the following Christian churches testified before the

Chicago City Council's Human Relations Committee for the inclusion of discrimination protection for gays and lesbians: United Methodist Church, Episcopal Diocese of Chicago, United Church of Christ, and Lutheran Church of America. Also testifying in support of discrimination protection for lesbians and gays were representatives of various Jewish organizations.

16. John Boswell, *Christianity, Social Tolerance, and Homosexuality: Gay People in Western Europe from the Beginning of the Christian Era to the Fourteenth Century* (Chicago: University of Chicago Press, 1980).

17. In re Jane B., 85 Misc. 2d 515, 380 N.Y.S. 2d 848 (1976); *see also* In re J. S. & C., 129 N.J. Super 486, 324 A. 2d 90 (1974). *See generally Sexual Orientation and the Law* (Cambridge, Mass.: Harvard University Press, 1990) (compiling and critically evaluating much of the law in this area), ch. 6.

18. Loving v. Virginia, 388 U.S. 1 (1967).

19. David P. McWhirter and Andrew M. Mattison, *The Male Couple: How Relationships Develop* (Englewood Cliffs, N.J.: Prentice-Hall, 1984), p. ix.

20. David F. Greenberg, *The Construction of Homosexuality* (Chicago: University of Chicago Press, 1988), p. 455. See *Sexual Orientation and the Law*, ch. 5.

21. Greenberg, *The Construction of Homosexuality*, pp. 470–71.

22. In re Baby "M," 109 N.J. 396, 537 A. 2d 1227 (1988) (in which the New Jersey Supreme Court held the biological father's constitutional right to privacy does not afford him custody of his child under a surrogate motherhood contract); Surrogate Parenting Associates v. Commonwealth, 704 S.W. 2d 209 (Ky. 1986) (in which the Kentucky Supreme Court held that a statute prohibiting the "purchase of any child for the purpose of adoption or any other purpose, including termination of parent rights" did not apply to the plaintiff's involvement in planning surrogate parenting); In re Adoption of Baby Girl, L. J., 132 Misc. 2d 972, 505 N.Y.S. 2d 813 (1986) (in which a lower court in New York upheld a $10,000 payment to a surrogate mother); Doe v. Kelley, 106 Mich. App. 169, 307 N.W. 2d 438 (1981), *cert. denied*, 459 U.S. 1183 (1983) (in which a Michigan Court of Appeals prohibited the exchange of money under a surrogate motherhood contract).

23. "The Rights of the Biological Father: From Adoption and Custody to Surrogate Motherhood," *Vermont Law Review* 12 (1987): 87–121, 100.

24. Ibid.

25. The couple may actually be infertile or perhaps may choose surrogate motherhood as a way to breed out a hereditary disease. There may also be other less serious reasons for entering into the contract.

26. *See generally* Catharine MacKinnon, "*Roe v. Wade:* A Study in Male Ideology," in *Abortion: Moral and Legal Perspectives,* ed. Jay L. Garfield and Patricia Hennessey (Amherst: University of Massachusetts Press, 1984), which discusses how privacy is used to preserve the dominance of male heterosexuality.

27. *See* Martha A. Field, *Surrogate Motherhood: The Legal and Human Issues* (Cambridge, Mass.: Harvard University Press, 1988), pp. 25–32.

28. Ibid., pp. 107–8; Sandra H. Johnson, "The Baby 'M' Decision: Specific Performance of a Contract for Specially Manufactured Goods," *Southern Illinois University Law Journal* 11 (1987): 1339–48, 1344; Sara Ann Ketchum, "Selling Babies and Selling Bodies: Surrogate Motherhood and the Problem of Commodification" (paper presented at the annual meeting of the Eastern Division of the American Philosophical Association, New York, December 20, 1988); Heidi Malm, "Comments on Ketchum's 'Selling Babies and Selling Bodies' " (paper presented at the annual meeting of the Eastern Division of the American Philosophical Association, New York, December 20, 1988).

29. For a contrary argument on this view, see Field, *Surrogate Motherhood.*

30. U.S. Constitution, Amendment Thirteen; *see* Slaughter House Cases, 16 Wall (83 U.S.) 36 (1873); *see also* Peonage Cases, 123 F. 671 (M.D. Ala. 1903).

31. Roe v. Wade, 410 U.S. 113 (1973).

32. "The Rights of the Biological Father," p. 105, n. 133.

33. While AIDS is not a so-called gay disease (in Africa, where it is believed to have originated, it is found almost exclusively among heterosexuals), in the United States gay men, intravenous drug users, and those who engage in frequent sexual contacts are the most susceptible. See W. Blattner, R. C. Gallo, and H. M. Temin, "HIV Causes AIDS," *Science*, July 29, 1988, 515.

34. "After the introduction of the AIDS antibody screening test in the United States, the transmission of HIV [the viral agent that most scientists believe causes AIDS] in the blood supply of the United States was reduced from as high as 1 in 1000 infected units in some high risk areas to less than an estimated 1 in 40,000 countrywide" (ibid., p. 515).

35. Although there is some scientific controversy, most scientists now seem to accept the view that human AIDS is caused by two viruses, HIV-1 and HIV-2 (Peter Duesberg, "HIV Is Not the Cause of AIDS," *Science*, July 29, 1988, p. 514; Blattner, Gallo, and Temin, "Blattner and Colleagues Respond to Duesberg," *Science*, July 29, 1988, pp. 514, 517; Blattner, Gallo, and Temin, "HIV Causes AIDS," p. 515; Peter Duesberg, "Duesberg's Response to Blattner and Colleagues," *Science*, July 29, 1988, pp. 515–16; Anthony Liversidge, "AIDS," *SPIN*, March 1989.

36. In states with donor-notification procedures, if a positive result on an antibody test is confirmed, the donor's name, social security number, and test results are logged into a computerized file that is usually inaccessible to all but top-ranking laboratory personnel. In all but one state, Connecticut, and some of the larger cities, the blood collection center will notify the donor whose blood has been confirmed to contain the AIDS antibody. One state, Colorado, has undertaken, and several other states are considering undertaking, regulations to require the re-

porting of all positive test results so that the state health department can monitor the donor's medical history. In addition, four states (Florida, Illinois, New Jersey, and Texas) and the District of Columbia all allow insurance companies to require that policy applicants be tested for the AIDS antibody. And forty states allow the use of ELSIA-related questions to be asked of insurance applicants. Only California and Wisconsin prohibit the use of ELSIA results as a determining factor for the granting or rejecting of insurance or employment applications. Robert Blau, "Blood Feud: A Test Called ELSIA Divides a Society Panicked by AIDS," *Chicago Tribune,* December 15, 1985, sec. 10.

37. Ibid., pp. 11–12.

38. Ibid., p. 12.

39. A recent study by Charles E. Lewis, M.D., professor of medicine at the University of California in Los Angles indicates that a significant number of hospitals in the United States have HIV testing policies that violate patients' rights. Many physicians and surgeons routinely order HIV tests of asymptomatic patients without their consent. *See AIDS Alert,* May 1990, pp. 81–86 (published by American Health Consultants, Atlanta, Ga.).

40. William F. Buckley, "Crucial Steps in Combating the AIDS Epidemic: Identify All the Carriers," *New York Times,* March 18, 1986, sec. 1.

41. "There is a period of about 4 to 8 weeks in which newly HIV-infected persons are capable of transmitting HIV, but have not yet developed antibodies" (Blattner, Gallo, and Temin, "HIV Causes AIDS," p. 515).

42. The study consists of volunteers from across the country who undergo confidential physical examinations for a period of years.

43. It has been suggested that spermicides containing Nonoxynol-9 may kill the AIDS virus. It is unclear how effective this method is and, therefore, it is usually suggested that the spermicide be used along with a condom.

44. Wayne Wooden and Jay Parker, *Men Behind Bars: Sexual Exploitation in Prison* (New York: Plenum, 1982).

45. To the extent that the testing may be used to weed out so-called undesirables who the military believes are morale problems, the burden is on the military to show why the morale problem could not be solved through better education of its members and strict enforcement of regulations designed to promote respect for the individual autonomy of all members of the armed forces.

46. *See generally* Robert Weiner, *AIDS: Impact on the Schools* (Arlington, Va.: The Education Research Group, 1986).

47. Doe v. Belleville Pub. School Dist., No. 118, 672 F. Supp. 342 (S.D. Ill. 1987); Ray v. School Dist. of Desoto County, 666 F. Supp. 1524 (M.D. Fla. 1987); Thomas v. Atascadero Unified School Dist., 662 F. Supp. 376 (C.D. Cal. 1986); District 27 Community School Bd. by Graniver v. Bd. of Educ. of New York City, 130 Misc. 2d 398, 502 N.Y.S. 2d 325 (1986); *see* Chalk v. United States Dist. Court, Cent. Dist. of Calif., 840 F. 2d 701 (9th Cir. 1988);

cf. New York State Assoc. for Retarded Children v. Carey, 612 F. 2d 644 (2d Cir. 1979) (involving an analogous situation where a student was a carrier of serum hepatitis B). *But cf.* Child v. Spillane, 866 F. 2d 691 (4th Cir. 1989) (which denied an award of attorney fees where the plaintiff had not proven that the filing of the lawsuit was what caused the school board to readmit the child).

48. Even in the case of a child who had bitten one of his classmates, the court noted that there is no reported case of the transmission of the AIDS virus in a school setting and that the overwhelming weight of medical evidence is that the AIDS virus is not transmitted by human bites, even bites that break the skin. *See* Thomas v. Atascadero Unified School Dist., 662 F. Supp. at 380.

49. *See* Chalk v. United States Dist. Court, Cent. Dist. of Calif., 840 F. 2d at 706–7.

50. In School Bd. of Nassau C. v. Arline, 480 U.S. 273 (1987), the Supreme Court held that a school teacher who contracted the contagious disease of tuberculosis was protected against discharge under Section 504 of the Rehabilitation Act of 1973, 29 U.S.C. sec. 794 (1982). In arriving at this decision, which has since been applied in AIDS cases (*see, e.g.*, Chalk v. United States District Court, Cent. Dist. of Calif., 840 F. 2d at 704–6), the court stated that in most cases there must be an individualized inquiry with appropriate findings of fact so that section "504 [may] achieve its goal of protecting handicapped individuals from deprivations based on prejudice, stereotypes, or unfounded fear, while giving appropriate weight to such legitimate concerns of grantees as avoiding exposing others to significant health and safety risks" (ibid., at 1131). The Arline decision requires trial courts to make findings of fact on four related factors: "(a) the nature of the risk (how the disease is transmitted); (b) the duration of the risk (how long is the carrier infectious); (c) the severity of the risk (what is the potential harm to third parties); and (d) the probabilities the disease will be transmitted and will cause varying degrees of harm" (ibid).

51. Susan Hooper and Gwendolyn H. Gregory, *AIDS and the Public Schools*, vol. 1 (Alexandria, Va.: National School Board Association, 1986).

52. Twenty-four states and the District of Columbia have sodomy statutes. These statutes are listed in the bibliography under the heading "Applicable State Criminal Statutes." Massachusetts' sodomy statute makes anal sex criminal (*see* Mass. Gen. L. ch. 272, § 34 (1986), but that statute may be invalid as applied to private consensual conduct by Commonwealth v. Balthazar, 366 Mass. 298, 302, 318 N.E. 2d 478, 481 (1974), which held that a companion statute making criminal "lewd and lascivious acts" was unconstitutional as applied to private, consensual adult behavior. *See generally, Sexual Orientation and the Law*, ch. 2.

A typical sodomy statute might read as the New York statute prior to its being held unconstitutional in People v. Onofre, 51 N.Y. 2d 476, 415 N.E. 2d 936, 434 N.Y.S. 2d 947 (1980).

§ 130.38 Consensual Sodomy:

A person is guilty of consensual sodomy when he engages in deviate sexual intercourse with another person.

§ 130.00 See offenses: definitions of terms.

The following definitions are applicable to this article: . . .

2. Deviate sexual intercourse means sexual conduct between persons not married to each other consisting of contact between the penis and the anus, the mouth and the penis, or the mouth and the vulva.

53. This argument could not be applied by way of extension to lifting restrictions on the availability of dangerous narcotics. However, the limitation is that such narcotics would have to be "dangerous" in the sense that there would be a high likelihood that they could injure a person either physically or mentally and further that they would likely be abused so as to make them a potential danger to society. Beyond this limitation, the only other restriction that could justifiably be placed on the availability of such drugs is that they not be allowed to reach the hands of minors, who may not be able to appreciate the danger involved.

54. Criminal statutes would presumably be available to cover the situation where the action was not consensual.

55. Obviously, there is a question of what should constitute adequate proof in this case. Indeed, the problem is somewhat analogous to the situation where the court is attempting to decide whether or not capital punishment should be allowed or whether or not separate but equal education is inherently unconstitutional. Since what is at stake is a restriction on a fundamental freedom, the standard of proof that should be required of the state should be the same as that which would be required to restrict any fundamental freedom. That is, the state should be required to prove beyond a reasonable doubt that a particular view of morality was in the interests of the citizens generally. The fact that so high a standard should govern what the state must prove reflects the fact that the right to privacy is viewed as a fundamental freedom.

56. Bowers v. Hardwick, 478 U.S. 186 (1986).

57. The pill RU 486, which was developed in France and is legal in much of Europe but not the United States, induces miscarriages in about six weeks and is thought by many to produce a fairly safe abortion.

58. Alan Gewirth, *Reason and Morality* (Chicago: University of Chicago Press, 1978), p. 27.

59. This reflects the fact that a fundamental question underlying the issue of abortion is not a privacy question but a question of personhood. The issue regarding the status of the unborn only relates to privacy insofar as it is a prior question. In other words, an answer to this question must at least be tentatively presupposed for privacy to be an issue.

60. Jay L. Garfield and Patricia Hennessey, eds., *Abortion: Moral and Legal Perspectives* (Amherst: University of Massachusetts Press, 1984).

61. In Roe v. Wade, 410 U.S. 113, 163 (1973), the Supreme Court held

that "with respect to the State's important and legitimate interest in potential life, the 'compelling' point is at viability."

62. Judith Jarvis Thompson, "A Defense of Abortion," *Philosophy and Public Affairs* 1 (Autumn 1971): 47–66.

63. See Nancy Davis, "Abortion and Self-Defense," *Philosophy and Public Affairs* 13 (Summer 1984): 175–207.

64. Thompson, "A Defense of Abortion," pp. 52–53.

65. *See generally* Phillip Kitcher, *Abusing Science: The Case Against Creationism* (Cambridge, Mass.: MIT Press, 1982) (in which creationism is shown to fail as a scientific theory).

66. Hyde, *Understanding Human Sexuality*, p. 20.

67. *"Summa Theologica": The Basic Writings of Saint Thomas Aquinas*, ed. Anton C. Pegis (New York: Random House, 1945), 2: 784–85.

68. Ibid.

69. Gewirth, *Reason and Morality*.

70. Webster v. Reproductive Health Services,—U.S.—, 109 S. Ct. 3040 (1989).

71. In Hodgson v. Minnesota, 58 U.S.L.W. 4957 (U.S. June 25, 1990) and Ohio v. Akron Center for Reproductive Health, 58 U.S.L.W. 4979 (U.S. June 25, 1990), the Court permitted states to require parental notification to one or both parents, at least where there is the alternative of a judicial hearing.

72. Bowers v. Hardwick, 478 U.S. 186 (1986).

73. Ibid., p. 10 (Blackmun, dissenting).

74. *See generally* MacKinnon, "*Roe v. Wade.*"

75. Quoted in David F. Linowes, "Must Personal Privacy Die in the Computer Age?" *American Bar Association Journal* 65 (August 1979): 1180.

76. U.S. Congress, Office of Technology Assessment, *Computer-Based National Information Systems: Technology and Public Policy Issues* (Washington, D.C.: Government Printing Office, 1981), p. 76.

77. Ibid., p. 77.

78. *See* U.S. Congress, Senate, Judiciary Subcommittee on the Constitution, *Preliminary Report by the Office of Technology Assessment on the Federal Bureau of Investigation National Crime Investigation Center Accompanied by Letters of Comments on the Draft Report*, 95th Cong., 2d sess., 1978.

79. John L. Wanamaker, "Computer and Scientific Jury Selection: A Calculated Risk," *University of Detroit Journal of Urban Law* 55 (Winter 1978): 345.

80. U.S. Congress, Office of Technology Assessment, *Computer-Based National Information Systems*, p. 78.

81. John T. Soma and Richard A. Wehmhofer, "Illegal and Technical Assessment of the Effect of Computers on Privacy," *Denver Law Journal* 60 (1983): 455.

82. A Bill to Safeguard the Privacy of Electronic Fund Transfers by Consumers, and for Other Purposes, S. 1929, 96th Cong., 1st sess., 1979.

83. The Fair Credit Reporting Act of 1970, 15 U.S.C. secs. 1681, 1681a–81t (1982) (requiring that credit investigation and reporting organizations make their records available to the data subject, providing procedures for correcting information, and permitting disclosure only to authorized customers); Justice System Improvement Act of 1979, 42 U.S.C. sec. 3789g (1982) (requiring that state criminal jury information systems developed with federal funds be protected by measures to insure the privacy and security of information); The Privacy Act of 1974, 5 U.S.C. sec. 522 (1982) (supplementing The Freedom of Information Act of 1966, 5 U.S.C. sec. 552 [1982] to protect the confidentiality of and provide access and a means for correction of personal information shared by federal agencies); The Family Education Rights and Privacy Act of 1974, 20 U.S.C. sec. 1232(g) (1982) (permitting federal funds to be terminated to any institution of higher education that releases the educational records of children to persons other than school officials "with a need to know," state or federal education officials, research organizations, or persons with a lawful subpoena, and guarantees the access to parents of such information); The Tax Reform Act of 1976, 26 U.S.C. sec. 7602 (1982) (exempting the Internal Revenue Service from statutes that deny access to an individual's personal records held by third parties); The Right to Financial Privacy Act of 1978, 12 U.S.C. secs. 3401–22 (1982) (imposing duty of confidentiality on institutions); The Electronic Fund Act of 1980, 15 U.S.C. sec. 1693b(d) (1982) (providing that electronic fund transfers or other such services notify their customers about third-party access to their accounts).

84. *See* the nineteen-point proposal in *National Commission on Electronic Funds Transfer* (Washington, D.C.: NCEFT, 1977).

85. Whalen v. Roe, 429 U.S. 589 (1977).

86. Ibid., p. 605.

87. Nixon v. Administrator of General Services, 433 U.S. 425 (1977).

88. Ibid., p. 465.

89. Fraternal Order of Police, Lodge No. 5 v. City of Philadelphia, 812 F. 2d 105 (3d Cir. 1987).

90. United States Dept. of Justice v. Reporters Committee for Freedom of the Press,—U.S.—, 109 S. Ct. 1468, 1473 (1989).

91. Ibid., p. 1476.

92. Ibid., p. 1480.

93. Ibid., p. 1485.

94. Stanley v. Georgia, 394 U.S. 557 (1969).

95. Ibid., p. 565.

96. Ibid., p. 559.

97. Osborne v. Ohio, 58 U.S.L.W. 4467 (1990).

98. Ibid., p. 4469.

99. Ibid.

100. The states having statutes prohibiting the possession of child pornography are Alabama, Arizona, Colorado, Florida, Georgia, Idaho,

Illinois, Kansas, Minnesota, Missouri, Nebraska, Nevada, Oklahoma, South Dakota, Texas, Utah, Washington, and West Virginia.

101. Osborne v. Ohio, 58 U.S.L.W. at 4477 (Brennan, J., dissenting). *But cf.* Irving Kristol, "Pornography, Obscenity and the Case for Censorship," in *Philosophy of Law,* 2d ed., ed. Joel Feinberg and Hyman Gross (Belmont, Calif.: Wadsworth Publishing Co., 1986) (arguing for censorship in order to create a society worthy of self-rule), pp. 246–52.

102. *See generally* Richards, *Sex, Drugs, Death and the Law,* pt. 2 (arguing that the right to drug use is associated with the control of consciousness).

103. William F. Buckley, "Firing Line Debate," WTTW–Channel 11, March 26, 1990, 9:00 P.M.

104. *See* Mayor Kurt Schmoke, "A War for the Surgeon General, Not the Attorney General," *New Perspectives Quarterly,* Summer 1989, p. 12; *see also* Nathan Gardels, "Comment: America's Domestic Quagmire," *New Perspectives Quarterly,* Summer 1989, p. 2, stating: "Already Washington, D.C., has the highest per capita incarceration rate of black males of any major city: 10,000 are in jail, the vast majority on drug-related charges."

105. *See* Schmoke, "A War for the Surgeon General," p. 13; *see also* Charles-Edward Anderson, "Uncle Sam Gets Serious," *American Bar Association Journal* 76 (1990): 62.

106. *See* Schmoke, "A War for the Surgeon General," p. 14.

107. *See* Barbara Flicker, "To Jail or Not to Jail?" *American Bar Association Journal* 76 (1990): 66.

108. *See* ibid., p. 64.

109. Sharyn Rosenbaum, "Is Legalization the Answer?" *Human Rights,* Spring 1989, p. 18.

110. *See* Lewis H. Lapham, "A Political Opiate," *Harper's,* December 1989, p. 45; *see also* Flicker, "To Jail or Not to Jail," p. 66.

111. *See* Arnold Trebach, "Why Not Decriminalize?" *New Perspectives Quarterly,* Summer 1989, pp. 43–44.

112. Michael S. Cerere and Philip B. Rosen, "Legal Implications of Substance Abuse Testing in the Workplace," *Notre Dame Law Review* 62 (1987): 859.

113. "Employee Drug Testing: Issues Facing Private Sector Employers," *North Carolina Law Review* 65 (1987): 832.

114. Cerere and Rosen, "Legal Implications of Substance Abuse Testing in the Workplace," p. 859.

115. "Drug Testing in the Workplace: The Need for Quality Assurance Legislation," *Ohio State Law Review* 48 (1987): 877–88. The usual methods employers use for screening for the presence of drugs are thin layer chromatography (TLC), enzyme immunoassay (EIA), and radioimmunoassay (RIA). Toxicologists and the manufacturers of these drugs recommend that all positive results be confirmed by another method in order to insure reliability.

116. Thomas L. McGovern III, "Employee Drug-Testing Legislation: Redrawing the Battlelines in the War on Drugs," *Stanford Law Review* 39 (1987): 1453, 1468–69.

117. Edward S. Adams, "Random Drug Testing of Government Employees: A Constitutional Procedure," *University of Chicago Law Review* 54 (1987): 1335; McGovern, "Employee Drug Testing Legislation," p. 1453; "Drug Testing in the Workplace," p. 877.

118. On September 15, 1986, President Ronald Reagan signed Executive Order 12,564 (3 C.F.R. 224 [1987]) authorizing the head of each executive agency to test employees for illegal drug use when "there is a reasonable suspicion that any employee uses illegal drugs" or as part of the investigation of an accident or unsafe work practice. This order applies to all employees of any "employing unit or authority of the federal government," except for the armed forces, Postal Rate Commission, and judicial and legislative branches. For a discussion of Fourth Amendment privacy protection, see Daniel P. Mazo, "Yellow Rows of Test Tubes: Due Process Constraints on the Discharge of Public Employees Based on Drug Urinalysis Testing," *University of Pennsylvania Law Review* 135 (1987): 1623.

119. *For example*, Division 241 Amalgamated Transit Union v. Suscy, 538 F. 2d 1264 (7th Cir.) (upholding mandatory blood and urine testing of employees involved in vehicle collisions or suspected of being under the influence of chemicals while on duty upon recommendation of two supervisors), *cert. denied*, 429 U.S. 1029 (1976).

120. Laws v. Calmat, 852 F. 2d 430, 433–34 (9th Cir. 1988) (upholding drug testing of drivers and other employees in building products company under management rights to "manage the plant" and implement safety rules under collective bargaining agreement); Rushton v. Nebraska Public Power Dist., 844 F. 2d 562, 566–67 (8th Cir. 1988) (upholding annual testing of nuclear power plant employees for alcohol and narcotics); National Treasury Employees Union v. Von Raab, 816 F. 2d 170, 179 (5th Cir. 1987) (upholding drug screens of customs officials within ambit of reasonable conditions of employment), *cert. granted,*—U.S.—, 108 S. Ct. 1072 (1988).

121. *For example*, Shoemaker v. Handel, 795 F. 2d 1136 (3d Cir.) (upholding random urine testing of jockeys and other racetrack employees), *cert. denied*, 479 U.S. 986 (1986).

122. David T. Lykken, "The Case Against the Polygraph in Employment Screening," *Personnel Administrator*, September 1985.

123. Cruzan v. Director, Missouri, Department of Health, 58 U.S.L.W. 4916 (U.S. June 25, 1990).

124. Ibid., p. 4917.

125. Bowers v. Hardwick, 478 U.S. 186 (1986).

126. Cruzan v. Director, Missouri, Department of Health, 58 U.S.L.W. at 4921.

127. Ibid., p. 4923 (O'Connor, concurring).

128. Ibid., p. 4929 (Brennan, dissenting).

129. Ibid., p. 4939 (Stevens, dissenting).
130. *See generally* Richards, *Sex, Drugs, Death, and the Law,* pt. 3 (arguing that the right to die is to be understood in the context of a contractarian notion of the right to life).
131. Cruzan v. Director, Missouri Department of Health, 760 S.W. 2d 408, 412 n.4, 413–18 (Mo. 1988) (en banc).
132. In re Quinlan, 70 N.J. 10, 355 A. 2d 647 (1976), *cert. denied,* 429 U.S. 922 (1976).
133. Ibid., p. 664.
134. Cruzan v. Director, Missouri, Department of Health, 760 S.W. 2d at 422.
135. For a good discussion of what characteristics define agency see Gewirth, *Reason and Morality,* pp. 31–42.
136. For a discussion of the distinction between potential and actual agents see ibid., p. 141.
137. Tamar Lewin, "Nancy Cruzan Dies, Outlived by Debate over Right to Die," *New York Times,* December 27, 1990, sec. A.

Epilogue

1. Alan Gewirth, *Reason and Morality* (Chicago: University of Chicago Press, 1978), pp. 138–39, 207, 256.
2. Marcus G. Singer, "Gewirth's Ethical Monism," in *Gewirth's Ethical Rationalism: Critical Essays, with a Reply by Alan Gewirth,* ed. Edward Regis, Jr. (Chicago: University of Chicago Press, 1984).
3. Alan Gewirth, "Replies to My Critics" in ibid., p. 203.
4. David A. J. Richards, *Sex, Drugs, Death, and the Law: An Essay on Human Rights and Overcriminalization* (Totowa, N.J.: Rowman and Littlefield, 1982), pp. 7–17. *See also* David A. J. Richards, *Toleration and the Constitution* (New York: Oxford University Press, 1986), pp. 229–81.
5. Ibid., p. 15.
6. Richard F. Hixon, *Privacy in a Public Society: Human Rights in Conflict* (New York: Oxford University Press, 1987), p. 137.
7. *See* Dronenberg v. Zech, 741 F. 2d 1388, 1392 (D.C. Cir. 1984) (Bork, J.). On questioning before Senate Judiciary Committee, Judge Bork admitted that while he thought a line of reasoning different from that in Griswold might lead to the same result, he had never in his two decades of criticizing the ruling suggested this before. Nina Totenberg, "The Confirmation Process and the Public: To Know or Not to Know," *Harvard Law Review* 101 (1988): 1213–29, 1221. *See generally* "The Bork Nomination," *Cardozo Law Review* 9 (1987): 1–530 (a collection of articles by different authors on the philosophy of Robert Bork and his nomination to the Supreme Court).
8. *See* Totenberg, "The Confirmation Process," p. 1228 (where a Gallup pole is cited for the proposition that the public had come to support most of the Court decisions in the areas of race, sex, speech, privacy, and abortion). *See also* "*New York Times*/CBS News Poll," *New*

York Times, April 26, 1989, sec. 1 (finding 49 percent support the legality of abortion, 39 percent want to restrict it only to instances of rape, incest, and danger to the mother's life, and 9 percent want it totally banned).

9. One example of a case I have in mind is Bowers v. Hardwick, 478 U.S. 186 (1986), which held that the constitutional right to privacy does not protect two adult gay persons who freely choose to have sex with one another inside their own home in a state that prohibits such activity.

10. *See, for example,* H. L. A. Hart, "Positivism and the Separation of Law and Morals," *Harvard Law Review* 71 (1958): 593; and Lon Fuller, "Positivism and Fidelity to Law: A Reply to Professor Hart," in *Harvard Law Review* 71 (1958): 630.

Selected Bibliography

Articles, Books, Papers, and Debates

Adams, Edward S. "Random Drug Testing of Government Employees: A Constitutional Procedure." *University of Chicago Law Review* 54 (1987): 1335–72.

AIDS Alert, May 1990, pp. 81–86. American Health Consultants, Atlanta, Ga.

Altman, Irwin. "Privacy: A Conceptual Analysis." *Environment and Behavior* 8 (1976): 7–29.

———. "Privacy Regulation: Culturally Universal or Culturally Specific?" *The Journal of Social Issues* 33 (1977): 68–84.

Anderson, Charles-Edward. "Uncle Sam Gets Serious." *American Bar Association Journal* 76 (1990): 60–63.

Baker, Tyler. "*Roe* and *Paris:* Does Privacy Have a Principle?" *Stanford Law Review* 26 (1974): 1161–89.

Beaney, William. "The Constitutional Right to Privacy in the Supreme Court." *The Supreme Court Review*, 1962, pp. 216–51.

Beardsley, Elizabeth. "Privacy, Autonomy, and Selective Disclosure." *Nomos XIII: Privacy*, edited by J. Roland Pennock and John Chapman. New York: Atherton Press, 1971.

Benn, Stanley I. "Privacy, Freedom, and Respect for Persons." In *Philosophical Dimensions of Privacy: An Anthology*, edited by Ferdinand D. Schoeman. New York: Cambridge University Press, 1984.

Berlin, Sir Isaiah. "Two Concepts of Liberty." In *Political Philosophy*, edited by Anthony Quinton. New York: Oxford University Press, 1967.

Beytagh, Francis. "Privacy and Free Press: A Contemporary Conflict in Values." *New York Law Forum* 20 (1975): 453–514.

Bickel, Alexander. *The Least Dangerous Branch: The Supreme Court at the Bar of Politics.* Indianapolis: Bobbs-Merrill, 1962.

Blackstone, William. *Commentaries on the Laws of England.* 4 vols. Chicago: University of Chicago Press, 1979.

Blattner, W., R. C. Gallo, and H. M. Temin. "HIV Causes AIDS." *Science,* July 29, 1988, p. 515.

———. "Blattner and Colleagues Respond to Duesberg." *Science,* July 29, 1988, p. 514.

Blau, Robert. "Blood Feud: A Test Called ELSIA Divides a Society Panicked by AIDS." *Chicago Tribune,* December 15, 1985, sec. 10.

Bloustein, Edward J. "Privacy as an Aspect of Human Dignity: An Answer to Dean Prosser." In *Philosophical Dimensions of Privacy: An Anthology,* edited by Ferdinand D. Schoeman. New York: Cambridge University Press, 1984.

Bork, Robert. "Neutral Principles and Some First Amendment Problems." *Indiana Law Journal* 47 (1971): 1–35.

———. *The Tempting of America: The Political Seduction of the Law.* New York: Free Press, 1990.

"The Bork Nomination." *Cardozo Law Review* 9 (1987): 1–530.

Bostwick, Gary L. "A Taxonomy of Privacy: Repose, Sanctuary, and Intimate Decision." *California Law Review* 64 (1976): 1447–83.

Boswell, John. *Christianity, Social Tolerance, and Homosexuality: Gay People in Western Europe from the Beginning of the Christian Era to the Fourteenth Century.* Chicago: University of Chicago Press, 1980.

Brown, D. G. "Mill on Liberty and Morality." *Philosophical Review* 81 (1972): 142–58.

Buckley, William F. "Crucial Steps in Combating the AIDS Epidemic: Identify All the Carriers." *New York Times,* March 18, 1986, sec. 1.

———. "Firing Line Debate." WTTW-Channel 11, March 26, 1990, 9:00 P.M.

Cerere, Michael S., and Philip B. Rosen. "Legal Implications of Substance Abuse Testing in the Workplace." *Notre Dame Law Review* 62 (1987): 859–78.

Clark, Don. *Loving Someone Gay.* New York: New American Library, 1977.

Cohen, Marshall, ed. *Ronald Dworkin and Contemporary Jurisprudence.* Totowa, N.J.: Rowman and Allanheld, 1984.

Countryman, Vern. "The Diminishing Right to Privacy: The Personal Dossier and the Computer." *Texas Law Review* 49 (1977): 837–971.

"Court Reaffirms Right to Abortion by Barring Variety of Local Curbs." *New York Times,* June 16, 1983, sec. 1.

Davis, Nancy. "Abortion and Self-Defense." *Philosophy and Public Affairs* 13 (Summer 1984): 15–207.

"Drug Testing in the Workplace: The Need for Quality Assurance Legislation." *Ohio State Law Review* 48 (1987): 877–95.

Duesberg, Peter. "HIV Is Not the Cause of AIDS." *Science,* July 29, 1988, p. 514.

———. "Duesberg's Response to Blattner and Colleagues." *Science,* July 29, 1988, pp. 515–16.

Dworkin, Ronald. *A Matter of Principle.* Cambridge, Mass.: Harvard University Press, 1985.

———. *Law's Empire.* Cambridge, Mass.: Harvard University Press, 1986.

————. *Taking Rights Seriously*. Cambridge, Mass.: Harvard University Press, 1977.

Ely, John Hart. *Democracy and Distrust: A Theory of Judicial Review*. Cambridge, Mass.: Harvard University Press, 1980.

————. "The Wages of Crying Wolf: A Comment on *Roe v. Wade*." *Yale Law Journal* 82 (1973): 920–49.

"Employee Drug Testing: Issues Facing Private Sector Employers." *North Carolina Law Review* 65 (1987): 832–47.

Feinberg, Joel. "The Nature and Value of Rights." In *Philosophy of Law*. 2d ed. Edited by Joel Feinberg and Hyman Gross. Belmont, Calif.: Wadsworth Publishing Co., 1980.

Feinberg, Joel, and Hyman Gross, eds. *Philosophy of Law*. 2d ed. Belmont, Calif.: Wadsworth Publishing Co., 1980.

————. *Philosophy of Law*. 3d ed. Belmont, Calif.: Wadsworth Publishing Co., 1986.

Field, Martha A. *Surrogate Motherhood: The Legal and Human Issues*. Cambridge, Mass.: Harvard University Press, 1988.

Flicker, Barbara. "To Jail or Not to Jail?" *American Bar Association Journal* 76 (1990): 64–67.

Freund, Paul. "Privacy: One Concept or Many?" In *Nomos XIII: Privacy*, edited by J. Pennock and J. Chapman. New York: Atherton Press, 1971.

Fried, Charles. *An Anatomy of Values*. Cambridge, Mass.: Harvard University Press, 1970.

————. "Privacy." *Yale Law Journal* 77 (1968): 475–93.

Fuller, Lon. "Positivism and Fidelity to Law: A Reply to Professor Hart." *Harvard Law Review* 71 (1958): 630.

Gardels, Nathan. "Comment: America's Domestic Quagmire." *New Perspectives Quarterly*, Summer 1989, pp. 2–3.

Garfield, Jay L., and Patricia Hennessey, eds. *Abortion: Moral and Legal Perspectives*. Amherst: University of Massachusetts Press, 1984.

Garrett, Roland. "The Nature of Privacy." *Philosophy Today* 18 (1974): 263–84.

Gavison, Ruth. "Privacy and the Limits of Law." In *Philosophical Dimensions of Privacy: An Anthology*, edited by Ferdinand D. Schoeman. New York: Cambridge University Press, 1984.

Gerety, Tom. "Redefining Privacy." *Harvard Civil Rights–Civil Liberties Law Review* 12 (Spring 1977): 233–96.

Gewirth, Alan. "The Basis and Content of Human Rights." *Georgia Law Review* 13 (1979): 1143–70. Article appears in *Nomos XXIII: Human Rights*, edited by J. Roland Pennock and John W. Chapman. New York: New York University Press, 1981. Also appears in *Human Rights*, edited by Alan Gewirth. Chicago: University of Chicago Press, 1982.

————. *Political Philosophy*. New York: Macmillan, 1965.

————. *Reason and Morality*. Chicago: University of Chicago Press, 1978.

Greenberg, David F. *The Construction of Homosexuality*. Chicago: University of Chicago Press, 1988.

Gross, Hyman. "The Concept of Privacy." *New York University Law Review* 42 (1967): 34–54.

————. "Privacy and Autonomy." In *Nomos XIII: Privacy*, edited by J. Pennock and J. Chapman. New York: Atherton Press, 1971.

Hamilton, Alexander, James Madison, and John Jay. *The Federalist Papers*, edited by Clinton Rossiter. New York: New American Library, 1961.

Hart, H. L. A. "Are There Any Natural Rights?" *Philosophical Review* 64 (1955): 175–91.

————. *The Concept of Law*. Oxford: Clarendon Press, 1961.

————. "Positivism and the Separation of Law and Morals." *Harvard Law Review* 71 (1958): 593–629.

Hart, H. L. A., and A. M. Honoré. *Causation in the Law*. Oxford: Oxford University Press, 1959.

Haworth, Lawrence. *Autonomy: An Essay in Philosophical Psychology and Ethics*. New Haven, Conn.: Yale University Press, 1986.

Henkin, Louis. "Privacy and Autonomy." *Columbia Law Review* 74 (1974): 1410–33.

Hirschleifer, Jack. "Privacy: Its Origin, Function, and Future." *The Journal of Legal Studies* 9 (1980): 649–65.

Hixon, Richard F. *Privacy in a Public Society: Human Rights in Conflict*. New York: Oxford University Press, 1987.

Hohfeld, Wesley N. *Fundamental Legal Conceptions*. Westport, Conn.: Greenwood Press, 1946.

Honderich, Ted. *Punishment: The Supposed Justifications*. London: Hutchinson and Co., 1966.

Hooper, Susan, and Gwendolyn H. Gregory. *AIDS and the Public Schools*. Alexandria, Va.: National School Board Association, 1986.

Hyde, Janet Shibley. *Understanding Human Sexuality*. 3d ed. New York: McGraw-Hill, 1986.

Ingham, Roger. "Privacy and Psychology." In *Privacy*, edited by John Young. New York: John Wiley and Sons, 1978.

Johnson, Dirk. "Opening Closets for Others in the Pursuit of Gay Rights." *New York Times*, March 27, 1990, sec. 1.

Johnson, Sandra H. "The Baby 'M' Decision: Specific Performance of a Contract for Specially Manufactured Goods." *Southern Illinois University Law Journal* 11 (1987): 1339–48.

"Justices, 6 to 3, Restrict Rights to Pornography." *New York Times*, April 19, 1990, sec. 1.

Kant, Immanuel. *Foundations of the Metaphysics of Morals*. Translated by Lewis W. Beck. Indianapolis: Bobbs-Merrill, 1959.

Katzner, Louis. "Is the Favoring of Women and Blacks in Employment and Educational Opportunities Justified?" In *Philosophy of Law*, 2d ed., edited by Joel Feinberg and Hyman Gross. Belmont, Calif.: Wadsworth Publishing, 1986.

Ketchum, Sara Ann. "Selling Babies and Selling Bodies: Surrogate Motherhood and the Problem of Commodification." Paper presented at annual meeting of the Eastern Division of the American Philosophical Association, New York, December 20, 1988.

Kitcher, Phillip. *Abusing Science: The Case Against Creationism.* Cambridge, Mass.: MIT Press, 1982.

Klipter, Peter, and Daniel Rubenstein. "The Concept 'Privacy' and Its Biological Basis." *The Journal of Social Issues* 33 (1977): 52–65.

Koch, Adrienne, and William Peden. *The Life and Selected Writings of Thomas Jefferson.* New York: Random House, 1944.

Konvitz, Milton. "Privacy and the Law: A Philosophical Prelude." *Law and Contemporary Problems* 31 (1966): 272–80.

Kristol, Irving. "Pornography, Obscenity, and the Case for Censorship." In *Philosophy of Law*, 2d ed., edited by Joel Feinberg and Hyman Gross. Belmont, Calif.: Wadsworth Publishing Co., 1986.

Kurland, Phillip B. "The Private I." *Chicago Magazine* 25 (Autumn 1976): 8.

Lapham, Lewis H. "A Political Opiate." *Harper's*, December 1989, pp. 43–48.

Laufer, Robert, and Maxine Wolfe. "Privacy as a Concept and a Social Issue: A Multidimensional and Developmental Theory." *Journal of Social Issues* 33 (1977): 22–42.

Levi, Edward H. *An Introduction to Legal Reasoning.* Chicago: University of Chicago Press, 1949.

Lewin, Tamar. "Nancy Cruzan Dies, Outlived by Debate over Right to Die." *New York Times*, December 27, 1990, sec. A.

Lewis, Charlton T., and Charles Short, eds. *A Latin Dictionary.* Oxford, Eng.: Oxford Clarendon Press, 1879.

Linowes, David F. "Must Personal Privacy Die in the Computer Age?" *American Bar Association Journal* 65 (August 1979): 1180–84.

———. *Privacy in America: Is Your Private Life in the Public Eye?* Urbana: University of Illinois Press, 1989.

Liversidge, Anthony. "AIDS." *SPIN*, March 1989, p. 54.

Locke, John. *Two Treatises on Government.* New York: Cambridge University Press, 1960.

Lykken, David T. "The Case Against the Polygraph in Employment Screening." *Personnel Administrator*, September 1985.

McCloskey, Robert G. *The American Supreme Court.* Chicago: University of Chicago Press, 1960.

McGovern, Thomas L., III. "Employee Drug-Testing Legislation: Redrawing the Battlelines in the War on Drugs." *Stanford Law Review* 39 (1987): 1453–69.

MacKinnon, Catharine. "*Roe v. Wade:* A Study in Male Ideology." In *Abortion: Moral and Legal Perspectives*, edited by Jay L. Garfield and Patricia Hennessey. Amherst: University of Massachusetts Press, 1984.

McWhirter, David P., and Andrew M. Mattison. *The Male Couple: How Relationships Develop.* Englewood Cliffs, N.J.: Prentice-Hall, 1984.

Malm, Heidi. "Comments on Ketchum's 'Selling Babies and Selling Bodies.' " Paper presented at annual meeting of the Eastern Division of the American Philosophical Association, New York, December 20, 1988.

Margulus, Stephen. "Conceptions of Privacy: Current Status and Next Steps." *Journal of Social Issues* 33 (1977): 5–19.

Marx, Karl, and Fredrick Engels. "Manifesto of the Communist Party." In *Basic Writings on Politics and Philosophy*, edited by Lewis S. Feuer. Garden City, N.Y.: Anchor Books, 1959.

Mazo, Daniel P. "Yellow Rows of Test Tubes: Due Process Constraints on Discharges of Public Employees Based on Drug Urinalysis Testing." *University of Pennsylvania Law Review* 135 (1987): 1623–56.

Mill, John Stuart. *On Liberty*. New York: Penguin Books, 1988.

Mohr, Richard D. *Gays/Justice: A Study of Ethics, Society, and Law*. New York: Columbia University Press, 1988.

Monagham, Henry Paul. "Of 'Liberty' and 'Property.' " *Cornell Law Review* 62 (1977): 405–44.

Murphy, Robert F. "Social Distance and the Veil." In *Philosophical Dimensions of Privacy: An Anthology*, edited by Ferdinand D. Schoeman. New York: Cambridge University Press, 1984.

National Commission on Electronic Funds Transfer. Washington, D.C.: NCEFT, 1977.

"New York Times/CBS Poll." *New York Times*, April 26, 1989, sec. 1.

Nowak, John E., Ronald D. Rotunda, and J. Nelson Young. *Handbook on Constitutional Law*. St. Paul, Minn.: West Publishing Co., 1978.

O'Brien, David. *Privacy, Law, and Public Policy*. New York: Praeger, 1979.

Olson, D. "Michigan Overturns Sodomy Laws: Similar Kentucky Decision Also Faces High Court Appeal." *Windy City Times*, July 19, 1990, sec. 1.

" 'Outing': An Unexpected Assault on Privacy: Gay Activists Are Forcing Others Out of the Closet." *Newsweek*, April 30, 1990, p. 66.

Parent, W. A. "Recent Work on the Concept of Privacy." *American Philosophical Quarterly* 20 (October 1983): 341–55.

Parker, Richard. "A Definition of Privacy." *Rutgers Law Review* 27 (1974): 275–96.

Pegis, Anton C., ed. *Summa Theologica, The Basic Writings of Saint Thomas Acquinas*. New York: Random House, 1945.

Perry, Michael J. *The Constitution, the Courts, and Human Rights: An Inquiry into the Legitimacy of Constitutional Policymaking by the Judiciary*. New Haven, Conn.: Yale University Press, 1982.

Polyviou, Polyvios G. *Search and Seizure: Constitutional and Common Law*. London: Gerald Duckworth, 1982.

Posner, Richard A. *The Economics of Justice*. Cambridge, Mass.: Harvard University Press, 1983.

———. *The Problems of Jurisprudence*. Cambridge, Mass.: Harvard University Press, 1990.

Prosser, William. *Handbook of the Law of Torts*. 4th ed. St. Paul, Minn.: West Publishing Co., 1971.

———. "Privacy." *California Law Review* 48 (1960): 383–423.

Rachels, James. "Why Privacy Is Important." In *Philosophical Dimensions of Privacy: An Anthology*, edited by Ferdinand D. Schoeman. New York: Cambridge University Press, 1984.

Rawls, John. *A Theory of Justice.* Cambridge, Mass.: Harvard University Press, 1971.

Rees, J. C. "A Re-Reading of Mill's *On Liberty.*" *Political Studies* 8 (1960): 113–29.

Regis, Edward, Jr., ed. *Gewirth's Ethical Rationalism: Critical Essays, with a Reply by Alan Gewirth.* Chicago: University of Chicago Press, 1984.

Reiman, Jeffrey H. "Privacy, Intimacy, and Personhood." In *Philosophical Dimensions of Privacy: An Anthology*, edited by Ferdinand D. Schoeman. New York: Cambridge University Press, 1984.

Richards, David A. J. *Sex, Drugs, Death, and the Law: An Essay on Human Rights and Overcriminalization.* Totowa, N.J.: Rowman and Littlefield, 1982.

————. *Toleration and the Constitution.* New York: Oxford University Press, 1986.

"The Rights of the Biological Father: From Adoption and Custody to Surrogate Motherhood." *Vermont Law Review* 12 (1987): 87–121.

"The Right to Privacy in Nineteenth Century America." *Harvard Law Review* 94 (1981): 1892–910.

Rivera, Rhonda R. "Our Straight-Laced Judges: The Legal Position of Homosexual Persons in the United States." *Hastings Law Journal* 30 (1979): 799–955.

Rosenbaum, Sharyn. "Is Legalization the Answer?" *Human Rights*, Spring 1989, pp. 18–19.

Rousseau, Jean-Jacques. *The Social Contract and Discourses on the Origin of Inequality.* Edited by Lester G. Crocker. New York: Washington Square Press, 1967.

Samar, Vincent J. "The Legal Right to Privacy: A Philosophical Inquiry." Ph.D. diss., University of Chicago, 1986.

Schauer, Frederick. *Free Speech: A Philosophical Enquiry.* Cambridge: Cambridge University Press, 1982.

Schmoke, Mayor Kurt. "A War for the Surgeon General, Not the Attorney General." *New Perspectives Quarterly*, Summer 1989, pp. 12–15.

Schoeman, Ferdinand D., ed. *Philosophical Dimensions of Privacy: An Anthology.* Cambridge: Cambridge University Press, 1984.

Schumpeter, Joseph. *Capitalism, Socialism, and Democracy.* 3d ed. New York: Harper and Row, 1950.

Sexual Orientation and the Law. Cambridge, Mass.: Harvard University Press, 1990.

Soma, John T., and Richard A. Wehmhofer. "Illegal and Technical Assessment of the Effect of Computers on Privacy." *Denver Law Journal* 60 (1983): 449–83.

"Summa Theologica": The Basic Writings of Saint Thomas Aquinas. Edited by Anton C. Pegis. New York: Random House, 1945.

Sunstein, Cass. "Sexual Orientation and the Constitution." *University of Chicago Law Review* 55 (1988): 1161–70.

Thompson, Judith Jarvis. "A Defense of Abortion." *Philosophy and Public Affairs* 1 (Autumn 1971): 47–66.

Thorne, Samuel E., et al. *The Great Charter: Four Essays on Magna Carta and the History of Our Liberty.* New York: Pantheon Books, 1965.

Totenberg, Nina. "The Confirmation Process and the Public: To Know or Not to Know," *Harvard Law Review* 101 (1988): 1213–29.

"Treating Adultery as a Crime: Wisconsin Dusts Off Old Law," *New York Times,* April 30, 1990, sec. 1.

Trebach, Arnold. "Why Not Decriminalize?" *New Perspectives Quarterly,* Summer 1989, pp. 40–44.

Tribe, Lawrence. *American Constitutional Law.* Mineola, N.Y.: Foundation Press, 1978.

U.S. Congress. Office of Technology Assessment. *Computer-Based National Information Systems: Technology and Public Policy Issues.* Washington, D.C.: Government Printing Office, 1981.

U.S. Congress. Senate. Judiciary Subcommittee on the Constitution. *Preliminary Report by the Office of Technology Assessment on the Federal Bureau of Investigation National Crime Investigation Center Accompanied by Letters of Comments on the Draft Report.* 95th Cong., 2d sess., 1978.

Van Den Haag, Ernest. "On Privacy." In *Nomos XIII: Privacy,* edited by J. Pennock and J. Chapman. New York: Atherton Press, 1971.

Wanamaker, John L. "Computer and Scientific Jury Selection: A Calculated Risk." *University of Detroit Journal of Urban Law* 55 (Winter 1978): 345–70.

Warren, Samuel D., and Louis D. Brandeis. "The Right to Privacy." *Harvard Law Review* 4 (1890): 193–220.

Wasserstrom, Richard. "The Legal and Philosophical Foundations of the Rights to Privacy." In *Bio-Medical Ethics,* edited by Thomas Mappes and Jane Zembaty. 2d ed. New York: McGraw-Hill, 1986.

———. "Privacy: Some Arguments and Assumptions." In *Philosophical Dimensions of Privacy: An Anthology,* edited by Ferdinand D. Schoeman. New York: Cambridge University Press, 1984.

Weiner, Robert. *AIDS: Impact on the Schools.* Arlington, Va.: The Education Research Group, 1986.

Westin, Alan. "The Origins of Modern Claims to Privacy." In *Philosophical Dimensions of Privacy: An Anthology,* edited by Ferdinand D. Schoeman. New York: Cambridge University Press, 1984.

———. *Privacy and Freedom.* New York: Atheneum, 1967.

Wittgenstein, Ludwig. *Philosophical Investigations.* 3d ed. Translated by G. E. M. Anscombe. New York: Macmillan Publishing Co., 1958.

Wooden, Wayne, and Jay Parker. *Men Behind Bars: Sexual Exploitation in Prison.* New York: Plenum, 1982.

Cases

Acanfora III v. Board of Educ. of Montgomery County, 359 F. Supp. 843 (D.C. Md. 1973), *aff'd* 491 F. 2d 498 (4th Cir.), *cert. denied,* 419 U.S. 836 (1974).

In re Adoption of Baby Girl, L. J., 132 Misc. 2d 972, 505 N.Y.S. 2d 813 (1986).

Akron v. Akron Ctr. for Reproductive Health, 462 U.S. 416 (1983).

Ashlie v. Chester-Upland School Dist., No. 78-4037, slip op. (E.D. Pa. May 9, 1989).

In re Baby "M," 109 N.J. 396, 537 A. 2d 1227 (1988).

Baker v. Wade, 553 F. Supp. 1121 (N.D. Tex. 1982).

Beck v. Ohio, 379 U.S. 89 (1964).

Berger v. New York, 388 U.S. 41 (1967).

Bowers v. Hardwick, 478 U.S. 186 (1986).

Breard v. Alexandria, 341 U.S. 622 (1951).

Brown v. Board of Education, 347 U.S. 483 (1954).

Carey v. Population Services Int'l, 431 U.S. 678 (1977).

Chalk v. United States Dist. Court, Cent. Dist. of Calif., 840 F. 2d 701 (9th Cir. 1988).

Child v. Spillane, 866 F. 2d 691 (4th Cir. 1989).

Chimel v. California, 395 U.S. 752 (1969).

Commonwealth v. Balthazar, 366 Mass. 298, 302, 318 N.E. 2d 478, 481 (1974).

Conway v. Hampshire County Bd. of Educ., 352 S.E. 2d 739 (W. Va. 1986).

Cruzan v. Director, Missouri, Department of Health, 760 S.W. 2d 408 (Mo. 1988) (en banc), *aff'd,* 58 U.S.L.W. 4916 (U.S. June 25, 1990).

District 27 Community School Bd. by Graniver v. Bd. of Educ. of New York City, 130 Misc. 2d 398, 502 N.Y.S. 2d 325 (1986).

Division 241 Amalgamated Transit Union v. Suscy, 538 F. 2d 1264 (7th Cir.), *cert. denied,* 429 U.S. 1029 (1976).

Doe v. Belleville Pub. School Dist., No. 118, 672 F. Supp. 342 (S.D. Ill. 1987).

Doe v. Commonwealth's Attorney, 403 F. Supp. 1199 (E.D. Va. 1975), *aff'd mem.,* 425 U.S. 901 (1976).

Doe v. Kelley, 106 Mich. App. 169, 307 N.W. 2d 438 (1981), *cert. denied,* 459 U.S. 1183 (1983).

Dronenburg v. Zech, 741 F. 2d 1388 (D.C. Cir. 1984).

Eisenstadt v. Baird, 405 U.S. 438 (1972).

Fraternal Order of Police, Lodge No. 5 v. City of Philadelphia, 812 F. 2d 105 (3d Cir. 1987).

Gaylord v. Tacoma School Dist., No. 10, 85 Wash. 2d 348, 535 P. 2d 804 (1975).

Gertz v. Robert Welch, Inc., 418 U.S. 323 (1974).

Griswold v. Connecticut, 381 U.S. 479 (1965).

Hodgson v. Minnesota, 58 U.S.L.W. 4957 (U.S. June 25, 1990).

In re Jane B., 85 Misc. 2d 515, 380 N.Y.S. 2d 848 (1976).

In re J. S. & C., 129 N.J. Super 486, 324 A. 2d 90 (1974).

Katz v. United States, 389 U.S. 347 (1967).

Kentucky v. Wasson, No. 86-X-48 (Cir. Ct., Fayette County, Ky., June 8, 1990).

Korematsu v. United States, 323 U.S. 214 (1944).

Lanz v. New York, 370 U.S. 139 (1962).

Laws v. Calmat, 852 F. 2d 430 (9th Cir. 1988).

Lord Byron v. Johnston, 2 Mer. 29, 35 Eng. Rep. 851 (1816).

Loving v. Virginia, 388 U.S. 1 (1967).

MacPherson v. Buick, 217 N.Y. 382, 111 N.E. 1050 (1916).

Mapp v. Ohio, 367 U.S. 643 (1961).

Martin v. Struthers, 319 U.S. 141 (1943).

Matter of Farber, 78 N.J. 259, 394 A. 2d 330 (1978), *cert. denied,* 439 U.S. 997 (1978).

Melvin v. Reid, 112 Cal. App. 285, 297 P. 91 (1931).

Michigan Organization for Human Rights (MOHR) v. Kelley, No. 88–815820CZ (Cir. Ct., Wayne County, Mich. July 9, 1990).

Minnesota v. Olson, 58 U.S.L.W. 4464 (1990).

Morrison v. State Bd. of Educ., 1 Cal. 3d 214, 461 P. 2d 375, 82 Cal. Rptr. 175 (1969).

National Gay and Lesbian Task Force v. Board of Educ. of City of Oklahoma City, 33 Fair Empl. Prac. Cas. (BNA) 1009 (W.D. Okla. 1982).

National Gay and Lesbian Task Force v. Board of Educ. of the City of Oklahoma City, 729 F. 2d 1270 (10th Cir. 1984), *aff'd* 470 U.S. 903 (1985).

National Treasury Employees Union v. Von Raab, 816 F. 2d 170 (5th Cir. 1987), *cert. granted,*—U.S.—, 108 S. Ct. 1072 (1988).

New York State Assoc. for Retarded Children v. Carey, 612 F. 2d 644 (2d Cir. 1979).

New York Times v. Sullivan, 376 U.S. 254 (1964).

New York v. Uplinger, 467 U.S. 246 (1984).

Nixon v. Administrator of General Services, 433 U.S. 425 (1977).

Ohio v. Akron Center for Reproductive Health, 58 U.S.L.W. 4979 (U.S. June 25, 1990).

Omstead v. United States, 277 U.S. 438 (1928).

On Lee v. United States, 343 U.S. 747 (1952).

Osborne v. Ohio, 58 U.S.L.W. 4467 (1990).

Palko v. Connecticut, 302 U.S. 319 (1937).

Paris Adult Theatre I v. Slaton, 413 U.S. 49 (1973).

Peonage Cases, 123 F. 671 (M.D. Ala. 1903).

People v. Onofre, 51 N.Y. 2d 476, 415 N.E. 2d 936, 434 N.Y.S. 2d 447 (1980), *cert. denied,* 451 U.S. 987 (1981).

People v. Roebuck, 183 N.E. 2d 166 (Ill. 1962).

Planned Parenthood Assn. v. Ashcroft, 462 U.S. 476 (1983).

Post v. State, 715 P. 2d 1105 (Okla. Crim. App.), *cert. denied,* 479 U.S. 890 (1986).

Public Utilities Commission v. Pollack, 343 U.S. 451 (1952).

In re Quinlan, 70 N.J. 10, 355 A. 2d 647, *cert. denied,* 429 U.S. 922 (1976).

Ray v. School Dist. of Desoto County, 666 F. Supp. 1524 (M.D. Fla. 1987).

Roberson v. Rochester Folding Box Co., 171 N.Y. 538, 64 N.E. 442 (1902).

Roe v. Wade, 410 U.S. 113 (1973).

Rushton v. Nebraska Public Power Dist., 844 F. 2d 562 (8th Cir. 1988).

Schneckloth v. Bustamonte, 412 U.S. 218 (1973).

School Bd. of Nassau C. v. Arline, 480 U.S. 273 (1987).

Semayne's Case, 5 Co. Rep. 91a, 77 Eng. Rep. 194 (1604).

Shoemaker v. Handel, 795 F. 2d 1136 (3d Cir.), *cert. denied,* 479 U.S. 986 (1986).

Sidis v. F-R Publishing Co., 113 F. 2d 806 (2d Cir. 1940).

Simopoulos v. Virginia, 462 U.S. 506 (1983).

Slaughter House Cases, 16 Wall (83 U.S.) 36 (1873).

Snydacker v. Brosse, 51 Ill. 357 (1869).

Snyder v. Massachusetts, 291 U.S. 97 (1934).

Stanley v. Georgia, 394 U.S. 557 (1969).

Surrogate Parenting Associates v. Commonwealth, 704 S.W. 2d 209 (Ky. 1986).

Terry v. Ohio, 392 U.S. 1 (1968).

Thomas v. Atascadero Unified School Dist., 662 F. Supp. 376 (C.D. Cal. 1986).

Thomas v. Winchester, 6 N.Y. 397 (1852).

Thornburgh v. American College of Obstetricians and Gynecologists, 476 U.S. 747 (1986).

Time, Inc. v. Hill, 385 U.S. 374 (1967).

Turnock v. Ragsdale, No. 88-790 (U.S. *cert. granted* July 3, 1989).

United States Dept. of Justice v. Reporters Committee for Freedom of the Press,—U.S.—, 109 S. Ct. 1468 (1989).

United States v. Leon, 468 U.S. 897 (1984).

United States v. Orita, 413 U.S. 139 (1973).

United States v. Reidel, 402 U.S. 351 (1971).

United States v. 12 200-Ft. Reels of Film, 413 U.S. 123 (1973).

United States v. Ventresca, 380 U.S. 102 (1965).

United States v. White, 401 U.S. 745 (1971).

Vale v. Louisiana, 399 U.S. 30 (1970).

Warden v. Hayden, 387 U.S. 294 (1967).

Webster v. Reproductive Health Services,—U.S.—, 109 S. Ct. 3040 (1989).

Weeks v. United States, 232 U.S. 383 (1914).

Whalen v. Roe, 429 U.S. 589 (1977).

Winterbottom v. Wright, 10 Meeson & Welsby 109, 152 Eng. Rep. 402 (1842).

Wolf Packing Co. v. Court of Indus. Relations, 262 U.S. 532 (1923).

Bills, Regulations, and Statutes

A Bill to Safeguard the Privacy of Electronic Fund Transfers by Consumers, and for Other Purposes, S. 1929, 96th Cong., 1st sess., 1979.

The Electronic Fund Act of 1980, 15 U.S.C. sec. 1693b(d) (1982).

Executive Order 12,564, 3 C.F.R. 224 (1987).

The Family Education Rights and Privacy Act of 1974, 20 U.S.C. sec. 1232(g) (1982).

The Fair Credit Reporting Act of 1970, 15 U.S.C. secs. 1681, 1681a–81t (1982).

The Freedom of Information Act of 1966, 5 U.S.C. sec. 552 (1982).

Justice System Improvement Act of 1979, 42 U.S.C. sec. 3789g (1982).

N.Y. Civil Rights Law, secs. 50–51 (McKinney 1948).

The Privacy Act of 1974, 5 U.S.C. sec. 522 (1982).

Rehabilitation Act of 1973, 29 U.S.C. sec. 794 (1982).

The Right to Financial Privacy Act of 1978, 12 U.S.C. secs. 3401–22 (1982).

The Tax Reform Act of 1976, 26 U.S.C. sec. 7602 (1982).

Applicable State Criminal Statutes

Ala. Code § 13A–6–65 (a) (3) (1982).

Ariz. Rev. Stat. Ann. § § 13–1411 to –1412 (Supp. 1988).

Ark. Stat. Ann. § 5–14–122 (1987).

D.C. Code Ann. § 22–3502 (1981).

Fla. Stat. § 800.02 (1987).

Ga. Code Ann. § 16–6–2 (1988).

Idaho Code § 18–6605 (1937).

Kan. Stat. Ann. § 21–3505 (Supp. 1987).

Ky. Rev. Stat. Ann. § 510.100 (Michie/Bobbs-Merrill 1985).

La. Rev. Stat. Ann. § 14:89 (West 1986).

Mass. Gen. L. ch. 272, § 34 (1986).

Md. Code Ann. art. 27, § § 553–554 (1987).

Mich. Comp. Laws § § 750.158, 750.388–.388(b) (1979).

Minn. Stat. § 609.293 (1988).

Miss. Code Ann. § 97–29–59 (1972).

Mont. Code Ann. § § 45–2–101, 45–5–505 (1987).

Mo. Rev. Stat. § 566.090 (1986).

Nev. Rev. Stat. § 201.190 (1987).

N.C. Gen. Stat. § 14–177 (1986).

Okla. Stat. tit. 21, § 886 (1981).

R.I. Gen. Laws § 11–10–1 (1986).

S.C. Code Ann. § 16–15–120 (Law. Co-op. 1985).

Tenn. Code Ann. § 39–2–612 (1982).

Tex. Penal Code Ann. § § 21.01(1), 21.06 (Vernon 1989).

Utah Code Ann. § 76–5–403 (Supp. 1988).

Va. Code Ann. § 18–2–361 (1988).

Index